The Power and Freedom of Black Feminist and Womanist Pedagogy

RACE AND EDUCATION IN THE TWENTY-FIRST CENTURY

Series Editors

Kenneth J. Fasching-Varner, University of Nevada, Las Vegas; Roland Mitchell, Louisiana State University; and Lori Latrice Martin, Louisiana State University

This series asks authors and editors to consider the role of race and education, addressing questions such as "how do communities and educators alike take on issues of race in meaningful and authentic ways?" and "how can education work to disrupt, resolve, and otherwise transform current racial realities?" The series pays close attention to the intersections of difference, recognizing that isolated conversations about race eclipse the dynamic nature of identity development that play out for race as it intersects with gender, sexuality, socioeconomic class, and ability. It welcomes perspectives from across the entire spectrum of education from Pre-K through advanced graduate studies, and it invites work from a variety of disciplines, including counseling, psychology, higher education, curriculum theory, curriculum and instruction, and special education.

Recent Titles in Series

The Power and Freedom of Black Feminist and Womanist Pedagogy

Still Woke

Edited by Gary L. Lemons and Cheryl R. Rodriguez

LEXINGTON BOOKS
Lanham • Boulder • New York • London

Published by Lexington Books
An imprint of The Rowman & Littlefield Publishing Group, Inc.
4501 Forbes Boulevard, Suite 200, Lanham, Maryland 20706
www.rowman.com

86-90 Paul Street, London EC2A 4NE

British Library Cataloguing in Publication Information Available

Library of Congress Cataloging-in-Publication Data

Names: Lemons, Gary L., editor. | Rodriguez, Cheryl Rene, 1952- editor.
Title: The power and freedom of Black feminist and womanist pedagogy : still woke /
    edited by Gary L. Lemons and Cheryl R. Rodriguez.
Description: Lanham : Lexington Books, [2023] | Series: Race and education in the
    twenty-first century | Includes bibliographical references and index.
Identifiers: LCCN 2022036905 (print) | LCCN 2022036906 (ebook) |
    ISBN 9781666925494 (cloth) | ISBN 9781666925517 (paper) | ISBN
    9781666925500 (ebook)
Subjects: LCSH: Women's studies--United States. | Women, Black--Study and teaching-
    -United States. | Racism--Study and teaching--United States. | Womanism--United
    States. | Feminism--United States. | Education and social justice--United States.
Classification: LCC HQ1181.U5 P69 2023 (print) | LCC HQ1181.U5 (ebook) | DDC
    305.420973–dc23/eng/20220913
LC record available at https://lccn.loc.gov/2022036905
LC ebook record available at https://lccn.loc.gov/2022036906

I write in honor of Septima Clark, Ida B. Wells, Ella Baker, Fannie Lou Hamer, and Audre Lorde, bell hooks, and many other Black feminist and womanist scholars and teachers whose courageous thoughts and words are the foundation of my teaching life.
Cheryl R. Rodriguez
In my longstanding calling to teach Black feminism and womanism in the college classroom, first and foremost, I have remained committed to demonstrating the self-liberating activism and the radical legacy of bell hooks. I am also forever thankful for the life-transformative activist academic and community-alliance building work(s) of Aaronette White, Beverly Guy-Sheftall, M. Jacqui Alexander, Alice Walker, AnaLouise Keating, Layli Marparyan, and Audre Lorde. Without them and my "womanist forefathers"—Frederick Douglass and W.E.B. Du Bois—I would not be the "woke" teacher I am today.
Gary L. Lemons

Contents

Preface

Reaffirming the Power and Joy of Black Feminist and Womanist Thought

Gary L. Lemons and Cheryl R. Rodriguez

In 1960, Ella Baker brought two hundred young people together at Shaw University, her alma mater in Raleigh, North Carolina. That historic gathering would lead to the founding of the Student Nonviolent Coordinating Committee, an organization that redefined activism and transformed the Civil Rights era. Beyond her role as an indefatigable activist, speaker, organizer and leader, Ms. Baker was also a mentor and teacher, who inspired the youth of that time to claim their place in an America that had made Black personhood synonymous with second class citizenship. Like many other Black women activist leaders, Ella Baker implemented a pedagogy of life[1] in which she taught resistance, determination and the true meaning of freedom. Her unequivocal message was always, "We who believe in freedom cannot rest." Guided by Ms. Baker's teachings, many young people committed themselves to dismantling America's very destructive social, political and economic inequalities. Their work in coalition building, democratic leadership, and in reaching out to local communities with humility is present in the Black Lives Matter movement and other contemporary movements for social change.

Remembering the powerful intellect that fueled Ella Baker's activism, we strive to be participants in social change through our work in classrooms and communities, hence, the title of our volume, *The Power and Freedom of Black Feminist and Womanist Pedagogy: Still Woke!* In honor of Ella Baker and many other womanist, activist teachers, each of the contributors to *Still Woke!* exclaims—in her/his own way—"We who believe in freedom and equality cannot rest until we have taught our students the complex meanings of freedom and equality." At this very critical moment in the history of Black revolutionary thinking, we recognize the importance of understanding the ways that our teaching supports contemporary movements against white supremacy, sexism, classism, homophobia, and all forms of oppression grounded in discrimination, hatred and ignorance. We also recognize that our teaching must be informed by a new movement for Black lives. Thus, police brutality, racist violence, and the disproportionate effects of poverty, loss, and illness on Black communities are all subjects that must be a part of our course content. Our pedagogical approaches to these and other social issues are informed by a deep connection to Black feminist and womanist pedagogical practices. That connection and its impact on our professional and personal lives is the subject of this book.

We began thinking about the foundations of Black feminist and womanist pedagogy by asking our wise mentor, Dr. Beverly Guy-Sheftall, how she became a Black feminist teacher. Her response is visionary and illuminating:

> I have been teaching for fifty-one years. My commitment to Black feminist pedagogy was perhaps unintentional when I began teaching English in 1969 at Alabama State University while completing a master's degree in English at Atlanta University. Two years later, I returned to my alma mater, Spelman College and began my more intentional journey as a Black feminist pedagogue and scholar. I did not have a road map, not having experienced classes as an undergraduate in the 60s (before Black Studies and Women's Studies) that included the writings or wisdom of Black women. My first scholarly project was *Sturdy Black Bridges: Visions of Black Women in Literature* (a co-edited anthology) whose purpose was making visible the extraordinary but largely invisible literary tradition of African American women writers. Becoming over time more knowledgeable about our robust Black feminist theorizing and activism since the early 1900s, my teaching became more radically feminist, more transgressive, more courageous. I became more intentional as I witnessed the profound changes my students at Spelman underwent as they acquired new knowledge and began seeing the world differently. This occurred as their analytical tools expanded around the intersections of race, gender, class and sexuality. I was transformed as well by my evolving and ever-expanding commitments to Black feminist pedagogy. I am convinced that I became a better teacher since that first year in 1969 as I struggled without the necessary tools and became a serious student of and contributor to the embryonic field of Black Women's Studies, and one of its most passionate advocates![2]

SPEAKING TRUTH TO POWER—TEACHING
FOR SURVIVAL ON AND ON . . .

As longstanding Black feminist-womanist professors affirming the radical legacy of Black Women's Studies, we have viewed our teaching as part of the historic struggle for social justice and transformative change in the United States and globally. Over the course of time, we have been led to link the evolution of our professional, pedagogical, and personal journeys to the visionary power of Black feminist and womanist intersectional theory and criticism. In this liberatory context, we labor in the classroom to contest *all* forms of oppression and social injustices. Conceptually, *Still Woke!* brings together teachers whose pedagogical approaches align with the liberating alliance of Black feminist-womanist professors and scholars who established and nurtured the field of Black Women's Studies. From its inception, the importance of pedagogical activist alliances—across differences of race, gender, class, sexuality, nationality, and abilities—has distinguished the life-saving value of this discipline. This book represents an alliance that continues and expands upon the tradition of sharing and exchanging radical pedagogical perspectives in the name of our own intellectual survival as well as toward the social and intellectual growth of our students.

Together we, as co-editors of *Still Woke!* along with our contributors, represent what it means to be critically conscious of the necessity of developing teaching strategies that embrace the (her)stories of Black feminist-womanists' survival against sanctioned and normative systems of social injustice(s). The editors and contributors to this project offer our personal experiences in classrooms reflecting on teaching as a bi-directionally transformative process. Not only do we feel compelled to enhance the critical consciousness of students' awareness of systemic and institutionalized oppression, but we also teach to demonstrate critical mindfulness of our own pedagogical self-survival in academia. In this anthology, the editors openly dialogue about ways we both teach, having survived varying institutional practices of white supremacy. We document our paths toward critical self-consciousness, linking our teaching and scholarly journeys to the (her)stories of Black/women of color struggles for social justice. As we shared out vision for the book, we challenged our contributors to profess their own struggles as Black feminist-womanist teachers and allies.

When reflecting on the Black feminist-womanist alliances we formed in this body of teaching narratives, we envision our collaborative effort toward the production of this book as a pedagogical sequel to *Building Womanist Coalitions: Writing and Teaching in the Spirit of Love.*[3] Comparatively, *Still Woke!* animates its mission by continuing to offer a strategic, collegial and scholarly platform for Black feminist-womanist pedagogical dialogues for social justice—across differences of race, gender, sexuality, and nationality. We intentionally align our voices with those of many noted Black feminists-womanists whose (her)stories of activism have stood the test of time in academia. This is precisely why *Still Woke!* not only affirms radical pedagogical praxes, but it also purposefully supports the labor of teachers willing to put their personal and professional lives "on the line." Reflexivity is the core principle of "autocritography" as defined by Michael Awkward:

> [It] is a self-reflexive, self-consciously academic act that foregrounds aspects of the genre typically dissolved into authors' always strategic self-portraits. Autocritography, in other words, is an account of individual, social, and institutional conditions that help to produce a scholar and, hence, his or her professional concerns. Although the intensity of investigation of any of these conditions may vary widely, their self-consciously interactive presence distinguishes [it] from other forms of autobiographical recall.[4]

Foregrounding our contributors' intersection of the personal with their "professional concerns" we invite readers to examine the critical importance of self-reflection in analyzing issues of social injustice(s). We contend that teaching for social justice and transformation must be linked to an ethic of critical self-consciousness. Absent this self-consciousness, students *and* teachers reinforce separatist notions of an integral relationship between the mind, body, and soul. In traditional mythology of higher education, the cognitive realm supersedes ethical principles of thinking for human rights—interconnected to inner-feeling/emotionality.

Thus, seriously considering the transformative innovation of self-reflection in academic professionalism, we underscore the liberating power of personal storytelling in the classroom. In this context, we and our contributors unapologetically defend and justify self-consciousness interrelated to academic professionalism. Once again, toward the production of this book, we worked very closely with each of our contributors to embrace the liberating legacy of Black feminist and womanist self-consciousness. As we continue to confront systemic and institutionalized oppression in classrooms *and* outside academia, we are inspired to be even more steadfast and unmovable in our allegiance to coalitional solidarity. Sometimes when teaching against the ubiquitous-ness of White supremacy, sexism, and classism, many of us have struggled with feelings of disillusionment, disappointment and ultimately discouragement. As Solomon and Rankin contend, "The fact is, White supremacy defines our current reality."[5] However, even as we witness visual media recordings of those who did not survive under the knee of social injustice, we must still teach for the hope that justice will prevail. So, as we teach on this journey of survival, we do not surrender the pedagogical standpoints we have taken. Telling our stories, we move forward against social injustice(s), as Alice Walker argues, *"Regardless."*[6] *Still Woke!* embodies the visionary writings of contributors committed to what bell hooks calls "education as the practice of freedom."[7] Together we envision, create, define, and delineate classroom spaces for self-transformation, intellectual transformation, and social transformation. In this volume, we hold up the banner of freedom—demonstrating the freedom and love for the spirit of justice for all from theory to pedagogical praxis.

WHEN THE REVOLUTION BEGAN: HONORING THE ACTIVIST SPIRIT OF "MAMA'S GENERATION [OF] HEADRAGGED GENERALS"

Alice Walker, Black feminist poet and righteous advocate for the use of the term "womanist," established a creative and intellectual foundation that supports Black women's activism historically and contemporarily. For example, the text, *All the Women Are White, All the Blacks Are Men, But Some of Us Are Brave: Black Women's Studies*[8] opens with Walker's evocative poem, "Women,"[9] which appears opposite a full-page photograph of an evicted Black woman sharecropper. This photographic image of one Black female homeless worker personfies the multitude of the women Walker envisions in her poem. While they, too, are invisible outcasts in America—still, they *own* themselves.

As Walker's poem illustrates, this generation of Black *mamas* also used their hands to guide the enslaved to freedom having led all kinds of "Generals" through precarious situations, including cotton fields and kitchens. Clearly, these women-warriors invoke the legacy of Harriet Tubman as "General" of the Underground Railroad liberation movement for the Africans enslaved on this land centuries earlier. The spirit of Tubman lives in the herstorical cohort of Walker's radical Black women, which includes not only Black women abolitionists but also Black women as important contributors to anti-lynching movements, Civil Rights activism, Black Panther Party activism and today's Black Lives Matter movement. Portraying her "mama's generation" as self-transformed *women* in the poem, Walker also demonstrates their deep-rooted and visionary knowledge as liberatory educators. Although laboring as enslaved domestic workers under a legal system of dehumanizing White supremacist oppression, they still understood the tools—books and desks—thought to be necessary for acquiring formal education. Unrelenting in their dreams for their children, these mothers made a place for their children and knew what their children had to know

Without knowing a page
Of it
Themselves.[10]

In the Introduction to the book *But Some of Us Are Brave*, entitled "The Politics of Black Women's Studies," Gloria T. Hull and Barbara Smith underscore the critical significance of Alice Walker's contribution to the establishment of Black Women's Studies. They indicate that Walker taught a groundbreaking course on Black women writers at Wellesley College in 1972. A year later, Walker broke more ground with the book, *In Search of Our Mothers' Gardens: Womanist Prose*. Walker's book opens with the definition of 'Womanist' in four distinct numbered statements. Opening with an explanation of the meaning of its *'womanish'* origin, she then personifies it in terms of 'A black feminist or feminist of color. From the black folk expression of mother to female children, 'You acting womanish,' i.e., like a woman.' Words like 'outrageous, audacious, courageous, or *willful*' illustrate a behavioral stance that would lead to a personal journey of self-reflection—wanting to know more and in greater depth than is considered 'good' for one." However, what appears most compelling in this opening statement about the sources of womanist identity is the idea of being interested in grown-up ideas. Once again, Walker articulates her definitional authority through Black vernacular stating, "You trying to be grown . . . Responsible. In charge. *Serious.*"[11]

In her second statement, Walker addresses what it actually means to be a womanist. First, she draws the reader's attention to a number of relevant and pervasive concerns that exemplify what a womanist is defined as, including the significance of her sexuality: "A woman who loves other women, sexually and/or nonsexually . . . Sometimes loves individual men sexually and/or nonsexually." Also, Walker defines a womanist related to "women's culture . . . emotional flexibility . . . and strength." Not only are these aspects central to her identity, but a notably radical element in Walker's womanist concept is also devotion to anti-racist alliance—rooted in the history of Black revolutionary struggle against slavery. A womanist is "committed to survival and wholeness of entire people, male and female."[12]

Advocating for social justice for all *othered,* excluded, and marginalized folks, and specifically focused on the role of gender in lived experiences, Alice Walker opposes separatism—except when needed for one's health. Today this particular womanist stance speaks to the urgency of understanding and being knowledgeable about racialized health disparities in the United States. Considering the convergence of the COVID-19 pandemic with the resurgence of a powerful, global movement against racism, we underscore womanism as a concept that embraces the "survival and wholeness" of Black/people of color in the United States in this day and time. Indeed, the discussions in this book about challenges we encounter teaching about race, racism, and social inequalities, also speak to professional environments that threaten our physical and mental health. There is a growing body of research documenting the traumatic generational history of Black physical, emotional, and mental well-being. Thus, today not only are Black people severely impacted the COVID-19 pandemic, statistics also reveal that Black death rates are three times higher than whites. Moreover, as is documented in varying social media platforms—concurrently Black folks (specifically in the United States) continue to confront the historically traumatizing and deadly power of systemic and institutionalized racism conceived in white supremacy.

Over the course of four centuries, Blacks in the United States having fought to survive through liberatory revolutionary movements to demonstrate—from the Underground Railroad (formed in the late 1700s) to the Civil Rights Movement (initiated in the 1950s) to the Black Power Movement (organized in the 1960s)—that Black Lives [*Still*] Matter. From the beginning of the insurgency of activist Black movements in the United States, education for social justice has served as a liberatory agent not only to enable Blacks to live in freedom, but ultimately to eradicate racism. A womanist defies the perpetuation of racism by calling into question the biologic superiority of the *white* race. Envisioned in a very brief conversation between a child *of color* and her/his mother, Walker demonstrates a womanist as capable of standing against the history of racist separatism in the United States. The child asks her/his mother a question about intra- and cross-racial skin color differences: "Mama, why are we brown, pink, and yellow, and our cousins are white, beige, and black?" Interestingly, the mother interprets the question through a visionary simile that is not only anti-racist, but also beautifully nature centered. In a world filled with *natural* colors, her response does not exclude the fact that skin color differences do matter. She says, "Well, you know the colored race is just like a flower garden, with every color flower represented." As a woman of color herself, Walker visually interconnects the beauty of the natural environment with that of the creation of humanity. As we each search for our mothers' gardens, we come to understand the biological inter-relationship of *all* skin color differences instead of thinking about the superiority of one over another. Clearly, as Walker prefaces the mother/child dialogue, a womanist is "[t]raditionally universal" affirming a worldwide inclusion of humanity across skin-color differences.[13]

Further contextualizing this heartfelt familial verbal exchange, the mother's seemingly simple lesson about race, color, and humanity is stunningly profound. As Walker further embodies her vision of a womanist as being "[t]raditionally capable," she connects the child's liberatory response to the mother's bio-multiracial view of the colored race. As the mother/child dialogue continues, without pause, the child immediately says, "Mama, I'm walking to Canada, and I'm taking you and a bunch of other slaves with me." The mother replies, "It wouldn't be the first time."[14] Clearly here, Walker strategically alludes to the historic Underground Railroad movement of enslaved Black people's revolutionary journey to freedom led by Harriet Tubman (whom the child would come to personify as a *capable* womanist). Through the critical self-consciousness of the *colored* mother and child in this brief radical narrative, anyone reading it should comprehend the lifesaving, herstorical lesson Walker teaches in her representation of *"womanish"* behavior. Moreover, anyone (student and/or teacher) studying it should also become critically aware that the eradication of racism *and* white supremacist ideology must be actively opposed by *all* races. In this viewpoint, a womanist—as Walker envisions—values *universal* love for humanity embracing struggle(s) committed to social justice.

In the third statement of Walker's characterization of a womanist, "love" lies at the core of what she stands for: she "[l]oves music. Loves dance. Loves the moon. *Loves* the Spirit. Loves love and food and roundness. Loves struggle. *Loves* the Folk. Loves herself. *Regardless.*"[15] Reaffirming the centrality of love in Walker's concept of womanism, AnaLouise Keating raises a series of questions that speak to "Alice Walker's love-saturated womanism":

> *What does transformation look like? What's the relationship between scholarship, research, pedagogy, and innovative social-justice work? How: can we use words, ideas, writing, and reading to promote progressive individual and collective change? How can we enact transformation in the various aspects of our lives—in our classrooms, our scholarship, our relationships, our daily practices?*[16]

We view this volume as a joyful response to these challenging and very necessary questions.

BIBLIOGRAPHY

Awkward, Michael. *Scenes of Instruction, A Memoir*. Durham: Duke University, 1999.
Brock, R. 2005. *Sista Talk: The Personal and the Pedagogical*. NY: Peter Lang, 2005.
Hobson, Janell. *Are All the Women Still White? Rethinking Race, Expanding Feminisms*. Albany: State University of New York, 2016.
hooks, bell. *Teaching to Transgress Education as the Practice of Freedom*. New York: Routledge, 1994.
Hull, Gloria, Patricia Bell Scott, and Barbara Smith. *All the Women Are White, All the Blacks Are Men, But Some of Us Are Brave: Black Women's Studies*. Old Westbury, NY: The Feminist Press, 1982.

Keating, AnaLouise. "Womanism for All! The Transformational Power of Radical Love." In *Building Womanist Coalitions: Writing and Teaching in the Spirit of Love,* edited by Gary L. Lemons, vii–xi. Urbana: University of Illinois Press, 2019.
Solomon, Akiba, and Kenrya Rankin. *How We Fight White Supremacy.* New York: Bold Type Books, 2019.
Walker, Alice. *In Search of Our Mothers' Gardens: Womanist Prose.* New York: Harcourt Brace & Co, 1983.

NOTES

1. Rochelle Brock, *Sista Talk: The Personal and the Pedagogical* (New York: Peter Lang, 2005).

2. Email communication with Professor Beverly Guy-Sheftall, May 20, 2020.

3. Gary Lemons, *Building Womanist Coalitions: Writing and Teaching in the Spirit of Love* (Urbana: University of Illinois Press, 2019).

4. Awkward, *Scenes of Instruction, A Memoir*, 7.

5. Solomon and Rankin, *How We Fight White Supremacy*, vii.

6. Walker, *In Search of Our Mothers' Gardens: Womanist Prose*, xii.

7. hooks, *Teaching to Transgress Education as the Practice of Freedom* (New York: Routledge, 1994).

8. Hull, Scott, and Smith, *All the Women Are White All the Blacks Are Men, But Some of Us Are Brave: Black Women's Studies* (Old Westbury, NY: The Feminist Press, 1982).

9. Alice Walker's poem "Women," in Hull, Scott, and Smith, *All the Women Are White, All the Blacks Are Men, But Some of Us Are Brave: Black Women's Studies*, xiii.

10. Alice Walker, "Women," xiii.

11. Alice Walker, *In Search of Our Mothers' Gardens: Womanist Prose*, xi.

12. Ibid., xi.

13. Ibid., xi.

14. Ibid., xi

15. Ibid., xii.

16. Keating, "Womanism for All! The Transformational Power of Radical Love," in *Building Womanist Coalitions: Writing and Teaching in the Spirit of Love*, ed. Gary L. Lemons (Urbana: University of Illinois Press, 2019), vii.

Introduction

Embracing Transformation: Welcoming Wholeness and Truth into Our Classrooms

Cheryl R. Rodriguez and Gary L. Lemons

The contributors to this anthology stand on the solid ground of pedagogical theory and praxis rooted in the legacies of Black women who fought for visibility and recognition of Black Women's Studies. Contemporarily, Black feminist, womanist-identified scholars, and our allies—including members of Latinx, Asian, and white communities, as well as cis-men, lesbians, non-binary, and gender non-conforming scholars—all embrace the transformational legacy of Black feminist and womanist pedagogical practices. Regarding allyship, Love and Jiggetts argue that through collaborative work, "we can make progress in ways that are not apparent when working in isolation and in separate communities."[1] Collectively, our pedagogical reflections in *The Power and Freedom of Black Feminist and Womanist Pedagogy: Still Woke!* personify individual and interconnected journeys for the liberation of students *and* teachers. Even in the complex multiplicity our differences, our mission remains the same: we are all committed to pedagogy for social justice, truth, and wholeness. We labor to transform classrooms into liberatory spaces dedicated to the realization of womanist love for the eradication of all forms of oppression.

PROFESSING OUR LOVE AND JOY
FOR SOCIAL JUSTICE

We could not have developed this project without having many animated discussions about the challenges of teaching for transformation and social justice. The contributors' pedagogical narratives and practices are intricately related to the work of courageous Black women and men activists, scholars, and teachers, including the historical groundings of Omolade[2] and a rich body of twenty-first-century scholarship that is profoundly enlightening, inspiring and intellectually energizing.[3] All of this work has inspired a radical vision of higher education that we share through personal and professional reflections.

The editorial production of *Still Woke!* has been an extraordinary journey of self-reflection shared with individuals who teach, instruct, and practice the transformative agency of critical consciousness. As every contributor to this volume illustrates, feminist and womanist teaching is not only about being conscientious, educationally prepared, and professionally responsible—it is also about embracing the wholeness of the human experience and teaching for freedom and social justice. In sum, it's about being critically aware of strategic ways to counter ideologies of domination—physically, emotionally, and mentally.

HOLDING UP THE BANNER OF FREEDOM
IN AND OUTSIDE THE CLASSROOM

Narrating (her)stories and (his)stories, as woke radical teachers confronting *and* contesting systemic and institutionalized oppression, we collectively join with our contributors to embody the visionary legacy of Black feminism *and* womanism. Thus, together we demonstrate how the classroom can be a life-saving space for spirited self-transformation. Acknowledging disciplinary boundaries many of us pedagogically transgress is one thing; acknowledging how our personal identities and often our actual physical bodies radically represent what we teach is quite another. This particular challenge has called for us to share our personal (her)stories and (his)stories with exceptional vulnerability. Narrative vulnerability acts as a strategic tool to reveal the willing sacrifices we offer in sharing our classroom experiences. In doing so, we create *room* for critical self-consciousness not only for our students, but for ourselves. In this visionary space, our pedagogical labor works for liberatory ideas of freedom *and* justice for all historically marginalized "Folks."

To the readers of our personal narratives and pedagogical strategies—including students in higher educational settings, along with teachers across instructional levels and disciplinary boundaries—we join together acknowledging that students cannot be challenged to transform their thinking without evoking passions and emotions that stretch us as well. In unity and solidarity, our voices speak to the complex dynamics of critical self-reflections that arise in our classes. Addressing them in our essays, we candidly admit our failures, successes, and personal ways of engaging them. Thus, envisioning the classroom as a space of liberatory transformation for students *and* teachers, we actively labor in pedagogical solidarity to promote the struggle for *pro*-feminist-womanist education. Together we continue the liberating and life-saving legacy of insightful, passionate, scholarly, and creative discussions about the politics of Black feminist-womanist pedagogy that began in the academic establishment of Black Women's Studies. Firmly grounded in Black feminist-womanist theory and practice, this book honors the *herstorical* labor of Black/women of color intellectual activists who have unapologetically held up the banner of freedom in academia.

PART I: "I AM"—PEDAGOGIES OF RESISTANCE, LIBERATION, AND TRANSFORMATION

What are the struggles of Black feminist and womanist scholars and teachers in the twenty-first century? How is a Black feminist and womanist vision communicated in our teaching? Is there a place for Black feminist and womanist pedagogy in every discipline? The essays in Part I address these questions from very distinctive perspectives. In these very personal and poignant essays, each of the contributors explores complex professional, political, social, and emotional issues that intersect with and challenge their relationships to teaching in the twenty-first century. These authors demonstrate a profound commitment to contribute to Black feminist thought and ultimately Black Women's Studies, regardless of the disciplines in which they teach.

The essays that comprise Part I grapple with the politics of teaching by examining the intricate intersections of personal identities, professional challenges, and political perspectives with course assignments and classroom dynamics. Cheryl Rodriguez opens with "The Radical Work of Teaching for Social Justice: Black Feminist Pedagogy for Twenty-First-Century Thought and Activism." In this essay, Rodriguez maintains that through knowledge production and teaching, Black feminist scholars make the radical commitment to show up for Black women and Black womanhood. Showing up for Black women and Black womanhood is a critical part of the justice-focused imperative of Black feminist thought. In the tradition of Hull, Scott, and Smith, who formally launched the discipline of Black Women's Studies with their classic text, *All the Women Are White, All the Blacks Are Men, But Some of Us Are Brave*, Rodriguez views Black Women's Studies as radical, analytical, courageous, transformative, and guided by Black women's lived experiences. Most importantly, she argues, the creation and development of Black Women's Studies reflects a passion for justice that must always be present in our scholarship and teaching.

Drawing upon her experiences as a scholar of Black women's community activism and as a Black feminist teacher, she includes examples of her justice-focused pedagogy. For Rodriguez, teaching for justice is a pedagogy of raising questions about power, equality, interactions, humanity, and community. Teaching for justice is a multivocalic pedagogy that welcomes the voices of a global community of Black women into college and university classrooms. Teaching for social justice is a humanistic pedagogy that shines a brilliant light on centuries of systemic oppression while also honoring histories and *her*stories of resistance.

Hanna Garth confronts historic and contemporary oppressive forces facing faculty of color at predominantly white universities (PWIs). In her deeply self-reflective essay—"Teaching as Liberatory Praxis: Learning to Shed Fear and Transcend Structures of Domination in the Classroom"—Garth discusses working in a climate of palpable racial hatred as white nationalist sentiments escalate on her campus. Motivated and empowered by her identity as a mother, Garth summons the courage to teach for her children and the generation of youth whose lives are threatened daily by the possibility of police brutality or random gun violence—in schools, in college campuses, and in most public spaces. She also examines the meaning of teaching for the self, which for her, means teaching for "a young, Black Queer woman-scholar." These powerful identities become tools for dismantling the insecurities of feeling unwanted by both her faculty community and the community of mostly white students in a large anthropology course on race and racism. Hence, self-knowledge, a commitment to self-love, and the determination to breathe a love of Blackness into her teaching, all help Garth to reshape, reinvent, and take charge of a course that does not appear to be a valued part of the anthropology curriculum.

Representing herself as a Vietnamese American woman of color professor in "Teaching Relationality: Pedagogies Across Asymmetries of Racialization and Colonization," Quynh Nhu Le writes about teaching in the fields of comparative race and Indigenous literary studies. She bases her essay on course content she teaches. The themes she engages all center around the mutual empowerment of Native and non-Native communities of color, with a specific attunement to women of color voices and critique. From this pedagogical standpoint, Le asserts:

[A] major goal in my courses is to highlight for students the long history of U.S. gendered racialization and settler colonization and their intimacies. That is, I specifically seek to make visible the critical differences between these two processes, of racialization and of colonization, which are all too often spoken in tandem in ways that conflate their varying logics and their varying effects on differently positioned communities. . . . This means not only centering the perspectives of marginalized communities in the selection of primary and critical readings that I include in a course, but to highlight specifically how these writers . . . the textures of their knowledge and experiences, speak to one another, to the students, and to me. Such a pedagogical mooring is deeply inspired by womanist/women of color and Indigenous feminist epistemologies and critique.

Moreover, Le maintains that central in the writings of both Native and non-Native feminists of color is the challenge towards "understanding the asymmetries and yet relationalities of struggles as they are informed by differences of race, colonial histories, gender, sexuality, class, ableism." She further asserts that for women of color feminist thinkers and teachers, it is particularly through this lens of *relational difference* that ethical engagement with one another and praxes of solidarity for dismantling the violence of white supremacist logics and colonial encroachment can be conceptualized and enacted. It is also through relational difference that an even deeper, perhaps more complicated, sense of shared goals can be reached. By introducing and examining the writings of women of color and queer writers of color, Le concludes that through relational difference a deeper and more complex sense of shared goals can be reached.

Clearly defining the disciplinary diversity and simultaneous interconnectivity between Black feminist and womanist thought, the contributors in Part I teach in varying disciplinary contexts, including anthropology, rhetoric and composition, literature, education/teacher preparation, and political science. Their essays illustrate ways in which their teaching methodologies are informed and sometimes confined by their disciplines. However, each writer employs the wisdom of Black feminist pedagogy to dismantle patriarchal disciplinary structures and transform curricula.

In a powerfully introspective essay, Kendra N. Bryant foregrounds the preeminent importance of identity and self-knowledge for Black feminist pedagogical practice. Thematically, "'I am that, *too*': Integrating the Black Woman into the *First Year Composition* Classroom" demonstrates the liberating authority of autobiographical rendering. This author recounts her struggles with embracing a feminist identity. She pinpoints the relevancy of the terms, Black feminism and womanism to her evolving personal and professional identities. While Bryant clearly identifies her authentic self as Black and lesbian, she argues that—until becoming more conscious about

Black feminist and womanist pedagogy—she had not invited those identities into her classroom, nor had she provided her students with opportunities to learn about Black women's genius and humanity.

Although Bryant's essay shares her coming to terms with womanism, her struggles reflect those of many Black women (of all ages) who remain uncomfortable with "feminism" and its generalist and colonized implications. The reality is that most disciplines of study have histories, canons, and tenets that thrive not only on patriarchal values but also racism, (hetero)sexism, and white intellectual elitism. As Black feminist and womanist practitioners in classrooms, we become scholars in these disciplines because of our interests and yet, we must work to transform traditional academic mores that restrict the voices we can, need—and must—bring to our *own* classrooms.

PART II. EDUCATION "AS THE PRACTICE OF FREEDOM" HOLDING ON TO BELL HOOKS'S PEDAGOGICAL LEGACY

In "Engaged Pedagogy," the opening chapter of her book *Teaching to Transgress: Education as the Practice of Freedom*, bell hooks writes: "To educate as the practice of freedom is a way of teaching that anyone can learn."[4] Both Cheryl and Gary assert that hooks's idea of "engaged pedagogy" is not only a way of teaching that is openly available to everybody, but that it is also an aspect of our vocation that is sacred. We love teaching in the "Spirit" of social justice.

Gary has continuously documented the self-transformative impact of hooks's pedagogical writings in his life and the lives of his students. Time and time again over the years, he has taught both *Teaching to Transgress: Education as the Practice of freedom* (1994) and *Teaching Community: A Pedagogy of Hope.*[5] Inspired by her writings in each book, he has remained committed to teaching "that embrace[s] the challenge of self-actualization . . . to live fully and deeply"[6] in resistance to systemic and institutionalized oppression. Having strategized this practice over the course of two decades in the college classroom, Gary has witnessed its self-liberating agency. Moreover, hooks underscores the self-transformative power of teaching for social justice uniting professors and students—across differences of race, gender, class, sexuality, and ability. Sharing with teachers the purpose of *Teaching Community,* in its "Preface" she says, " . . . in these essays, I hope to illuminate the space of the possible where we can work to sustain our hope and create community with justice as the core foundation."[7] This is precisely the intention of the writings produced by all four of the contributors in Part II. At one or more points in their academic career paths, each contributor to this part of the book was a student in one or more of the courses Gary taught. Now, as teachers, the four individuals address the groundbreaking legacy of bell hooks as a radical Black feminist professor.

Reflecting upon their longstanding individual coursework with him, Gary has become even more critically aware of the revolutionary currency of bell hooks's unwavering labor devoted to "self-actualization" for students *and* teachers. Thus, each contributor's written work is a testament to the life-transforming power of "education as the practice of freedom." To begin, in "Still Becoming Me: My Journey through bell hooks's Vision of 'Engaged Pedagogy,'" La-Toya Scott (as one of the few Black female graduate students Gary has taught whose work centered on literature by Black women writers) claims her identity as a Black feminist scholar and teacher. In this essay, Scott writes about the power of Black female self-reclamation. She grounds her essay in bell hooks's idea of teaching practices devoted to student-teacher self-actualization. Mapping the evolution of her own experiences as a student in a HBCU and a PWI, she shares her journey toward becoming an instructor at a community college where she taught students with particular learning disabilities. In this context, she proclaims:

> At the end of the day, I am secure in the fact that I know I want to practice 'engaged pedagogy.' As a radical form of teaching, it reaches, touches, and transforms the lives of *all* people in and outside academic institutions. It is critically important that we as educators—across differences of gender, race, ethnicity, class, sexuality, *and* abilities—remember that we are much more than intellectual figures in the classroom. We not only possess the power to become bridges to sharing a wealth of knowledge, but we—teachers and students can be facilitators of life-changing conversations focused on what it means *to be* as people. This is a vision of the classroom that we need to foster in order to move forward—promoting social justice and human rights for our students and for ourselves—particularly reflecting on what it means to enact Black feminist and womanist pedagogy in the college classroom. I am still *becoming me.*

Maggie Romigh situates herself "as a white female committed to radical pedagogy" in "I Ain't No Damned Pedagogue: Reevaluating my Stance in the Classroom from a Black Feminist Perspective and Reclaiming my Mother Tongue." She unrelentingly questions institutionalized notions of academic authority, reaffirming the life-transforming influence of her study of bell hooks's pedagogical standpoint represented in *Teaching to Transgress*. About her personal enlightenment, Romigh writes, "[this work] compelled [me] to reevaluate my own teaching practices, reconceptualize the value of [the] vernacular, and reconsider the ways that my working-class background sometimes makes me feel marginalized but also offers me a platform for empowerment in the hallowed halls of academia." As she personally reveals, reading hooks's work is always engaging, often eye-opening, and liberating for teacher and student.

Moreover, Romigh discloses, "In reading hooks, I position myself as the child of a peanut sharecropper to explore the ways my own highly irregular and broken path to academia has affected the ways I teach and engage with my students and work to subvert [systems of domination]." Exposing the ways she internalized and normalized ideologies of a dominant culture, Romigh concludes that her introduction to Black feminist theory transformed her classroom persona.

Freeing himself from the shackles of what hooks calls "imperialist white supremacist patriarchy," Gary Lemons has also continued to promote hooks' teaching strategies for *self-decolonization*. In 2009, he taught his first graduate class called "Feminist Theory" in the English department where he currently teaches. To his surprise, this class would come to represent a radical teacher-student mentoring relationship he had not envisioned nor planned. Additionally, in 2015, Gary would begin teaching a graduate course focused on the writings of hooks. He titled the course "bell hooks and Autocritography."

Committed to teaching for social justice, Gary's pro-womanist pedagogical practice would also manifest itself in the academic career path of Paul T. Corrigan. Before acquiring his doctorate in literature, he enrolled in a graduate course with Gary called "Literature by Women of Color." Paul contacted him in spring 2019 requesting that the two of them meet for a dialogue about the self-empowering influences of Black feminist and womanist pedagogy in each of their lives. Meeting in Gary's office on campus, they talked for hours—recalling and mapping the evolution of their teacher-student relationship. As recorded in "You Poured Your Soul into This Work: A Dialogue about *Black Male Outsider* and Teaching Womanist Writings" personifies the transformative legacy of Black feminist and womanist pedagogical practices.

Openly talking back to each other, the Corrigan-Lemons dialogue covers a range of topics—including the relationship between teacher and student; the power of writing by women of color to transform lives (including the lives of male and white readers); the value of dialogue on topics of race, gender, and other categories so often used to exclude and/or marginalize certain people; the "autocritigraphical" method for analyzing and responding to literature; the high quality of work students often produce in writing rigorously about things that matter for their lives; the relative absence of men (including both white men and men of color) in classrooms focused on feminism/womanism; the challenges of student resistance and the joy of student "hunger" for difficult conversations calling into question the perpetuation of systemic oppression; and higher education for survival, liberation, and transformation.

Also in 2009, Gary met Scott Neumeister in the same "Feminist Theory" class. From that class on, Gary would work with Scott, who identifies "as a cisgender, white male pro-feminist/womanist ally." Over the course of eight years, Gary became his "major" professor as Scott journeyed to acquire an MA and PhD in multicultural literary studies. Scott composed "Teaching to Progress: bell hooks, Radical Roots and Branches." The essay contextualizes a longstanding student-teacher relationship. Scott writes about it as a testament to the life-transforming power of radical learning and teaching *rooted* in hooks's belief teaching. Before finishing doctoral work, Scott would unapologetically prompt Gary to teach a graduate course on the writings of hooks. Accepting his request in 2015, it would be the first time in his professional career that Gary would teach a course focused on the writings of hooks. He titled the course—"bell hooks and Autocritography." To this day, these two— pro-feminist/womanist identified men—have co-authored an article, a book chapter, and a book (*Let Love Lead on a Course to Freedom*, 2019) based on their pedagogical collaboration together. They call themselves "Brothers of the Soul."

PART III. BLACK MALE RADICAL (HIS) STORIES: TEACHING TO SURVIVE

In "Remembering *Intersectional* Interventions: Teaching to Reclaim Human Rights Legacies" M. Thandabantu Iverson (an independent labor and human rights activist educator) examines the content, pedagogical relevance, and intervention of a workshop he conducted at the 2015 FIHRE (Fighting Injustice through Human Rights Education) Program of the U.S. Human Rights Network. He titled the workshop "From Sojourning for Rights to Black Lives Matter: Remembering Intersectional Lessons, Reclaiming Human Rights Legacies." Rooted in Black feminist and womanist thought, his essay details how the workshop provided social justice activists in the United States with strategic ways to strengthen their commitment to and struggle for social justice. Enabling them to comprehend possibilities of a human rights framework based on an intersectional and people-centered lens, Iverson critiques concepts of human rights conceptualized in "politically correct" liberalism.

In fact, Iverson's instructional setting is the historic Highlander Center, a site specifically created as a retreat for social justice activists. During the Civil Rights era, for example, activists such as Rosa Parks and Fannie Lou Hamer traveled to Highlander for respite. Recounting his experiences leading a workshop for human rights activists with Black women's activism as the focus of his pedagogy, Iverson discusses the concept of intersectionality and the ways in which it can be operationalized in social movement contexts. As the central concept of his workshop, he offered his participants an insightful vision of Black women's contributions to the theory and practice of intersectionality. While Iverson facilitated the workshop in a non-traditional, non-academic setting, its concept underscored the transformative impact of Black feminist pedagogical practice. Engaging his students in critical discussions about their lived experiences as human rights activists, he passed on the legacy of Black women as agents of change rather than as victims of human rights abuses. Iverson concludes, "Human rights activists can learn much from careful study of the [herstories of] Black radical women."

The legacy of radical Black women's herstories strategically grounds the pedagogical "his-story" of Marquese McFerguson. In his autoethnographic essay "Working Overtime: My Mother and Black Feminists' Embodied Narrative Inheritance," McFerguson focuses on the life-transforming ways his mother's employment as a working-class Black woman impacted his behavior, from childhood to adulthood. McFerguson documents his path to higher education, as a student _and_ instructor, integrally linked to his mother's personal stories of survival and "of growing up in the Jim Crow South [preparing him] for moments of being 'othered' within higher education." Specifically, he writes: " . . . even though my mother never had the opportunity to attend college, it was her narrative inheritance . . . sharing [her] stories [provided him] a keen sense of understanding the ways in which Black bodies are [interpreted] within racialized spaces." In sum, McFerguson argues that his mother's life experiences would become the root of his "pedagogical and performative template for navigating [his experiences in] predominately white academic institutions as a Black man."

In "A Pedagogical Awakening: My Pro-Womanist His-Story," Vincent Adejumo writes about the impact of Black feminist thought in the evolution of his pedagogical standpoint. He notes that in 2017, he received a grant to teach a course he titled "Black Wall Street." It focuses on the history of the historic Black business district in Tulsa, Oklahoma, established in the early 1900s. His concept for this course—grounded in the significance of black feminist thought—was originally inspired by his grandmother. He explains that it was her entrepreneurship as the owner of a restaurant in the 1960s in Tampa, Florida. As he writes, his grandmother's wisdom not only motivated Adejumo to create the course, but also enabled him to conceptualize the course strategies. As his vision for the course evolved, he recounts that his frequent conversations with his grandmother related to her commercial pragmatics. The Black female entrepreneurial lessons he learned from her moved him to incorporate her vision of Black female business ownership. As such, Adejumo created a specific womanist-centered pedagogy for the course. It would be steeped in practical strategies for the students to not only master the material of the course, but also to conceptualize the possibility of future personal enterprises they envisioned while taking the class. Looking back over the course of his own life as a Black male student, from boyhood to manhood, Adejumo reflects about lessons of survival he learned from Black women inside and outside of his family. He concludes and confesses that these life-transforming lessons have enabled him to teach to from a "radical" and "woke" Black feminist perspective. In his words, "'Black Wall Street' challenges traditional patriarchal business ownership ideology in the U.S. I specifically focus on Black female entrepreneurship—a subject that is traditionally not focused upon in academia."

Addressing another subject not traditionally discussed in academia, Roderick A. Ferguson's essay, "The Past and Future Diversities of HBCUs: Queerness and the Institutional Fulfillment of Black Studies," begins:

> Unlike the days in which Black LGBTQ students primarily existed within the closets of historically Black colleges and universities (HBCUs), those students are often now visibly apart of HBCU environments. For teachers and leaders within those institutions, the presence of LGBTQ students should not simply be regarded as a demographic fact, however. Indeed, in the spirit of this volume, the presence of queer and trans students on HBCU campuses should provoke us to exercise an aspect of Black feminism and womanism, that element of its vision that sees gender and sexual embodiment as reasons for intellectual and institutional insurrections. Looked at this way, the fact of Black LGBTQ difference as it is lived at HBCUs can be a way of deepening our pedagogical and scholarly engagements with the intersections of race, gender, sexuality, class, and so on.

Ferguson asserts that the inclusion of Black LGBTQ students is "actually consistent with the critical vision of black studies," particularly related to Black feminist and womanist thought. Moreover, he aligns this standpoint with the idea that Black studies is not only about the intellectual and political relevance of Black struggle for social justice, but also essentially interrelated to institutional imperative(s) for inclusion. Affirming the representation of gender and sexual diversity in HBCUs as a visionary undertaking, Ferguson states that, "The circumstances of Black queer students become the reason to revive this powerful feature of Black studies . . . in order to build academic institutions that affirm gender and sexual diversity we must address the gendered history of Black studies—that is, its masculinist foundations—and put forth a version of Black Studies first articulated by Black feminist intellectuals."

Collectively—as the contributors to this volume boldly address the intersectionality of systemic and institutionalized oppression rooted in racism, sexism, classism, heteronormativity and ableism, as well as other forms of

domination—we demonstrate an unwavering commitment to teaching critical awareness and social justice for the oppressed and marginalized. From
this standpoint, we carry forward the visionary legacies of Black feminism
and womanism. Ultimately, we are scholars, learners, thinkers, activists who
dream of changing the world through the power of teaching.

BIBLIOGRAPHY

Evans, Stephanie, Andreas D. Domingue, and Tania D. Mitchell, eds., *Black Women and Social Justice Education: Lessons and Legacies*. New York: State University of New York Press, 2019.

Gutiérrez y Muhs, G.G., Niemann, Y.F., González, C.G., and Harris, A.P., eds., *Presumed Incompetent: The intersections of race and class for women in academia*. Boulder: University Press of Colorado, 2012.

hooks, bell. *Teaching Community: A Pedagogy of Hope*. New York: Routledge, 2003.

hooks, bell. *Teaching to Transgress*. New York: Routledge, 1994.

Lemons, Gary L. *Black Male Outsider, a Memoir: Teaching as a Pro-Feminist Man*. New York: State University of New York Press, 2008.

Love, Barbara J., and Valerie D. Jiggetts. "Black Women Rising: Jumping Double-Dutch with a Liberatory Consciousness," in *Black Women and Social Justice Education: Legacies and Lessons*, edited by Evans, Domingue and Mitchell. New York: State University of New York Press, 2019.

Love, Bettina L. *We want to do more than survive: Abolitionist teaching and the pursuit of educational freedom*. Boston: Beacon Press, 2019.

Omolade, B. "A Black feminist pedagogy." *Women's Studies Quarterly 15*, no 3/4: 32–39. 1987.

Perlow, O.N., Wheeler, D.I., Bethea, S.L., and Scott, B.M. eds., *Black Women's Liberatory Pedagogies: Resistance, Transformation, and Healing Within and Beyond the academy*. Springer, 2017.

Ross, Sabrina. "Matters of Life and Love: Some Preliminary Mappings of Feminist Pedagogical Futures." *Educational Studies* 57, no. 3: 224–37, 2021.

NOTES

1. Barbara J. Love, and Valerie D. Jiggetts, "Black Women Rising: Jumping Double-Dutch with a Liberatory Consciousness" (Albany: State University of New York Press. 2019), Foreword, Kindle.

2. B. Omolade, "A Black feminist Pedagogy," *Women's Studies Quarterly* 15, no. 3 & 4 (1987): 32.

3. See the important work of Stephanie Evans, Andreas Domingue, and Tania Mitchell 2019; Bettina Love 2019; Perlow, Wheeler, Bethea, and Scott 2017; Ross 2021; and Gutiérrez y Muhs, Niemann, González, and Harris 2012.

4. bell hooks, *Teaching to Transgress* (New York: Routledge, 1994), 13.

5. See bell hooks, *Teaching Community: A Pedagogy of Hope (2003) and Teaching to Transgress* (1994).

6. bell hooks, *Teaching to Transgress* (New York: Routledge, 1994), 22.

7. bell hooks, *Teaching Community: A Pedagogy of Hope* (New York: Routledge, 2003), xvi.

PART I

"I Am"

Pedagogies of Resistance, Liberation, and Transformation

Chapter One

The Radical Work of Teaching for Justice

Black Feminist Pedagogy for Twenty-First-Century Thought and Activism

Cheryl R. Rodriguez

On December 12, 2017, Black women's political participation in Alabama made Doug Jones the first Democrat elected to the U.S. Senate from that state since 1997. In a special election for the U.S. Senate seat vacated by Jeff Sessions, Jones defeated Republican Roy Moore in a very heated race that captured national attention. Jones's historic triumph, in the Republican stronghold of Alabama, was largely attributed to massive Black voter turnout. In particular, 98 percent of Black women turned out and ushered Jones to victory. Jubilant responses to the election results included many accolades to Black women on social media such as #ThankBlackWomen and in some news outlets Black women were praised for "saving America."[1] However, many of us who have committed our intellectual energies to the theory and pedagogy of Black womanhood understood that Black women in Alabama used their votes to save their communities and themselves from the ongoing brutality of patriarchy, racism, and the deepening poverty that stifles and strangles too many southern Black families. As a scholar who has studied and written about Black women's community activism, I know that Black women's contemporary activism is a part of a courageous legacy of resistance and struggle.[2] A diverse national community of Black women in America votes in the names of many other known and unknown Black women who risked their lives for the right to vote, including Sojourner Truth, Frances Ellen Watkins

Harper, Ida B. Wells, Ella Baker, Fannie Lou Hamer, and Annell Ponder, among many others. No one should have been surprised that Black women in Alabama supported a moderate Democrat with a respectable civil right record over a racist Republican who had been credibly accused of sexual assault and who had publicly praised the era of slavery as a time of family unity.[3] Black women have always understood and resisted threats to Black survival. As the Combahee River Collective asserts, "Black women have always embodied, if only in their physical manifestation, an adversary stance to white male rule and have actively resisted its inroads upon them and their communities in both dramatic and subtle ways."[4] Black women vote in the name of Black people and Black communities. Most importantly, Black women organize and vote in the name of justice—a concept and idea that is the foundation of Black freedom movements, including Black feminist thought and action.

Media responses to the election in Alabama are examples of the many ways that journalists and other writers underestimate, misrepresent and simplify Black women's thoughts and actions. As James contends, "What often distracts attention from the fruits of black women's labors are depoliticizing representations that obscure their contributions to democratic politics."[5] Similarly, I argue for deeper perspectives on Black women's lives and political actions that move us beyond the monolithic image of Black women as sacrificial, morally superior beings. Like other stereotypical images created to perpetuate the "strong Black woman" myth, the #ThankBlackWomen meme suggests that Black women have power in a racist and sexist system that was created to destroy them. It is certainly important to celebrate political victories, but it is also critical that we celebrate within the contexts of Black women's stark historical, social and political realities.[6] In their classic 1978 Black Feminist Statement, the Combahee River Collective express the importance of refuting shallow, simplifying, dehumanizing notions of Black womanhood: "We reject pedestals, queenhood, and walking ten paces behind. To be recognized as human, levelly human, is enough."[7] Contemporarily, Doreen St. Felix expresses that same idea when she writes about Black women and the 2018 special election: "Critical nuances—aspects of class and region, especially—are lost when black women become icons, forever trapped in a cycle of ennoblement, flattening and dehumanization."[8] As other online supporters posted well-meaning, appreciative notes to Black women of Alabama, many supporters echoed the sentiment of Black feminists like Ijeoma Oluo, who asserted, "If you appreciate black women, don't just appreciate when we show up for you in a world that has never shown up for us. Try showing up with us instead. Every day."[9]

In this essay, I argue that through knowledge production and teaching, Black feminist scholars make the radical commitment to show up for Black women and Black womanhood. As members of the academy and as participants in varied national and international Black communities, the major component of our work is a pedagogy guided by a search for truth and a vision of engagement, equality and justice. In this essay, I explore the ways in which Black feminist pedagogy is a justice-focused endeavor. I examine my journey into Black feminist pedagogy by recounting my experiences with the first text that formally launched the discipline of Black Women's Studies entitled, *All the Women Are White, All the Blacks Are Men, But Some of Us Are Brave.* This profoundly influential text named and described a field of study that privileged the historical, cultural, intellectual, political, and activist voices of Black women. The authors of this groundbreaking volume, Hull, Scott, and Smith, argued unapologetically that Black Women's Studies had to be feminist, radical, analytical, courageous, transformative, and guided by Black women's lived experiences.[10] Most importantly, the creation and development of Black Women's Studies reflects a passion for justice that must be present in our scholarship and teaching, regardless of the subject matter.

While Black women have always faced brutal oppressive forces, the rise in state-sanctioned racism, misogyny, sexism, and hatred, has injected an element of urgency to my own pedagogical mission. That urgency should push us to move beyond the formidable boundaries imposed by academic institutions and to reconnect with a Black feminist and womanist mission to teach for justice. I think of justice as a concept that requires me to consider the humanity of those who have been socially, economically, and politically brutalized by state powers. As a Black feminist teacher, my justice-focused curriculum must present the raw truth and encourage new and productive ways of looking at the world. My discussion of teaching for justice is inspired by the reflections and theorizing of M. Jacqui Alexander, whose book, *Pedagogies of Crossing: Meditations on Feminism, Sexual Politics, Memory and the Sacred* challenged me to think deeply about my interactions and ways of being in the classroom, including thinking of pedagogy as:

> . . . something given, as in handed, revealed; as in breaking through, transgressing, disrupting, displacing, inverting inherited concepts and practices, those psychic, analytic and organizational methodologies we deploy to know what we believe we know so as to make different conversations and solidarities possible.[11]

For me, this definition argues that teaching for justice calls out patriarchy, hegemony, colonialism, racism, sexism, and militarism, and shows how these constructs have stood in the way of freedom for marginalized populations. Further, as Evans, Domingue, and Mitchell argue, Black women's herstories, lived experiences and narratives bring human rights and social justice to the educational process: "Black women's educational philosophies and pedagogical values provide primary source material to advance education about social justice, human rights and civil rights that can be useful inside and outside of the classroom."[12] My own awakening to social justice through Black feminism and Black Women's Studies was the catalyst for a life of learning, teaching, and activism.

RADICAL LEARNING: BLACK WOMEN'S STUDIES AND WOKENESS

I will never forget the day that I happened upon the anthology, *All the Women Are White, All the Blacks Are Men, But Some of Us Are Brave*. Just reading that audacious title left me breathless. Standing in a Chicago bookstore in the early 1980s, I was overwhelmed with curiosity and anticipation about what I would find in the dangerous pages of this radical, provocative volume. I remember feeling rather shocked to find this extraordinary book placed unceremoniously among stacks of other books on feminist theory. I felt that it should have had its own singularly majestic and celebratory display on a well-lit stand calling out to women like me who had been awaiting a publication that would set our intellectual lives on fire. I knew nothing about the backstory on this book. In the pre-internet 1980s, there were no online book reviews to alert me of upcoming publications, particularly those I sought in order to feed my hungry intellect and nurture my feminist soul. Of course, a book like this one would not have been reviewed in traditional, patriarchal newspapers or magazines. So, there I stood in the bookstore with a million questions swirling through my brain about the book's origins, editors, and contributors.

Always in search of feminist literature, I was fascinated with "women's" bookstores even though the few independent, feminist bookstores that dotted the urban landscapes in my world focused primarily on writings by and about white women. But this book, with the rich green background and the stunning subtitle, *Black Women's Studies*, was much more than I could have expected on that day. Before I turned back the crisp cover of this volume that would inaugurate a new discipline, I knew this book would be much more than I had ever experienced in my very limited life as a Black feminist thinker. And it was. I also knew it would change my life. And it did.

My love affair with this publication led me to seek out other powerful Black feminist writing and resources and I became fluent in the language and transformative knowledge of Black Women's Studies. While it was not the first influential feminist anthology to address political, intellectual, social, and cultural issues in Black women's lives, *But Some of Us Are Brave* took on the task of identifying the basic tenets of the emerging discipline of Black

Women's Studies. One of the most distinctive, memorable, and moving assertions in this book is Hull and Smith's bold statement on self-definition and autonomous thinking for Black women: "Like any politically disenfranchised group, Black women could not exist consciously until we began to name ourselves. The growth of Black Women's Studies is an essential aspect of that process of naming."[13] This volume, which is a foremother to many other anthologies that contributed to the foundation and ongoing evolution of Black Women's Studies, continues to resonate with students and scholars.[14]

When I began my doctoral studies in anthropology, I committed myself to engaging in research that explored Black feminism and the multilayered realities of Black women's lives. I made this commitment even though I had no professors with expertise in Black feminist thought who could help me to process my ideas and contribute to my development as a Black feminist thinker. Moreover, when I began teaching in Africana Studies and Women's Studies, I had to face the stark reality that Africana Studies was deeply patriarchal, and Women's Studies was overwhelmingly white. As Hull and Smith pointedly assert in their Introduction, "Because of white women's racism and Black men's sexism, there was no room in either area for a serious consideration of the lives of Black women."[15] In the early 1990s, this was still the case. Hence, there was little departmental validation for my ambitions to develop knowledge on Black womanhood. For years I worked in isolation. Nevertheless, I resolved to be a mentor for students who were interested in Black feminism. Most importantly, one of my major pedagogical goals was to have students be touched and affected by the rich, diverse, and creative learning experiences that are possible in Black Women's Studies.

In the 1980s, Hull and Smith were adamant that an emergent Black Women's Studies be feminist, radical, analytical, and intricately connected to the politics of Black womanhood. In the twenty-first century we witness a prolific and vibrant Black Women's Studies that has transformed scholarship on race, gender, class, and sexuality. Black Women's Studies has expanded and reconceptualized feminist thought by relentlessly developing scholarship that explores and boldly illustrates the complexity of Black womanhood. Black Women's Studies is a force that has interrupted patriarchal and hierarchical structures within the discipline of Black Studies and racism within the discipline of Women's Studies. Black Women's Studies is a fire that has inspired innovative and creative interdisciplinary scholarship by generation after generation of thinkers. As such, Black Women's Studies is foundation, fire, and fuel for Black feminist pedagogy—a pedagogy of theory, action, transformation, and justice.

BLACK FEMINIST PEDAGOGY:
TEACHING FOR JUSTICE

In her discussion of Black feminist pedagogy as a political and liberatory practice, Joseph contends, "Education has always been central in antiracist struggle."[16] As a Black feminist and womanist practice, teaching "has histori-cally been an integral part of Black women's struggle for social justice."[17] From slavery until the present day, education has been a formidable activist tool for a national community of Black women and men in search of freedom. During the eighteenth and nineteenth centuries, underground schools were created to educate enslaved Blacks. Learning to read and write gave enslaved people hope and even the intellectual ammunition for escape or fomenting rebellions. During the Reconstruction era and well into the twentieth century, the building of Black schools, Black institutions of higher learning and the training of Black teachers were major endeavors toward Black autonomy and self-determination. In the 1950s, activist and educator Septima Clark created Citizenship Schools throughout the South. These schools brought literacy to poor rural Blacks and played a major role in voting rights activism. Clark had a very radical and broad view of the power and purposes of education. She conceptualized pedagogy as "an active, communal, democratic and dialectical process involving all different types of learners and society as the classroom."[18] Citizenship Schools served as a model for the Freedom Schools created in the 1960s during the Civil Rights era in order to prepare Black people for the struggle to gain the right to vote. It is very encouraging to note the return of the Freedom School in the post-2016 election era. In the summer of 2019, Marian Wright Edelman and the Children's Defense Fund revisited the Freedom School concept and developed a training program for youth who attended the camp and returned to their home communities as teachers and social justice activists.[19] These examples illustrate a long history of Black people utilizing education and knowledge as powerful forces for social change. Black feminist pedagogy is very much a part of that political, liberatory, and revolutionary history. Courageous, independent, and visionary Black women like Mary McLeod Bethune, Anna Julia Cooper, and Septima Clark—who built schools, who risked their lives to teach, who were intel-lectual leaders and undaunted warriors for Black women's freedom—all laid the foundation for the development of Black feminist thought, "a theory of change with black feminist pedagogy being the change agent in and outside of the classroom—wherever education takes place."[20]

Black feminist pedagogy is theory, methodology, and praxis. Theorizing is a form of agency[21] that allows Black women to conceptualize and deconstruct social phenomena that impact their lives. Black feminist theory is rooted in

Black women's lived experiences as individuals, as members of families and as participants in communities. Regarding the relationship between pedagogy and theory, Alexander argues, "Pedagogic projects are not simple mechanistic projects, for they derive from theoretical claims about the world and assumptions about how history is made, in other words, pedagogy and theory are mutually related."[22] Indeed, pedagogy and theory are both important interventions through which scholars and learners can raise questions, challenge oppressive social structures, change ways of thinking, and explore novel possibilities. Further, Black feminist pedagogy is intricately connected to key theories on the simultaneity of oppressions in Black women's lives, shaped and developed by scholar-activists such as Anna Julia Cooper, the Combahee River Collective, and Kimberlé Crenshaw. These scholars and their theoretical perspectives make up the fabric of what we know as the curriculum of Black Women's Studies. As a methodology, Black feminist pedagogy is a courageous and radical force that encourages students and scholars to reexamine and view the world through a conscious, liberatory and revolutionary lens.[23] As praxis, Black feminist pedagogy is concerned with the impact of "domination and hierarchy"[24] on those we teach. Through teaching and community engagement, Black feminists seek "the establishment of just societies where human rights are implemented with respect and dignity."[25] Hence, our overarching mission is to teach for justice. This is a personal, political, and professional mission that can take many forms in the classroom.

As a Black feminist teacher, I understand teaching for justice as a pedagogy of raising questions about power, equality, interactions, humanity, and community. While traditional pedagogic practices often communicate to students the idea that their work as learners is to answer questions, Black feminist pedagogy challenges the notion of "answers." Black feminist pedagogy encourages students to see themselves as people who are capable of developing new questions about power, equality, fairness, peace, access to resources, human relationships to the natural world, and many other issues that challenge our existence on planet earth. The problems of the world evolve; solutions and answers can become obsolete. Rather than thinking of answers as final solutions to problems, Black feminist pedagogy challenges students to think about collaboration and diversity of thought. One of the courses that I teach requires students to develop research questions that will facilitate their understandings of peoples' connections to their communities. As students work through their research questions, they realize the power of questions and the potential instability of what we think of as answers. Thus, teaching for justice means taking the risk of posing difficult questions even when we cannot provide simple answers to these questions.

In their introduction to *But Some of Us Are Brave*, Hull and Smith underscored the importance of including multiple voices and experiences in the

Black feminist classroom. "A descriptive approach to the lives of Black women, a 'great Black women' in history or literature approach, or any traditional male-identified approach will not result in intellectually groundbreaking or politically transforming work."[26] Hence, I think of teaching for justice as a pedagogy that welcomes the voices of a grand, extraordinary and global community of Black women into our courses. Opening the curriculum to the multiple voices of Black women is critical to dispel the limiting and damaging stereotypes historically associated with Black womanhood. Some of these stereotypes—like the Mammy and Jezebel images—are visibly and viscerally objectionable to students. But do students critically analyze the contemporary forms of these stereotypes such as the #ThankBlackWomen meme? Also, by opening the curriculum to multiple voices, students can begin to understand the contributions of academic and nonacademic women to their learning experiences. Alexander suggests that it is hypocritical to promote our own desire to teach for justice without including these voices. She asks, "what might we learn from women who have discovered a yearning for justice in their new work sites, which only appear to be different from the work site of the academy?"[27] When I began my career as a cultural anthropologist, I knew that I wanted to study Black women's grassroots activism. I understood that through their work as grandmothers, mothers, sisters, and aunts, Black women nurtured their families and also did the arduous political work of advocating for their communities. The insights gleaned from my interviews with Black women who are public housing advocates, gay and lesbian rights activists, and leaders of local social justice organizations, are invaluable to my teaching. I enthusiastically agree with Lindsey, who argues "some of the most significant theorizing and practice of Black feminism occurs outside of the ivory tower."[28]

Teaching for justice is also a humanistic pedagogy that reinforces the inherent value of Black women's lives. Guided by my passion for honoring invisible Black women, I always begin the first session of my Black Women in America course with stories of my grandmothers. My maternal grandmother, Mittie Mae, was a very beautiful and dignified woman, who—in the 1940s and 1950s—rode a city bus across town every day and cleaned houses in the homes of white families. After work, she would ride the bus back home to our apartment in a Black housing project. Although she shared very little with me about her work life, sometimes in quiet moments she would tell me stories about some of the subtle ways in which she resisted the blatant, daily racism of her employers. My paternal grandmother, Caridad Lavin, was an immigrant from Cuba who worked in a cigar factory and saved as much of her small salary as possible so that her three children would grow up and attend college. Because of her determination, my father and his two siblings each graduated from Florida A and M in the 1940s, when few Black people had that privilege. Both of my grandmothers had visions of life beyond kitchens and factories for their children and grandchildren. Because I benefited tremendously from the backbreaking work that my grandmothers did on behalf of their families and because I was enriched and encouraged by their hopes, dreams and visions, I introduce myself as the granddaughter of women who cleaned houses and rolled cigars. I want my students to understand that my professional achievements are directly connected to women who did not have the luxury of buying or reading books. Because of racism and poverty, my grandmothers were not formally educated but they understood the value of education for their children and grandchildren. Through my lived experiences and through my research, I can offer my students knowledge about women whose work and lives often remain invisible because of the times in which they lived and because their work has not been valued. When students awaken to the inherent value of Black women's lives, they awaken to the need for justice, equality and freedom in societies all over the world.

Teaching for justice means shining light on centuries of injustices that have oppressed people in Black communities throughout the United States. However, teaching for justice also means illustrating the ways in which Black people actively participate in struggles to dismantle oppression. When we teach about contemporary social issues we are teaching for justice. Although it is difficult, disconcerting, and uncomfortable to teach about racism, sexism, homophobia, classism, and violence, it is critical to provide platforms for students to discuss these issues safely. For example, it is important that we raise questions about the intersection of race, gender and sexuality in deaths of Black women at the hands of police and in the murders of Black trans women across the United States. As Lindsey argues, "The rapidly growing numbers of Black women and girls, victims of anti-Black state violence in the twenty-first century, illuminates a new chapter in racial terror and subjugation."[29]

Teaching for justice offers students conceptual maps to explore an increasingly globalized world. Today's technologies may allow us to witness cultural realities of others, but these technologies do not always encourage the kind of understanding we need in order to create just societies. When we are threatened by difference, we fail to see the humanity in others. Teaching for justice is a pedagogy that deconstructs social phenomena such as mass immigration, resistance to immigration of Black and Brown people, and some of the very personal, painful, and desperate reasons for crossing national boundaries. Teaching for justice helps our students to understand the impact of displacement on individuals and communities and the meaning and urgency of spatial justice. Black feminist pedagogy, a pedagogy of justice, counters hegemonic thinking that allows people of privilege to ignore the very human plights of those who cross geographic boundaries in search of peace and freedom.

Teaching for justice is not simply a pedagogy but a way of seeing and a way of being. As Alexander tells us, "Thinking justice, teaching for justice, and living justice means that we continually challenge each other to enunciate our vision of justice."[30] My vision of justice is one that guides my life and my teaching.

BLACK FEMINIST PEDAGOGY AND TEACHING FOR JUSTICE IN THESE TUMULTUOUS TIMES

We are now well into the twenty-first century, and from my own experiences as a faculty member in an established Africana Studies degree program, I would not describe today's Black Women's Studies as being firmly rooted in the curriculum. In fact, in twenty-first-century America most universities do not offer degrees in Black Women's Studies and most Black feminist scholars do not and cannot work within the parameters of an academic department called Black Women's/Black Feminist Studies. However, Black Women's Studies is very much alive in the academy, nurtured and cultivated by an impressive and growing cadre of Black feminist scholars representing the Social Sciences, Humanities, Literary Studies, Education, the Natural Sciences, Cultural Studies, Performance Studies, Religious Studies, and other disciplines. In the introduction to *But Some of Us Are Brave*, Hull and Smith assert:

> The very fact that Black women's studies describes something that is really happening, a burgeoning field of study, indicates that there are political changes afoot that have made possible that growth. To examine the politics of Black women's studies means to consider not only what it is, but why it is and what it can be.[31]

There was then and is now so much joy and optimism in this statement. As I grew in my knowledge of Black feminist theory and praxis, I internalized that joy, optimism, hope, and passion for Black Women's Studies and now, nearly forty years later, I continue to joyfully celebrate the resiliency of this profoundly important discipline. However, maintaining that joy and hope during the post-2016 election, in these times known as the "post-truth" era, remains a formidable challenge. Post-truth is a ludicrous term, but it is one way of describing a time when the leaders of the United States very publicly proclaim statements that are blatantly untrue. Teaching the next generation that lying is a legitimate leadership strategy is very destructive to our educational system and to the global community! This post-truth era is also a time when multiple forces are attempting to delegitimize the work we do as scholars and teachers. There are so many ways in which Black feminist scholars and teachers are denied legitimacy and autonomy. In our classrooms scholarly books are often too expensive for our students to purchase, so we cannot require them to read materials that we deem important. Moreover, we continue to work in a culture of justification in which we are required to show that the study of Black women's histories, writings and theories are worth supporting.

In the sacred spaces of our classrooms, other problems occur including overt demonstrations of racism by students. We also must contend with the increasing presence of white nationalism on campuses. Even feminist classrooms can feel emotionally threatening for faculty and students. Cespedes, Evans, and Montiero discuss experiences in a Black feminist course in which "hegemonic feminists" often attempted to decenter race and deny the racialized experiences of Black women in the classroom, arguing that sexism and heterosexism were the dominant forces with which all women should be concerned. Further, they argue that in this particular situation, the decentering of blackness allowed white feminists to "avoid accountability from their complicity in racial oppression while exploiting black women for their knowledge, experiences, and labor."[32] All of these issues present complicated and sometimes traumatic challenges to our roles as scholars and teachers. Sadly, these issues affect students' desires to participate fully in learning processes.

And yet, despite feelings of despair at our national condition, the urgency and commitment to reach and teach our students does not wane. Hence, regardless of its disciplinary or curricular positionality in academia in the twenty-first century, Black Women's Studies remains an intellectual space for the creation and development of theories and concepts that systematically analyze the complexities of Black women's lives in a turbulent world. Over time, this intellectual space has been shaped and influenced by a dynamic and productive range of scholars in many disciplines. We have named ourselves. We know who we are, and we still bravely contribute to Black Women's/ Black Feminist Studies through scholarship, community engagement and teaching. As twenty-first-century Black feminist scholar Brittany Cooper asserts, "Black women's intellectual leadership traditions are long, robust, multigenerational, and continuing."[33]

That very powerful truth guides me back to my original copy of *All the Women Are White, All the Blacks Are Men, But Some of Us Are Brave*. It has traveled with me and held a place of honor in every office or dwelling that I have called my own. The cover is quite faded and tattered as any illustriously revered book should be. The binding has come apart and some of the pages hang precariously loose. Underneath the audaciously and provocatively long title is a vintage photograph of two young Black women who stare back at me each time I pick up the book. They are standing side by side next to a clapboard house wearing Sunday hats and matching three-piece gingham outfits.

The only description of the photo is that they are two young women, probably somewhere in Virginia around 1910, the year my maternal grandmother was born. Every time I look at the photograph, I imagine the two women on their way to church or a meeting and pausing to be photographed in their very snazzy outfits. Looking straight at the camera, they appear to indulge the photographer while also maintaining serious, composed expressions.

This photo reminds me of how little we still know about the daily lives of Black women in the early 1900s. It is tragic that we do not know the names of these women. It is tragic that the camera did not—and could not—stop very often to capture the faces and feelings of these extraordinary women who probably wanted more out of life than could ever be offered to them. Who, I wonder as I study the photograph looking for clues, was each woman on her way to becoming? How did these women define their lives in the early twentieth century just forty-five years after the end of slavery? What did they know of the thoughts and dreams of Black women who had lived hundreds of years before their births? What were their own thoughts and dreams? I cannot answer these questions with any coherent words. And yet, I allow myself to imagine that the proud and confident women in that photograph were women who would want us to keep asking questions about Black women's lives. They would want Black feminist thinkers to fill libraries with our scholarly thoughts and creative works. They would want us to continue educating our students in ways that promote and encourage responsibility to humanity and the building of a just world. These modest women would want Black Women's Studies to prevail and continue honoring their legacies of survival as well as their unknown suffering and sacrifices. I believe they would want Black feminist scholars and teachers to continue showing up for Black women. Finally, I passionately believe we can honor these women and many others by living and developing our own unique liberatory pedagogies grounded in Black feminist knowledge, hope, light and a never-ending commitment to justice for everyone.

BIBLIOGRAPHY

Alexander, M. J. *Pedagogies of Crossing*. Durham: Duke Univ. Press. 2005.

Cespedes, K. L., Evans, C. R., and Monteiro, S. "The Combahee River Collective Forty Years Later: Social Healing within a Black Feminist Classroom." *Souls* 19 no.3 (2017): 377–89.

Combahee River Collective. "The Combahee River Collective Statement." In *Home Girls: A Black Feminist Anthology*, edited by Barbara Smith, 272–82. New York: Kitchen Table Women of Color Press, 1983.

Cooper, Brittney. *Beyond Respectability the Intellectual Thought of Race Women.* Chicago: University of Illinois Press, 2017.

Evans, Stephanie Y., Andrea D. Dominigue, and Tania D. Mitchell. "Black Women's Educational Philosophies and Social Justice Values of the 94 Percent." In *Black Women and Social Justice Education: Legacies and Lessons*, edited by Evans, Dominigue, and Mitchell, 1–20. New York: SUNY, 2019.

Hull, G., Patricia Bell Scott, and Barbara Smith. *All the Women Are White, All the Blacks Are Men, But Some of us Are Brave.* Old Westbury: Feminist Press, 1982.

Hull, Gloria T., and Barbara Smith, "Introduction: The Politics of Black Women's Studies," in *All the Women Are White, All the Blacks Are Men, But Some of us Are Brave*, edited by Hull, Scott, and Smith, xvii–xxxii. Old Westbury: Feminist Press, 1982.

James, Joy. "Resting in the Gardens, Battling in the Deserts," in *Still Brave the Evolution of Black Women's Studies*, edited by James, Foster, and Guy-Sheftall, 363–71. New York: The Feminist Press, 2009.

James, Stanlie. "Introduction," in *Theorizing Black Feminisms*, edited by Stanlie James and Abena Busia, 1–12. New York: Routledge, 1993.

Joseph, G. "Black Feminist Pedagogy and Schooling in Capitalist White America," in *Words of Fire an Anthology of African-American Feminist Thought*, edited by Beverly Guy-Sheftall, 462–71. New York: The New Press, 1995.

Lindsey, T. B. "A Love Letter to Black Feminism." *Black Scholar,* 45, no.4 (2015):1–6.

Oluo, I. "Don't Thank Black Women for Roy Moore's Loss. Fight for Us Every Day." NBCNews.com, 2017. https://www.nbcnews.com/think/opinion/don-t-thank-black -women-roy-moore-s-loos-fight-ncna829681.

Perlow, Wheeler, Bethea, and Scott. "Introduction," in *Black Women's Liberatory Pedagogies*, edited by Perlow, Wheeler, Bethea, and Scott, 1–18. NY: Palgrave MacMillan, 2018.

Rodriguez, C. 2003. "Invoking Fannie Lou Hamer: Research, Ethnography and Activism in Low-income Communities." *Urban Anthropology,* 32, no.2 (2003): 231–51.

Rodriguez, C. "'We Came with Truth': Black Women's Struggles against Public Housing Policy," in *Homing Devices: Poor People and Public Housing Policies*, edited by Marilyn Thomas-Houston and Mark Schuller, 81–98. Lexington, MA: Lexington Press, 2006.

St. Felix, D. "How the Alabama Senate Election Sanctified Black Women Voters." *The New Yorker (Online),* December 14, 2017. https://www.newyorker.com/news/daily -comment/how-the-alabama-senate-election-sanctified-black-women-voters.

NOTES

1. Jarvie, Finnegan, and Mark Barabak. 2017. In *Alabama and Across the Country, Pride Swells as Black Female Voters Show They Matter*. Retrieved from https://search .proquest.com/docview/1977231514.
2. For example, see Rodriguez, "Invoking Fannie Lou Hamer: Research, Ethnography and Activism in Low-Income Communities," 231–51, and Rodriguez, "'We Came With Truth': Black Women's Struggles against Public Housing Policy," 81–89.
3. https://time.com/5062625l/doug-jones-alabama-senate-results-upset/   How Doug Jones Won the Alabama Senate Election | Time.
4. Combahee River Collective, "The Combahee River Collective Statement," 273.
5. James, "Resting in Gardens, Battling in Deserts, Black Women's Activism," 363.
6. In her article, "Don't Thank Black Women for Roy Moore's Loss. Fight for Us Every Day," Oluo includes very disquieting statistics on U.S. Black women's economic and health status in the twenty-first century.
7. Combahee River Collective, "The Combahee River Collective Statement," 275.
8. St. Felix, "How the Alabama Senate Election Sanctified Black Women Voters."
9. Oluo, "Don't Thank Black Women for Roy Moore's Loss."
10. Gloria Hull, Patricia Bell Scott, and Barbara Smith, *All the Women Are White, All the Blacks Are Men, But Some of Us Are Brave: Black Women's Studies* (Old Westbury, NY: The Feminist Press, 1982).
11. M. Jacqui Alexander, *Pedagogies of Crossing* (Durham: Duke University Press, 2005), 7.
12. Evans, Dominique, and T. Mitchell, "Black Women's Educational Philosophies and Social Justice Values of the 94 Percent," 4.
13. Gloria Hull and Barbara Smith, "Introduction: The Politics of Black Women's Studies," xvii.
14. These anthologies, for example, focused on African American feminism and womanism: *Home Girls: A Black Feminist Anthology* (1983), edited by Barbara Smith; *Theorizing Black Feminisms* (1993), edited by James and Busia; *Words of Fire: An Anthology of African-American Feminist Thought* (1995), edited by Guy-Sheftall; *Still Brave: The Evolution of Black Women's Studies* (2009), edited by James, Foster and Guy-Sheftall; *Are All the Women Still White?* (2016), edited by Janell Hobson; and *The Crunk Feminist Collection* (2017), edited by Cooper, Morris, and Boylorn.
15. Gloria Hull and Barbara Smith, "Introduction: The Politics of Black Women's Studies," xxi.
16. Gloria Joseph, "Black Feminist Pedagogy and Schooling in Capitalist White America," 463.
17. Perlow, Wheeler, Bethea, and Scott, "Introduction," 2.
18. Perlow, Wheeler, Bethea, and Scott, "Introduction," 4.
19. https://www.npr.org/2019/08/02/747504742/childrens-defense-fund-trains-new -activists.
20. Gloria Joseph, "Black Feminist Pedagogy and Schooling in Capitalist White America," 468.
21. James, "Introduction," 2.

22. M. Jacqui Alexander, *Pedagogies of Crossing*, 91–92.

23. Joseph, "Black Feminist Pedagogy and Schooling in Capitalist White America," 467.

24. Alexander, *Pedagogies of Crossing*, 5.

25. James, "Introduction," 3.

26. Hull and Smith, "Introduction: The Politics of Black Women's Studies," xxi.

27. Alexander, *Pedagogies of Crossing*, 92.

28. Lindsey, "A Love Letter to Black Feminism," 2.

29. Lindsey, "A Love Letter to Black Feminism," 1.

30. Alexander, *Pedagogies of Crossing*, 116.

31. Hull and Smith, "Introduction: The Politics of Black Women's Studies," xvii.

32. Cespedes, Evans, Monteiro, "The Combahee River Collective Forty Years Later: Social Healing within a Black Feminist Classroom," 381.

33. Brittney Cooper, *Beyond Respectability: The Intellectual Thought of Race Women*, 152.

Chapter Two

Teaching as Liberatory Praxis

*Learning to Shed Fear and
Transcend Structures of
Domination in the Classroom*

Hanna Garth

I used to be afraid. I was afraid of making people mad, upsetting people. It is hard to be a people pleaser and a professor. It is even harder to be a people pleaser and teach on the topic of race. Although I had developed a teaching philosophy that upheld liberatory pedagogy, an open and inclusive classroom, and critically engaged learning, I had also developed a fear that students at a predominantly white institution (PWI) would be hostile toward a woman-of-color professor teaching in a way that exposed ongoing forms of racism, heteropatriarchy, and called out white supremacy. These fears made me instinctively want to close off my teaching style, construct ridged boundaries, and feel in complete control of the classroom. Nevertheless, I was there to teach a course on "Race and Racism," and I felt that I had to figure out a way to do it that upheld my teaching philosophy and made me more at ease in the classroom. As I elaborate below, I started my first faculty position at a time when media outlets were reporting that the reason that faculties were not more diverse was that faculty of color simply were not wanted. In this context, as many of my colleagues saw things I was "hired to teach Race and Racism," a large lecture course offered several times a year by our department that meets the university Diversity, Equity, and Inclusion undergraduate course requirement. The enrollees consist largely of non-majors who sought a relatively easy way to meet this requirement. The double burden of being "unwanted faculty" teaching a group of students who were begrudgingly taking my course was a huge obstacle to surmount.

This essay is a self-reflexive examination of the challenges and opportunities of using Black feminist pedagogy in a large lecture course on "Race and Racism" at a PWI. I reflect on my experience teaching this course during a time of political and racial turmoil in the United States, and the ways in which my role as a Black mother influenced the way that I developed and taught the course. I detail my orientation to the course and how I used an emancipatory approach in preparing the syllabus and lectures. I then connect this approach with the ways it can be used to break down Eurocentric masculinist approaches to education and wear down the forms of domination and the depersonalization of education more broadly. Finally, I conclude by reconnecting my approach to the classroom with key life practices and the ways the pedagogical is personal.

"WE SIMPLY DON'T WANT THEM"

The start of my first faculty position coincided with a flurry of media attention over a statement made by Marybeth Gasman, professor of higher education at the University of Pennsylvania. Gasman's answer to the question "Why aren't college faculties more racially diverse?" sparked national attention, when she stated, "The reason we don't have more faculty of color among college faculty is that we don't want them. We simply don't want them."[1] Gasman's remarks may have seemed offensive, but many people have praised her honesty. She exposed the forms of prejudice and discrimination that go on in the hiring process and concluded that the underlying cause of the lack of faculty diversity is simply that majority-white departments do not want to hire faculty of color.[2]

A few months later the climate would change even more after November 8, 2016, when Donald Trump was elected president of the United States. Trump's election fueled many hate groups across the nation, emboldening white nationalists and other racists to speak out and carry out acts of violence and hate crimes. In the months leading up to the election and those that would follow there were a series of racist incidents on our campus, including students writing in chalk "Build the Wall," and "Deport Them All" among other things along highly trafficked campus sidewalks.[3] While the University spoke out against such acts, the climate of racial hate was palpable.

At the outset, the emboldening of campus racists coupled with the awareness that faculty of color were deeply unwanted filled me with fear. I was afraid that my classroom would be filled with White, conservative Trump supporters who constantly fought me, offended me, and intimidated me. I dreaded the idea of getting up in front of a room of people who absolutely did not want to be there, but the university was making them take this course.

I feared that I would pander too much to this audience and in turn fail the students of color in the room, fail the students who were there to learn, fail the students who wanted tools to fight racism. There were moments when I resented that my White colleagues had hired me, the only Black person in the department, to teach this large, required diversity course. I felt that in many ways it could be better for a senior White male to be teaching this topic. I did not feel that I was "presumed incompetent," but instead presumed to only be competent at teaching race or to be naturally suited to teaching about race and racism because of other people's assumptions about my own identity.[4] However, there was not much I could do about the situation, and—in many ways—I was very pleased with the job overall. So, I resigned myself to just suck it up and teach the course. I decided that the easiest thing to do would be to teach it as my colleagues had done previously with just a few updates to the readings.

Then, as I was trudging along through my avoidance approach, Armound Brown, a twenty-five-year-old young man with an intellectual disability was shot and killed by police officers on January 23, 2017. Brown was said to be holding a "deadly weapon," which was later determined to be a butter knife. As I read about this killing, I found myself weeping at my desk. This murder made the many that came before, run through me like poison. Philando Castile—murdered in a city where I once lived. Alton Sterling. Sandra Bland. The Charleston Nine. Freddie Gray. Ezell Ford. Michael Brown. Eric Garner. Tamir Rice. Trayvon Martin. I found myself pouring over news articles and videos of the murders, testimonies of the families, and I read about acquittal after acquittal after acquittal of police officers. In her blog post, Adrienne Maree Brown contends, "I feel black grief permeate my dreams and thicken in my mouth before I even hear the news. some days even the sun is heavy, even the pale blue sky looks guilty."[5] When I thought of my own sons living in this context, I found myself inconsolable. As a Black mother, I realized I was tethered to what Christen Smith calls the "sequelae" of "gendered necropolitics"; I was and continue to "face the dragon" as I navigate Black motherhood under the conditions of anti-black state violence where "raising our children and simply surviving is a perilous game."[6] I felt pulled into what Christina Sharpe calls "the wake," a state of "keeping watch of the dead" and living in the afterlife of slavery. Sharpe asks, "what kind of mother/ing is it if one must always be prepared with knowledge of the possibility of violent and quotidian death of one's child?"[7] I was living within the wake, a state that requires constant "wake work."[8]

Inconsolable, stuck sitting within a seemingly all-encompassing state of anti-Blackness, as a part of living in the wake and doing "wake work" I resolved to teach the course for myself. To teach it for who I am today as something that I could get behind politically, as something that I would enjoy preparing, and I aspired to have every lecture be something that felt good, felt necessary, and energized me as I taught it. I resolved to teach it for my children; to envision and think through other worlds, a future where Black is beautiful everywhere. I also resolved to be bold in calling out racism, to not be afraid of my audience but to fearlessly give them my honest truth about racism in the US today. The course became wake work. No sugarcoating, no rose-colored glasses. Yet, I also knew that I could not live with the weight of the world on my shoulders.

I resolved to focus on teaching to the marginally racist students, who would certainly not call themselves racist in a way that might push them toward anti-racism, and the ability to talk to their peers and parents about race in a way that would incite them to care and maybe even make them a little less racist. To create this kind of emancipatory learning environment, I knew that I had to turn to Black feminist pedagogy.[9] As fate would have it, when I turned to the sample syllabi that my department chair had provided me, I stumbled upon a syllabus created six years earlier by my white, male colleague Joseph Hankins. As I skimmed through Joe's syllabus, I fixated on one particular paragraph in which he wrote: "Black feminist thinker bell hooks talks about using the classroom to create a learning community. This is a community dedicated to transforming everyone in it—teachers and students alike. It is a community that comes together to share new knowledge but also to transform behaviors, to challenge each other, to take risks, to express and address conflict, and to support each other. It is a community that takes trust and work. I want you to think of your participation in this class in terms of responsibility not simply to yourself but to a learning community."[10]

While I had previously had my own ideas about creating inclusive classrooms and teaching in a way that was attuned to student needs, I was struck by my colleague's use of bell hooks and goal to create a transformative learning community. Joe's use of hooks caused me to turn to hooks's Teaching to Transgress. Although I had read hooks at previous points in my life, first through the 2003 Rock My Soul: Black People and Self-Esteem, I had never read Teaching to Transgress, or hooks's other pedagogically oriented works, such as Teaching Community or Teaching Critical Thinking. hooks contends that "to educate as a practice of freedom" is a sacred part of our vocation, that more than merely sharing information we promote "intellectual and spiritual growth."[11] However, "Engaged pedagogy is more demanding than conventional critical or feminist pedagogy" and "[t]his means that teachers must be actively committed to a process of self-actual inaction that promotes their well-being if they are to teach in a manner that empowers students."[12] hooks draws on the wisdom of Buddhist teacher Thich Nhat Hanh, who says that "the practice of a healer, therapist, teacher, or any healing professional should be directed at his or herself first, for if the healer is unhappy he or she cannot help many other people."[13] Thich Nhat Hanh and bell hooks engaged in another conversation about love. hooks pointed out that one of the great things about the civil rights movement was that it centered around love and forgiveness. Hanh reminds us of the importance of loving ourselves as well as others, and hooks reminds us that Martin Luther King Jr. said that one must have courage in order to love.[14]

From then on, I had this idea to teach the course "for myself" by which I meant several things. Teaching "for myself" meant teaching for a young, Black, Queer woman-scholar, it meant working to liberate myself from the confines of White supremacy, from toxic masculinities, from heteropatriarchy, from the many ways in which the academy was not made for me, not made for Black Queer, non-male, young "folx." I was influenced by Alexis Pauline Gumbs, Adrienne Maree Brown, and Black feminist public scholars who were succeeding in bringing Afro-futurism, speculative imaginings, and the possibilities of envisioning and living out forms of utopic worlding that center Blackness as beautiful. For Gumbs, "Black feminism is a practice of putting love first and knowing the at a profound love, a deep love, an actualized love, an accountable love is the only thing that will break through what the Combahee River Collective calls the 'interlocking' forms of oppression."[15] Gumbs uses an intentional practice of loving Black women as a way of learning to "breathe love, learning to live a life that is an act of love designed to empower all oppressed people and to be a gift to our species and to the universe that holds us."[16] In my teaching what this has meant is to always breathe a love of Blackness into my lectures and assignments, to make the course ooze with a love of Blackness and by extension all people of color as an antidote to anti-Blackness and the myriad forms of prejudice and discrimination that people of color face. This also necessitated an ongoing practice of self-love. With this approach, I would join a long legacy of Black women educators engaging in liberatory pedagogies.[17] I would rely upon this legacy by thinking of liberatory pedagogy as "wake work."

WAKE WORK IN SYLLABUS PREPARATION

Increasingly Black feminist scholars are doing "wake work" in research.[18] I have found that teaching and syllabus preparation can also serve as wake work, which in turn is central to the process of self-reflection, integrally linking the life-transforming power of pedagogy rooted in an emancipatory vision of human rights and social justice. The first step for me in this process was the creation of a genuine course description. I sat down and reflected on what I needed to work through and talk through to sit well with teaching a course on race at the predominantly white institution. The following was the description I used in my first syllabus for the course:

> This course is a deep reflection on the question: What is race? Through readings and class discussions we will delve into historical and present-day understandings of race and how our understanding of race influences forms of racism. We will explore related questions such as: In what ways do race and racism affect how people live their lives? What tools does anthropology provide for understanding the changing impact of race and racism in the United States and around the globe? How is race-related to other forms of identity such as gender, religion, or disability? How is racism linked to similar concepts like prejudice or discrimination? This course has a particular focus on race and racism as they are used and understood within the social sciences, specifically anthropology, but we also use the anthropological lens to see how race and racism are understood in the sciences, medicine, law, and policy. We will investigate the lived and practical effects of linkages among talking, acting, and being when it comes to race, how those presumed links have changed over time, how they sit alongside other categories like gender, ethnicity, and citizenship, and how they relate to racism, and the unequal distribution of power via authority, respect, economic and political resources, security, and health across different racial groups. The course focuses on concepts of race both within and beyond the United States to understand race and racism globally.

This description of the course was how I was able to meet the needs of teaching a large lecture course with my critical Black feminist approach to pedagogy. I had to cover certain material, but I could do it in a way that was more amenable to liberatory praxis. Then, in truly following a Black Feminist approach that moves away from a "banking" approach to learning toward a critical, reflexive approach, I addressed how I understood assignments as part of critical engagement with the material, not a bank of knowledge or recitation of "facts." To that effect, I included the following statement in my syllabus:

> The assignments for this course are meant to serve as ways for you to reflect upon and synthesize what you have learned in the lectures, discussions, and course readings. The goal of this course is for you to understand, process, and critically reflect on the material, not to memorize or repeat what was said in class or the readings.

Rather than stating concise learning objectives, I wanted to be clear that this was a chance for students to think beyond the bounds of their current understanding, to expand their notions and definitions of race, to think critically about how racism functions, and to do this in ways that are not easily captured by learning objectives. To ensure that students understood the type of classroom environment I was creating I used a lot of space in the document to make clear my stance on etiquette and accommodations as part of Black feminist praxis. These practices are part of understanding the student as a whole person, which I convey in the following statements:

> I consider this classroom to be a place where you will be treated with respect, and I welcome individuals of all ages, backgrounds, beliefs, ethnicities, genders, gender identities, gender expressions, national origins, religious affiliations, sexual orientations, ability–and other visible and nonvisible differences. All members of this class are expected to contribute to a respectful, welcoming, and inclusive environment for every other member of the class.

As part of Black feminist praxis, I honored students' intersectional identities to the best of my ability and made that intention explicit in the syllabus with the following two statements:

> I will gladly honor your request to address you by your name or gender pronoun. Please advise me of this preference early in the quarter so that I may make appropriate changes to my records.

> Students who miss work for the purpose of religious observance are permitted to make up this work.

Finally, a critical element of Black feminist syllabus creation lies in the selection of course texts. For this course, I was committed to using the work of scholars of color. I selected Audra Simpson's Mohawk Interruptus: Political Life Across the Borders of Settler States (2014) as a difficult book that would force students to read and push their ability to engage with a text. I used L. Kaifa Roland's Cuban Color in Tourism and La Lucha: An Ethnography of Racial Meanings (2011), which functioned to demonstrate the myriad ways in which race is experienced in the United States and transnationally. Finally, we read Anthony Christian Ocampo's The Latinos of Asia: How Filipino Americans Break the Rules of Race (2016), another text that cuts race in a nuanced way by demonstrating how Filipino Americans align more with Latino communities than Asian communities. These texts work to push the boundaries of race studies, demonstrating how people do not neatly conform to checkboxes. The texts work both to expand students' understanding of the topic at hand and to slowly break down Eurocentric, masculinist forms of categorization that do not align with the epistemologies of communities of color.

SELF-LOVE IN LECTURE WRITING

My approach to course planning begins like many aspects of my work life, by consulting the National Center for Faculty Development & Diversity Directed by Kerry Ann Rockquemore. I am committed to using their course planning guide because if I really follow the steps, it ensures that I cannot spend too much time on course preparation. Concise course preparation is essential not only for research productivity but also for work/life balance and self-care—aspects that are particularly important for scholars of color who may undertake disproportionate amounts of university service. Course planning for a large lecture course, with a majority of non-major students, is a difficult task. I needed to make sure that I covered enough basic information that those who had no background would not be completely lost without boring those who already knew a great deal.

At first, I was attempting to cater to everyone in the class. However, my approach quickly shifted when during Week 1 I was pleasantly surprised at the number of students who told me that they were taking the course because they were interested in the topic, not because it was a requirement (many had already fulfilled the requirement). I estimate about twenty of 230 students were taking the course because they were really interested in learning about the topic. Those students tended to sit near the front of the classroom, came to almost every lecture, and would usually participate in the discussions. I began to really enjoy interacting with these students and shifted from thinking of teaching just for myself to teaching for these twenty or so students and myself. The other 210 would probably derive some benefit from whatever level of listening they were doing. Teaching to the 10 percent of the class that was excited to be there was much more fulfilling for me and inspired me to teach a more engaging and dynamic course. While teaching to the 10 percent of already engaged students had benefits for my well-being and a potential trickle-down effect, it also meant that I was not meeting the majority of the class at their level of need. Learning from this experience, I have since incorporated engaged pedagogical techniques that target those who might be less interested or has less baseline knowledge of the topic. In other classes, think-pair-share activates, small group work, and in-class analysis of current events from different perspectives have allowed me to harness the knowledge of eager students to engage the rest of the class.

LECTURE WRITING AS LIBERATORY PRAXIS

While many pedagogical techniques have proven to work as liberatory praxis in smaller classroom settings, teaching a large lecture course that fulfills a campus-wide requirement necessitates its own approach. By lecture course, I mean a class that is structurally and institutionally designed for the professor to deliver content via spoken discourse in front of the class, often behind a podium. Usually, lecture classes have high enrollments and take place in large halls where it is difficult to conduct discussions or facilitate group work. First, the large lecture course requires balancing the desire to steer clear of "pedagogical structures mired in structures of domination,"[19] while at the same time maintaining control over a classroom where highly sensitive topics were being discussed in a diverse classroom. I found three strategies helped me to maintain a Black feminist pedagogical praxis while balancing the needs of a large lecture 1) a consciously engaged process of lecture writing, by lecture here I mean a written set of comments or thoughts that I deliver orally before the class; 2) careful incorporation of media into the course; 3) active learning strategies for the large lecture.

To maintain my Black feminist teaching philosophy, I knew that I would need a different approach to lecture writing. Previously I had written lectures quickly before class—focusing on connecting the readings with my learning outcomes. This approach often did not allow for critical reflection on how students resonate with the material personally and emotionally. However, in a large lecture, I could not feasibly allow all the students to voice and share their reflections. Instead, my approach to writing lectures shifted to include my personal and emotional resonance with the material. Before writing a lecture, I would read the selected pieces, select videos, and music that connected me with the material emotionally, and incorporate those into my lectures. I would then use media and my own analysis to connect the work to core concepts in anthropology, which would ensure that I covered the learning outcomes. The additional step of self-reflexivity and the connection to music and media added a more personal element to the course.

Instead of quickly writing my lectures before class, I began to write my lectures immediately after class. I would often find myself very emotionally charged after discussing the topics we cover in "Race and Racism," and I would use this emotion to fuel writing my next lecture. This had the effect of ensuring that the themes of the course were nicely interwoven and that overall, the course flowed together well. After class, I would sit with music, find sources of media, and plan engaged classroom activities that brought together the nexus of emotions that the previous class had drawn out. This process of lecture writing became cathartic, allowing me to both process my own emotional response to the material and to enliven my future lectures with my own passion for the material and the effects of liberatory pedagogy.

One dilemma that I faced in the process was whether to include the racist canon of Anthropology in the course. Early anthropologists produced great deals of research and writing to show that indigenous and Black people were intellectually inferior; this was used as a rationalization for settler colonialism and slavery. I was hesitant both because I did not want students to come away with the impression that this was correct information, that anthropology still perpetuated these narratives, nor did I want to give time or space in my course and my life to these racist scholars. Ultimately, I decided that explaining the racist history of anthropology was important for showing students how far we have come and to make it clear that even the way that we think of race today is still changing. Nevertheless, teaching a racist cannon is extremely difficult, it is hard to explain their logics and the update of those narratives without becoming angry and making sure it is absolutely clear that new data shows that these logics were deeply flawed. On the other hand, working through difficult topics and a racist cannon is also a central part of racial justice and Black feminist praxis in that it is a part of providing access to resources, representation, and demonstrating how racist narratives can be reclaimed, rejected, and reformulated as a way of empowering anti-racism and its related causes.

TEACHING AS HEALING PRAXIS

hooks has also noted the detrimental effects of attempts to force people to "conform to someone else's image of who and what [we] should be."[20] In 2010 I published a paper based on ethnographic research among a group of thirty people who had recently applied to graduate programs in anthropology. Based on this research, I found that applicants to graduate school systematically felt that they had to mold themselves into the ideal graduate student even if that was not who they really were.[21] Instead, they listened to what their mentors told them to write in their applications, who they should work with, and the kinds of words they should use to describe their interests. Further, the students in this research told me they felt the process caused them to lose some of their sense of self. I also found that in many ways the application to graduate school mirrors the experience in graduate school.

Although I did not follow up with these students on this topic specifically, I imagine that graduate training also slowly strips away one's sense of self over time. This common experience in graduate school is part of what Patricia Hill Collins has described as a "Eurocentric masculinist knowledge validation process"[22] where obedience to authority is to be upheld, and any personal, ethical, or emotional stance toward the work that deviates from this validation process is considered to be incorrect and is to be eschewed. hooks has described a related "dis-ease among professors when students want us to see them as whole beings rather than simply as seekers after compartmentalized bits of knowledge,"[23] in turn, there is a "dis-ease" when faculty present themselves as whole people with personal lives, emotions, and ethics.

Black Feminist pedagogy often constitutes a move away from the "Eurocentric masculinist knowledge validation process" as a central part of teaching as self-emancipatory. That is, through this liberatory praxis, we work to shed the structures of domination and hierarchy that may have become ingrained in us at previous moments in our education or early career. In turn, once we begin to liberate ourselves from toxic pedagogies, we can begin to develop our critical consciousness in a way that will allow us to share it with others. By making clear why what we teach matters, why it is meaningful to us, through our vulnerability and willingness to open our personal and emotional lives to the classroom we can empower ourselves and others. This Black feminist and womanist approach is a foundation for eradicating systematic and institutionalized oppression. The classroom can become a space to confront the interlocking forms of oppression we face.

Beyond the capacity to liberate the educator, this approach to Black Feminist Pedagogy has the potential to allow students who have become disengaged from higher education to reconnect to their education through their own sets of liberatory praxis that the classroom fosters. This is particularly true for Black female students, who have been found to "feel neglected by education reform efforts" when such efforts "disregard unique race-gender stigmatization."[24] Through this approach to liberatory praxis as educators, we can illuminate how people of color generally, and Black women specifically, are more than "multiply burdened" but also "characterized by a multiplicity of strength, love, joy, and transcendence."[25] That is to say, Black feminist pedagogy can become a practice that demonstrates the beauty and strength of Blackness itself. This orientation can be a form of "worlding" or "conceptualizing analytic possibilities"[26] and "envisioning a world where our experience was standard."[27] This pedagogical orientation is a momentary rearrangement of institutional hierarchies, whereby the classroom and scholarship of faculty of color are not (only) understood through the white gaze but can also be seen through a lens of Black self-definition. This experience is rare for students at PWIs, but it is vital to their growth, learning, and well-being.

Conclusions

My dear friend Jess has a tattoo on the forearm that reads: "If I didn't define myself for myself, I would be crunched into other people's fantasies for me

Hanna Garth

and eaten alive." I am sometimes brought to tears when I see these words from Audre Lorde. I often wonder if I am in the midst of being eaten alive, and if I have ever been defining myself for myself or if I have whether or not I will be able to sustain this in the face of the ever-encroaching pressures to succumb to others' expectations. I have to remind myself of another Audre Lorde quote: "When I dare to be powerful, to use my strength in the service of my vision, then it becomes less and less important whether I am afraid."[28]

However, I know that the classroom is where I can continue to take the time to define myself for myself, it can be my space for cultivating a pedagogical praxis that is part of a racial revisioning of higher education and learning more broadly. In this current political moment in the United States, it is crucial to cultivate a classroom where students were not passive consumers but active participants who were enabled to understand why race and racism matter for everyone, and not just people who experience the most egregious racism, prejudice and discrimination. Black feminism and Black radical resistance are foundational to some of our most "courageous acts of rebellion,"[29] which are central to ongoing efforts to eradicate systematic and institutional oppression of all people. The personal is pedagogical, as being in the wake and doing wake work shows us. We can only create an emancipatory learning environment if we are vulnerable and open to the possibility of self-actualization and transformation in the classroom.

BIBLIOGRAPHY

Brown, Adrienne Maree. "what it takes to look." 2011. http://adriennemareebrown .net/2016/09/21/what-it-takes-to-look/.

Collins, Patricia Hill. *Black Feminist Thought: Knowledge, Consciousness, and the Politics of Empowerment*, Routledge: New York and London, 1990.

Diehl, Caleb. Racist, pro-Trump chalk messages found at UC San Diego. *USA Today.* April 11, 2016. http://college.usatoday.com/2016/04/11/racist-pro-trump-chalk -messages-found-at-uc-san-diego/.

Evans, Stephanie Y., Andrea D. Domingue, and Tania D. Mitchell, editors. *Black Women and Social Justice Education: Legacies and Lessons.* New York: SUNY, 2019.

Fordham, Signithia. "'Those loud Black girls': (Black) women, silence, and gender 'passing' in the academy." *Anthropology and Education Quarterly*, 24, no. 1 (1993): 3–32.

Garth, Hanna. "Lost and Delirious in the Anthropology Graduate Application Process: Negotiations of the Self in early Graduate Socialization." *Michigan Discussions in Anthropology,* 18 no.1 (2010): 39–69.

Gasman, Marybeth. "The five things no one will tell you about why colleges don't hire more faculty of color." *The Hechinger Report: Covering Innovation and*

Inequality in Education. Sept 20, 2016. http://hechingerreport.org/five-things-no -one-will-tell-colleges-dont-hire-faculty-color/.

Gasman, Marybeth. "An Ivy League professor on why colleges don't hire more faculty of color: 'We don't want them.'" *Washington Post*, Sept 26, 2016. https://www .washingtonpost.com/news/grade-point/wp/2016/09/26/an-ivy-league-professor -on-why-colleges-dont-hire-more-faculty-of-color-we-dont-want-them/?utm_term =.ded9e4fba125.

Goodman, Trudy. "A Note from Trudy: A conversation with bell hooks & Thich Nhat Hanh." 2018. https://insightla.org/Media/Blog/PostId/34/a-note-from-trudy-a -conversation-with-bell-hooks-thich-nhat-hanh.

Gumbs, Alexis Pauline. "Black Feminism." 2011. http://alexispauline.com/ blackfeminism.html.

Hankins, Joseph D. *Race and Racism Syllabus.* Anthropology Department. University of California San Diego. Microsoft Word File. 2011.

Guy-Sheftall, Beverly, ed. *Words of Fire: An Anthology of African American Feminist Thought.* New York: The New Press, 1995.

hooks, bell. *Teaching to Transgress: Education as the Practice of Freedom.* New York: Routledge, 1994.

Lane, Monique. "Reclaiming Our Queendom: Black Feminist Pedagogy and the Identity Formation of African American Girls." *Equity & Excellence in Education*, 50, no.1 (2017):13–24.

Morris, E. W. "'Ladies' or 'loudies'? Perceptions and experiences of Black girls in classrooms." *Youth and Society*, 38, no.4 (2007): 490–515.

Muhs, Gabriella Gutiérrez y, Yolanda Flores Niemann, Carmen G. González, Angela P. Harris. *Presumed Incompetent: The Intersections of Race and Class for Women in Academia.* Logan: Utah State University Press, 2012.

Ocampo, Anthony Christian. The Latinos of Asia: How Filipino Americans Break the Rules of Race. Redwood City, CA: Stanford University Press, 2016.

Perlow, Olivia N., Durene I. Wheeler, Sharon L. Bethea, Barbara M. Scott. *Black Women's Liberatory Pedagogies: Resistance, Transformation, and Healing Within and Beyond the Academy.* Cham, Switzerland: Palgrave Macmillan, 2018.

Preston, Ashley Robertson. "A Seat at the Table: Mary McLeod Bethune's Call for the Inclusion of Black Women During World War II." In *Black Women and Social Justice Education: Legacies and Lessons*, edited by Stephanie Y. Evans, Andrea D. Domingue, and Tania D. Mitchell, Kindle Edition. New York: SUNY, 2019. Kindle.

Rankine, Claudia. *Citizen: An American Lyric.* Durham: Duke University Press, 2014.

Roland, Kaifa. Cuban Color in Tourism and La Lucha: An Ethnography of Racial Meanings. Oxford: Oxford University Press, 2011.

Sharpe, Christina. *In the Wake: On Blackness and Being.* Durham: Duke University Press, 2016.

Simpson, Audra. *Mohawk Interruptus: Political Life Across the Borders of Settler States.* Durham: Duke University Press, 2014.

Smith, Christen A. "Facing the Dragon: Black Mothering, Sequelae, and Gendered Necropolitics in the Americas." *Transforming Anthropology* 24, no. 2 (2016): 31–48.

Wing, Adrien Katherine. "Brief reflections toward a multiplicative theory and praxis of being." *Critical race feminism: A reader,* edited by Adrien K. Wing, 27–34. New York: New York University Press, 1997.

Wolf-Meyer, Matthew. 2010. "Thinking Through Other Worlds: An Interview with Mei Zhan." *Somatosphere.* May 30, 2010. http://somatosphere.net/2010/05/thinking-through-other-worlds-interview.html.

NOTES

1. Gasman, "An Ivy League professor on why colleges don't hire more faculty of color."

2. Gasman, "The five things no one will tell you about why colleges don't hire more faculty of color."

3. Diehl, "Racist pro-Trump messages found at UC San Diego."

4. Muhs, Niemann, González, and Harris, *Presumed Incompetent.*

5. Brown, "what it takes to look," http://adriennemareebrown.net/2016/09/21/what-it-takes-to-look/.

6. Smith, "Facing the Dragon."

7. Sharpe, *In the Wake*, 78.

8. Sharpe, *In the Wake*, 14.

9. Resources on this include Perlow et al., 2018; Evans et al., 2019; and Muhs et al. 2012.

10. Quote from syllabus of the class "Race and Racism."

11. hooks, *Teaching to Transgress*, 13.

12. hooks, *Teaching to Transgress*, 15.

13. Thich Nhat Hanh, quoted in hooks, *Teaching to Transgress*, 15.

14. Goodman, "A note from Trudy," https://insightla.org/Media/Blog/PostId/34/a-note-from-trudy-a-conversation-with-bell-hooks-thich-nhat-hanh.

15. See Gumbs's 2011 blog post, http://alexispauline.com/blackfeminism.html.

16. Gumbs, "Black Feminism," blog post.

17. Preston, "A Seat at the Table."

18. See, for example, Rankin, *Citizen: American Lyric*, and Sharpe, *In the Wake.*

19. hooks, *Teaching to Transgress*, 18.

20. hooks, *Teaching to Transgress*, 4.

21. Garth, "Lost and Delirious in Anthropology."

22. Patricia Hill Collins, *Black Feminist Thought.*

23. hooks, *Teaching to Transgress*, 15.

24. Lane, "Reclaiming Our Queendom," 14. See also Forham 1992, and Morris 2007.

25. Wing, "Brief reflections toward a multiplicative theory and praxis of being," 31.

26. Wolf-Meyer, "Thinking Through Other Worlds: An Interview with MeiZhan."

27. Wing, "Brief reflections toward a multiplicative theory and praxis of being," 31.
28. Audre Lorde, Second Sex Conference, New York, 1979.
29. Guy-Sheftall, "Introduction," 2.

Chapter Three

Teaching Relationality

Pedagogies Across Asymmetries of Racialization and Colonization

Quynh Nhu Le

As a Vietnamese American, woman-of-color professor, teaching in the fields of comparative race, Asian American, and Indigenous literary studies, my goals in the classroom space are manifold and contingent on the level and topic of the course. However, the course content that I teach and the themes that I engage all center around the mutual empowerment of Black, Indigenous, and People of Color, with a specific attunement to women-of-color voices and critique. This means not only centering the perspectives of marginalized communities in the selection of primary and critical readings that I include in the class, but to highlight specifically how these writers and characters, the textures of their knowledge and experiences, speak to one another, to the students, and to me. Such a pedagogical mooring is deeply inspired by Black womanist, and Indigenous feminist, and women of color epistemologies and critique. Central in their writings is this push toward understanding the asymmetries and yet relationalities of struggles as they are informed by differences of race, colonial histories, gender, sexuality, class, ableism. For Black, Indigenous, and women-of-color feminist thinkers, it is particularly through this lens of *relational difference* that ethical engagement with one another and praxes of solidarity for dismantling white supremacy, gendered violence, and colonial encroachment can be conceptualized and enacted. It is also through relational difference that an even deeper, perhaps more complicated, sense of shared goals can be reached. Indeed, as bell hooks writes: "When women actively struggle in a truly supportive way to understand our differences, to change misguided, distorted perspectives, we lay the foundation for the

35

experience of political solidarity. solidarity is not the same thing as support. To experience solidarity, we must have a community of interests, shared beliefs and goals around which to unite, to build Sisterhood. Support can be occasional. It can be given and just as easily withdrawn. Solidarity requires sustained, ongoing commitment."[1] It is through understanding differences and articulating "shared beliefs and goals" out of the asymmetries that sustained and more occasional moments of solidarity can be possible.

Given the potentiality of centering relational difference, a major goal in my courses is to highlight for students the long history of U.S. gendered racialization and settler colonization and their intimacies.[2] That is, I specifically seek to make visible the relationship and critical differences between these two processes, of racialization and of colonization, which are all too often spoken in tandem in ways that conflate their varying logics and their varying effects on differently positioned communities. BIPOC scholars and activists have long worked to highlight the connections and yet differences between the two processes. In regard to the connections, Jodi Byrd elaborates:

> The two processes of domination have often been conflated (making racism colonialism and vice versa) within the critiques of empire by U.S. postcolonial, comparative area, and queer studies—and for good reason. Racialization and colonization have worked simultaneously to other and abject entire peoples so that they can be enslaved, excluded, removed, and killed in the name of progress and capitalism. These historical and political processes have secured white property, citizenship, and privilege, creating a 'racial contract,' as Charles W. Mills argues that orders 'a world which have been foundationally shaped for the past five hundred years by the realities of European domination and the gradual consolidation of global white supremacy. Racialization and colonization should thus be understood as concomitant global systems that secure white dominance through time, property, and notions of self[3] (xxiii)

While both racialization and colonization are "concomitant global systems" towards the consolidation of white personhood and property, Byrd and other scholars maintain that the settler colonialism in the United States is attached specifically to the seizing of North American Indigenous lands and the logics of elimination and knowledge production that work to elide this violent theft. Because of this, Indigenous formations are structured by, entangled with, but also disarticulated from processes of racialization. Indigenous community organizing with regards to the United States often center issues of territoriality, land/water rights, sovereignty, recognition, and treaties relations. Thus, similar to hooks's warning about the problematics of conflating the struggles of women across such vast differences, Byrd suggests that the conflation of colonization and racialization can elide the different specificities and goals of Indigenous struggles. Byrd maintains:

the conflation of racialization into colonization and indigeneity into racial categories [. . .] masks the territoriality of conquest by assigning colonization to the racialized body, which is then policed in its degrees from whiteness. Under this paradigm, American Indian national assertions of sovereignty, self-determination, and land rights disappear into U.S. territoriality as indigenous identity becomes a racial identity and citizens of colonized indigenous nations become internal ethnic minorities within the colonizing nation-state (xxiv).

This conflation can also elide the role of different communities of color in the continued reproduction of settler colonialism. This is not to say that there can be no solidarity between the struggles of differently positioned communities, but to note that recognizing the differences can provide a necessary blueprint for the common goals and the tensions that might exist in solidarity work. Given the conflation of racialization and colonization in critical theory and ethnic studies writ large, it becomes all the more imperative, and yet all the more difficult, to draw their differences in the classroom space.

In this essay, I elaborate on how this lens of relational difference informs my course content and pedagogical goals and practices in the classroom space. I share the challenges that emerge in the classroom space when discussing these asymmetrical yet intersecting histories and presences. At the same time, I highlight the critical possibilities for generative ethical engagement (by student and teacher) when attending to the relational histories of and ongoing work by communities of color in the Americas. Structured into three sections, I first begin by discussing the difficulties that come with having students grasp the theory and praxis of relational difference. Such difficulties emerge out of the production of Western colonial knowledge at the turn of the fifteenth century and its inheritance in the neoliberal multicultural present. Given such difficulties, I discuss how I come to see that the work toward relational difference emerges through a form of collective *un*learning that is crucial in the classroom space and dynamic. I then move into a discussion of how my strategies of critical juxtaposition (in course readings, content, and dialogue) provide an anchoring methodology that moors me through the intricacies and specificities of each classroom space, student, and classroom text. I conclude with an example of how this pedagogical practice emerges in a specific readings and topics that I often assign for my courses.

Before proceeding, I want to elaborate on my history as a teacher in the university setting. I have been teaching at the University of South Florida for the past few years as a tenure track (and now tenured) professor in English after graduating with a PhD at the University of California, Santa Barbara. While I had taught a few individual courses at UCSB, it has really been at USF where I worked out and refined the specific content and methodologies of the courses I have come to teach over the years. While a multiracial and economically diverse campus, reflected in the demographics of the Tampa Bay area, the classroom space in upper division level courses are often major- ity white students. Often, the classes have an equal number of women and men enrolled. This is different when I teach courses such as "Literature, Race, and Ethnicity" where there is often a greater number of students of color. I see more women, and particularly women of color enroll in these courses over other courses that do not center communities of color. For the most part, however, women of color are still largely underrepresented in my classes. As I teach mostly upper division and graduate level classes, the majority of students are English majors. The difficulties of and my own strategies for conveying the course agenda is thus very specific to the demographics of the student population in USF and their specific experiences living in, moving to, and among people in the Tampa Bay area.

Moreover, like many metropolitan cities, Indigenous peoples are often either completely erased from dominant rhetoric or cordoned materially and metaphorically into reservations. Having lived in different settler spaces such as Denver, Colorado; Santa Barbara, California; Los Angeles, California; and now Tampa, Florida, I see this continued elision of Indigenous presence in the "common sense" rhetoric on race and relations. Given the black/white binaries which inform histories of the South, and its intersections with the Caribbean, the mainstream discussion that centers on race in Florida writ large often effaces the struggles of the Seminole and Miccosukee communi- ties. I see this elision in the classroom space where students provide honest feedback about the lack of knowledge or overdetermined stereotypes that they sometimes carry in regard to Indigenous communities. These dominant social discourses and erasures no doubt affect the outcomes of the courses and student reactions.

COLLECTIVE UNLEARNING

While concepts of relational difference, intersectionality, and the differences between racialization and colonization are central in Black, Indigenous, and women-of-color feminist theories and praxes, it is less prevalent in the University setting writ large and in many English department curriculum and classrooms. Such absence leads to a settler and racial common sense that disallows students to grasp conceptually and affectively the intertwined con- ditions out of which heteropatriarchal, racial, and settler colonial values and institutions emerge.[4] As such, when I am introducing the groundwork theory that centers relational difference, I often anticipate a dissonance that students might experience between grasping the concept and how such concepts are activated on the ground.

This dissonance is connected to the deep entrenchment of racial and colonial production of knowledge and their legacies in the (neo)liberal multicultural moment. Because of such entrenchment, I find that one key element towards the work of relational difference is to engage with a collective *un*learning surrounding heteropatriarchal and colonial knowledge about racialized and colonized communities. Such work begins with unlearning that white writers and thinkers are somehow centers and innovators of critical knowledge and that non-white people are merely objects of study. While the liberal multicultural moment provides the possibilities for a limited celebration of "difference," institutional biases and unchanging curriculum can continue to arbitrate these deeply entrenched racialized and colonial understandings about knowledge as a domain of whiteness. In a similar track, liberal gestures towards forms of inclusion, through tokenization or emphases on diverse representations, still repeat negative and stereotypical renderings (so-called scientific knowledge) of Black, Indigenous, and communities of color in ways that spur scholars like Linda Tuhiwai Smith to proclaim that "research is one of the dirtiest words in Indigenous peoples' vocabulary," and bell hooks to illuminate how schooling in the desegregated South was not "about the practice of freedom."[5] It is toward the work of collectively unlearning the knowledge that situate communities of color as objects of study that one can come to centering such communities as what Lisa Lowe calls subjects of critique.[6] Lowe argues that as subjects of critique, differently racialized and colonized communities can expose the productions of power and concomitant white supremacist logics which undergird histories of racialized and gendered devaluation.

In the classroom space, I seek not only to emphasize the unlearning of white supremacist knowledge that devalue communities of color, but also to emphasize the unlearning of surface (neo)liberal multicultural celebrations of diversity and cultural difference. Indeed, such celebrations of diversity, perhaps the status quo or common sense naturalized under liberal rhetoric, can coopt traditions of resistance into cultural and material capital. In so doing, these seemingly positive gestures towards inclusion support corporate structures and elide the material inequities that continue to persist under racialized, settler colonial, and gendered domination in the United States. Such celebrations of diversity are also especially discordant with Native American/ Indigenous struggles that center around sovereignty, self-determination, territory, and decolonizing epistemologies. The goals of (neo)liberalism flatten the asymmetrical histories of communities of color, and of women of color, and assume that the dismantling of heteropatriarchal colonial systems of power can be enabled under the auspices of national inclusion. In the classroom space, I ask students to query the efficacy of celebrating difference if it cannot attend to the continuation of material inequities across divisions of race, gender, ethnicity, and sexuality.

While the movement from white centered knowledge toward an increasingly multicultural framework can look and feel like a radical shift, they often connect under the common link of liberal capitalism which relies on what Lisa Lowe calls the "intimacies of four continents" or the accumulation of colonial wealth through the co-constitution of colonialism, empire, slavery, cheap labor, and capitalism. Dependent upon these intimacies, liberal capitalism persists through the elisions of these connections and relationalities.[7] This elision of the intimacies of four continents is undergirded by Western epistemologies that posit the self and the other as discrete essentialized entities. For scholars such as Grace Hong and Roderick Ferguson, these epistemological divisions of the self and other make possible both white supremacist and liberal multicultural ideologies. That is, these epistemological divisions make invisible the particularities and yet co-constitution out of which racialized and gendered divisions emerge.[8] Where connections are made, as in the case between racialized and colonized communities, they are registered as simply the same. By relying on these missed dialogues across communities of difference, liberalism builds on what Jodi Byrd calls the "cacophony of empire" where incommensurate dialogue across differently situated communities prevent critical intervention and radical disruptive strategies to take place.

For scholars like Hong and Ferguson, the work of women of color and queer of color critique are crucial to destabilizing such facets through the centering of a relational and shifting analytic. Here, the crucial task of unlearning white supremacist and liberal multicultural epistemologies is replaced by adopting a lens of intersectionality and relationality as a shifting "blueprint." They take Cherríe Moraga's famous train ride, which she discusses in detail in *This Bridge Called My Back*, as illuminative of WOC and QOC critique. In the anthology, Moraga calls for a malleable blueprint that can allow her to trace the relational dynamics of power and privilege, and her placement therein, as she as she takes a tense train ride through the city. Connecting her own light-skin "privilege" to the surveillance of a young Black man on the train, and her friend Julie's racial profiling in the suburbs, Moraga observes: "I want a movement that helps me make some sense of the trip from Watertown to Roxbury, from white to Black. I love women all the way."[9] Of this ride, Hong and Ferguson observe, their relationality is constantly shifting, as Moraga notes when she contrasts Julie's hypervisibility within a white suburb to her invisibility on the subway and when she then juxtaposes Julie with herself and the boy on the train. Moraga's "unmolested" passage through the city, her "protected" status, is complexly determined by, and determining of, the surveillance and disciplining the boy undergoes, as well as the brutal state repression that ends the life of another racialized boy.[10] This shifting blueprint provides an efficacious lens that highlight the asymmetries of inequities and privilege across difference and punctuate how such asymmetries have a shifting relationship to one another. This critical unlearning about the discrete delineations between self/other has an imperative role in the classroom space in order to have students come to the recognition of their own shifting relationship to the continuation of heteropatriarchal colonial and racist power. This is especially pertinent so that students do not so easily detach their own lives as if it were radically unconnected from the lives of communities represented in the texts that I teach. Such unlearning also provides the grounds upon which to activate uncommon dialogue across communities that are often either conflated, seen solely in conflict, or not seen in any crucial or logical relationship at all.

Indigenous epistemologies and Indigenous studies theorizing also provide a crucial groundwork for enabling a critical lens and praxis of relational difference. Here, I draw from Indigenous feminist scholars like Aileen Moreton Robinson and Jodi Byrd, who center Indigenous notions of what Robinson calls inter-substantiation to Indigenous struggles for sovereignty. For such scholars, Indigenous knowledge and stories, long the target of annihilation by colonists, carry important ethical visions/lenses with which to relate with human and non-human others. Given that such knowledge is continually under duress under settler colonialism, the work of sovereignty is linked deeply to the maintenance of worldviews that counteract the destructive white supremacist colonial way of thinking. Robinson writes:

Our sovereignty is embodied, it is ontological (our being) and epistemological (our way of knowing), and it is grounded within complex relations derived from the intersubstantiation of ancestral beings, humans and land. In this sense, our sovereignty is carried by the body and differs from Western constructions of sovereignty, which are predicated on the social contract model, the idea of unified supreme authority, territorial integrity, and individual rights.[11]

Robinson's quote is especially meaningful for me given how any goals toward achieving forms of relational difference is critically bound with the goal toward Indigenous sovereignty and self-determination. Thus, the analytic that Moraga sets up not only needs to attend to the different bodies in city spaces, but also on whose *grounds* such spaces emerge.

CRITICAL JUXTAPOSITION

This kind of collective unlearning does not come instantaneously or solely from an instructor centered or a lecture heavy model. As bell hooks convincingly suggests, "it is rare that any professor, no matter how eloquent a lecturer, can generate through his or her actions enough excitement to create an exciting classroom. Excitement is generated through collective effort. Seeing the classroom always as a communal place enhances the likelihood of collective effort in creating and sustaining a learning community."[12] In my own classes, the project of unlearning dominant paradigms and embodying relational difference often emerges through the critical juxtaposition of people, communities, readings, activities, assignments, and discussions. I speak about "critical juxtaposition" here as a methodology that infuses its way into the construction of my syllabi, the in-class activities, presentations, and discussions, and the kinds of assignments that are created. I do so by often placing two or more (often unrelated) communities, works, or discourses in adjacency in order to generate a kind of productive tension or friction where previously submerged conversations or knowledge can arise. This notion of critical juxtaposition provides an anchoring point in drawing me and the classroom consistently toward the main imperatives of relational difference that inform my courses.

I believe that critical juxtaposition is inherent in any collective space, where different worldviews meet, connect, and collide. I work to nourish this space through the integration of professor and student-lead discussions, presentations, and activities. The assignments also reflect critical juxtaposition by allowing students to read, and integrate, multiple texts and contexts beyond disciplinary boundaries. Here, I invest in sharing and having students share news stories, images, music, political cartoons, social media stories, that might pertain to the critical topic or readings for the day. I see that when students are invited to share their varied knowledge, they create points of access (and necessary points of productive tension) for other students (and for myself) to destabilize common sense worldviews.

I find that when students are comfortable in sharing with one another, open to destabilizing rigid ideologies, that my role in the classroom is to have students come in contact with voices that are not as readily representable in the discussion. For example, given how normalized settler colonial occupation has become in the Américas, my role is often to ask students to confront directly how Indigenous land and sovereignty are erased in any discussions of social justice. In the construction of course syllabi, I consistently place BIPOC texts in conversation whether through the inclusion of primary and/ or secondary works. For example, in an "Asian American Literature" class, I include both primary or critical texts that draw out the conversations about cross-racial relationalities. Novels like Karen Tei Yamashita's *Through the Arc of the Rain Forest*, for example, work well as it directly conveys the relationship between Asian racialization, anti-blackness, and Indigenous dispossession across the hemisphere. I also include critical works that might draw out cross-community conversations in texts that do not readily give way to such discussion. When having students read Lois Ann Yamanaka's *Blu's Hanging*, a novel about a Nikkei (persons of Japanese descent) family set in Hawai'i, I have students also read Haunani Kay Trask's and Candace Fujikane's works, both of which analyze the erasures of Indigenous presence even in fiction by communities of color. I find it generative to have the class query why there are gaps and erasures in the texts themselves and to question Western epistemologies that make these erasures a common phenomenon.[13]

In all my classes, I work to include BIPOC women's voices in both primary and secondary readings. These selections are important to have students attend to the differences across women of color communities. For example, the experiences of Native American/Indigenous women are effects of a gendered settler colonial imposition and thus the mobilization of decolonial efforts must also attend to these distinct histories. Native women in the United States and Canada were often subject to anti-miscegenation laws that stripped them of Indian status were they to marry outside of the tribe. These laws impacted the strength and sovereignty of Indigenous nations given the many Native nations with matriarchal structures and the centering of Native women as leaders in their communities.[14] Gendered violence of Indigenous women are thus both the effects of a white supremacist racial structure as well as of genocidal logics tied to settler colonial investment in land and property. This investment in settler colonial land, property, and personhood is also enacted (albeit differently) through settler violence on Black women's bodies. As scholar Tiffany Lethabo King writes in regards to Black fungibility, "While Black slave labor and other forms of exploited labor are constitutive of the political economy, the slave is essential as an object of negation for the construction of the master's notion of self. As what Wilderson would describe as 'accumulable' and what Hartman would call a 'fungible' object, the slave is a Spillerian open space of sensual pleasure to be used indefinitely."[15] King continues with regards to Native women: "within Native feminism, one finds another unflinching interrogation of how the conquistador human produces "flesh." Flesh in the form of the "scalp,' 'the sq—,' and the Indigenous woman's womb becomes space that confronts the violence of murder and conquest every day. The flesh and the violence of making flesh is a grammatical system that circulates within both Native feminist and decolonial thought and Black studies."[16] Citing missing and murdered Indigenous women (MMIW) such as Marlene Bird of Saskatchewan and Tina Fontaine in Winnipeg, Manitoba, King reveals the ongoing legacy of violence against Black and Indigenous women from the beginnings of conquest (which she cites as 1441) to today. Indigenous Latinx women are also among the missing and murdered when we consider the femicides in Ciudad Juarez. In the class, I seek to connect this with the violence on Asian/Asian American women's bodies produced out of U.S. imperial wars in Asia. Seeing the links and yet differences between forms of gendered violence across BIPOC communities can provide a basis to think beyond liberal frameworks of settler colonial inclusion and can provide potent critical language through which to imagine otherwise.

CRITICAL REFUGEE LITERATURE
THROUGH RELATIONAL DIFFERENCE

To illuminate how both collective unlearning and critical juxtaposition occurs in my classes, I now turn to a specific example. A key element to engaging critical juxtaposition in the classroom space is the sharing of *my own* iden- tifications and positionality in relation to the class, the readings, and our conversations about these intersecting histories. As a Vietnamese American, heterosexual, cis-gendered woman, I usually try to include refugee narratives centering specifically on Southeast Asian refugee subjects when the course topic permits. Students are often quite compelled by the history of the Vietnam War given its legacy in popular U.S. memory. Because of the overdetermina- tion surrounding narratives of the Vietnam War and its continued legacies today, I begin any discussions about a Vietnamese American literary work by asking students what they know about Vietnam. With variation, students often rehearse dominant discourses about Vietnam being a "difficult war," one that demonstrates U.S. weakness and violence, and one that many try to forget.[17] When it is remembered in dominant discourse, it is often conjured as a spectral presence that haunts contemporary U.S. military operations, for example in regard to the Iraq War. Sometimes, students bring up the violence of the My Lai Massacre and the institutional and social abandonment of U.S. soldiers when they come home. What usually gets elided, at least in the initial discussion, is the fact that Vietnam is not a war, but a country. In addition, discussions of the Vietnam War center on the violent collisions between the United States and Vietnam, but often erase the war's haunting aftermath in the case of the mass movements of Vietnamese refugees via boat to the United States in the post-1975 era or legacies of chemical warfare on the lands and bodies of the people.

While the discussion of Vietnamese refugees, and their often traumatic experiences, will disrupt Euro-American-centric narratives about Vietnam, I also want to be careful that such discussion not spillover into renderings of refugees as abject or passive figures who are in need of saving by the United States.[18] As scholar Yen Le Espiritu argues, such liberal discourse work to re-narrate U.S. loss in Vietnam as an ultimate victory through the triumph of the liberal United States as a savior and a humanitarian nation. Through critical juxtapositions of primary and secondary readings, with in-depth ques- tions and discussions that center the Vietnamese refugee racialized experi- ences in the United States, the class begins to collectively unlearn dominant

Euro-American-centric and liberal narratives of the war and their concomitant structures of feeling.

For me, however, the story cannot end there. In engaging in such texts, I also ask students to critically juxtapose Vietnamese refugee experiences in relation to the experiences of other BIPOC during the time period. Here, Vietnamese American narratives often fall short as they can invoke white/Asian or immigrant/citizen paradigms central in earlier Asian American works. For example, Lan Cao's *Monkey Bridge*, one of the earliest novels about the war by a Vietnamese American woman, does important and crucial work of centering Vietnamese refugee traumatic experiences during the war and ambivalence arriving to the United States. The novel also recenters Vietnamese women's experiences of war and their aftermaths through its depiction of a mother and daughter's relationship after arrival to the United States. This facet of the novel intervenes in dominant renderings of the war that highlights the impact of the war on the male soldiers deployed to fight for the United States. Despite its gendered intervention, the narrative often binds to racial binaries (White/Asian) which obscures the impact of the war on other BIPOC in the United States. In addition, Vietnamese arrival in the United States can take as a given the settler sovereignty of the state without question, thus indirectly reinvoking settler norms that erase Indigenous communities. This repetition of a static racial binary erases BIPOC war veterans as well as the politics of refugee resettlement on occupied Indigenous lands. In the case of Cao's novel, the centering of placemaking as a refugee enterprise can reveal the ways that the gendered dimensions of creating a "home" relies on settler spaces and logics.

By querying these erasures through an ethical anchoring of relational difference, with the centering on gendered representations, students not only connect Vietnamese refugee experiences with the experiences of BIPOC, but also to the potential lacuna of knowledge which haunts any understanding of "Vietnam." Reading the novel through the centering of black womanist, critical race, and Indigenous studies perspectives provide opportunities for students to think through how Vietnamese refugee women's experiences are always already entangled in a broader inheritance and dynamic of settler colonialism, anti-blackness, and asymmetrical forms of racialization. In revealing these entanglements through literature, I engage students in the process of tracing forms of gendered resistance embedded in the narrative that might otherwise be erased.

CONCLUSION

While the work in the classroom space is limited given the time constraints, my goal is for the class members to create a deep enough impression among each other that when they leave the class, they continue to work toward investing in the work to dismantling the complex and vexed systems of power that maintain privilege and capital for so few at the cost of non-human and human communities. That is, I encourage students to draw from the inspiration of Black and Indigenous women who have, as scholars Olivia N. Perlow, Durene I. Wheeler, Sharon L. Bethea, and BarBara M. Scott suggest, "historically been at the forefront of liberation efforts through both formal and informal education where they have engaged in what Rochelle Brock has termed a 'pedagogy of life,' teaching resistance in various capacities."[19] While student responses to my classes, whether formal or informal evaluations, show that they do leave with paradigm shifting views and impressions, I can only know so much of what kind of impact can be made. What I do know (and this provides me with some understanding of the crucial work of the classroom as spaces of freedom and radical liberatory visions) are the ways that students also change and challenge my worldviews. Their knowledge, when in productive tension with each other and with my own, allows me to engage with the elisions that structure my own understanding of the world. Having taught in Tampa now several years (after living primarily in the Southwest/Western regions of the United States) has led me to understanding the specificities of racial formations and settler colonialism in this part of the United States all the more. Literary and theorical readings can only do so much in informing any knowledge about the processes of power and its impact and effects on different communities. The students give me the language, the feeling, and texture of their worlds in ways that allow me to imagine new ways to practice pedagogies that center decolonization, antiracism, and social justice.

BIBLIOGRAPHY

Byrd, Jodi. *The Ends of Empire*. Minneapolis: University of Minnesota Press, 2011.

Espiritu, Yen Le. *Body Counts: The Vietnam War and Militarized Refugees.* Berkeley: University of California Press, 2015.

Fujikane, Candace, and Jonathan Y. Okamura. Eds. *Asian Settler Colonialism: From Local Governance to the Habits of Everyday Life in Hawai'i*. Honolulu: University of Hawai'i Press, 2008.

Hong, Grace Kyungwon, and Roderick Ferguson. *Strange Affinities: The Gender and Sexual Politics of Racialization.* Durham: Duke University Press, 2011.

hooks, bell. *Teaching to Transgress*. New York: Routledge, 1994.

hooks, bell. "Sisterhood: Political Solidarity Between Women." *Feminist Review* 23.1 (1986): 125–38.

King, Tiffany Lethabo. *The Black Shoals: Offshore Formations of Black and Native Studies*. Durham: Duke University Press, 2019.

Lawrence, Bonita. *"Real" Indians and Others: Mixed-Blood Urban Native Peoples and Indigenous Nationhood.* Lincoln: University of Nebraska Press, 2004.

Lowe, Lisa. *The Intimacies of Four Continents*. Durham: Duke University Press, 2015.

Moraga, Cherríe, and Gloria Anzaldúa. *This Bridge Called My Back*. New York: Kitchen Table, 1983.

Perlow, Olivia N., Durene I. Wheeler, Sharon L. Bethea, and BarBara M. Scott. Eds. *Black Women's Liberatory Pedagogies: Resistance, Transformation, and Healing Within and Beyond the Academy*. London: Palgrave MacMillan, 2017.

Robinson, Aileen Moreton. *Sovereign Subjects: Indigenous Sovereignty Matters.* Crows Nest NSW: Allen and Unwin, 2007.

Rifkin, Mark. *Settler Common Sense: Queerness and Everyday Colonialism in the American Renaissance.* Minneapolis: University of Minnesota Press, 2014.

Trask, Haunani Kay. "Settlers of Color and 'Immigrant' Hegemony." *Amerasia Journal* 26.2 (2000):1–24.

NOTES

1. bell hooks, "Sisterhood: Political Solidarity Between Women," *Feminist Review* 23, no. 1 (1986): 138.

2. Here, I use the term "intimacies" to reference Lisa Lowe's discussion about the interrelatedness of these histories. See, Lisa Lowe, *The Intimacies of Four Continents* (Durham: Duke University Press, 2015).

3. Jodi Byrd, *The Ends of Empire* (Minneapolis: University of Minnesota Press, 2011): xxiii.

4. For a discussion of "settler common sense," see Mark Rifkin, *Settler Common Sense: Queerness and Everyday Colonialism in the American Renaissance* (Minneapolis: University of Minnesota Press, 2014).

5. Linda Tuhiwai Smith, *Decolonizing Methodologies* (New York: Zed Books, 1999): 1; bell hooks, *Teaching to Transgress* (New York: Routledge, 1994): 3. As Smith attests: "When mentioned in many indigenous contexts, it stirs up silence, it conjures up bad memories, it raises a smile that is knowing and distrustful. It is so powerful that indigenous people even write poetry about research. The ways in which scientific research is implicated in the worst excesses of colonialism remains a powerful remembered history for many of the world's colonized peoples. It is a history that still offends the deepest sense of our humanity. Just knowing that someone measured our 'faculties' by filling the skulls of our ancestors with millet seed to the capacity for mental thought offends our sense of who and what we are" (1).

6. Lisa Lowe, *Immigrant Acts: On Asian American Cultural Politics* (Durham: Duke University Press, 1996). Lowe speaks on subjects of critique specifically in the Asian American context. She writes: "[Their] distance from the national culture

constitutes Asian American culture as an alternative formation that produces cultural expressions materially and aesthetically at odds with the resolution of the citizen in the nation. Rather than expressing a 'failed' integration of Asians into the American cultural sphere, this distance preserves Asian American culture as an alternative site where the palimpsest of lost memories is reinvented, histories are fractured and retraced, and the unlike varieties of silence emerge into articulacy" (6).

7. Lisa Lowe, *The Intimacies of Four Continents*, 39. As Lowe suggests: "Colonized peoples created the conditions for liberal humanism, despite the disavowal of these conditions in the European political philosophy on which it is largely based. Racial classifications and an international division of labor emerged coterminously as parts of a genealogy that were not exceptional to, but were constitutive of, that humanism. 'Freedom' was constituted through a narrative dialectic that rested simultaneously on a spatialization of the 'unfree' as exteriority and a temporal subsuming of that unfreedom as internal difference or contradiction. The 'overcoming' of internal contradiction resolves in 'freedom' within the modern Western political sphere through displacement and elision of the coeval conditions of settler dispossession, slavery, and indentureship in the Americas. In this sense, modern liberal humanism is a formalism that translates the world through an economy of affirmation and forgetting within a regime of desiring freedom" (39).

8. Grace Kyungwon Hong and Roderick Ferguson, *Strange Affinities: The Gender and Sexual Politics of Racialization* (Durham: Duke University Press, 2011): 10.

9. Cherríe Moraga and Gloria Anzaldúa, *This Bridge Called My Back* (New York: Kitchen Table, 1983): xlv.

10. Grace Kyungwon Hong and Roderick Ferguson, *Strange Affinities*, 10.

11. Aileen Moreton Robinson, *Sovereign Subjects: Indigenous Sovereignty Matters* (Crows Nest NSW: Allen and Unwin, 2007): 211.

12. bell hooks, *Teaching to Transgress*, 8.

13. See Haunani Kay Trask, "Settlers of Color and 'Immigrant' Hegemony," *Amerasia Journal* 26:2 (2000):1–24. See also, Candace Fujikane and Jonathan Y. Okamura, *Asian Settler Colonialism: From Local Governance to the Habits of Everyday Life in Hawai'i* (Honolulu: University of Hawai'i Press, 2008).

14. See Bonita Lawrence's *"Real" Indians and Others: Mixed-Blood Urban Native Peoples and Indigenous Nationhood* (Lincoln: University of Nebraska Press, 2004) for a discussion of gendered restrictions through the Indian Act in Canada.

15. Tiffany Lethabo King, *The Black Shoals: Offshore Formations of Black and Native Studies* (Durham: Duke University Press, 2019): 61.

16. Tiffany Lethabo King, *The Black Shoals: Offshore Formations of Black and Native Studies* (Durham: Duke University Press, 2019): 55. I have crossed out the word "sq---."

17. See Yen Le Espiritu's *Body Counts: The Vietnam War and Militarized Refugees* (Berkeley: University of California Press, 2015) for a discussion about popular media depictions of the Vietnam War.

18. See Yen Le Espiritu's *Body Counts: The Vietnam War and Militarized Refugees* for a discussion of the refugee figure as passive and abject. For Espiritu, the rendering of the refugee figure as a passive and abject figure feeds into the narrative of U.S.

Page

dominance and might. Refugees, Espiritu suggests, are often beholden to the feeling of gratitude for being rescued.

19. Olivia N. Perlow, Durene I. Wheeler, Sharon L. Bethea, and BarBara M. Scott, eds., *Black Women's Liberatory Pedagogies: Resistance, Transformation, and Healing Within and Beyond the Academy* (London: Palgrave MacMillan, 2017): 1.

Chapter Four

I am that, *too*

Integrating the Black Woman into the First Year Composition Classroom

Kendra N. Bryant

In a pedagogical context, I was stumped when I was invited to compose an essay describing my feminist classroom. *"My feminist classroom?"* I asked—to which editor Gary Lemons responded: *Yes. I'd like you to write an essay explaining how you integrate feminism into your composition classroom.* My immediate response to myself was: *"Holy shit. I don't."* However, as a tenure track assistant professor who had worked at three different universities—and was beginning a new contract at the fourth—I was eager for a publication that would maintain my relevance and scholarly track record: I had to produce at least one publication a year, especially since I was moving from one university to the next searching for my academic "home." With that endeavor in mind, coupled with my own surprise (and embarrassment) regarding the absence of a feminist agenda in my composition courses, I set out to compose an essay about *my* "feminist" classroom—much of which I thought would be bullshit. But I needed a publication, so I was willing to wade in the stench.

I began my research by first reading a few of the Black feminist scholars I knew of and who were leading "experts" in the field: bell hooks, Patricia Hill Collins, and Beverly Guy-Sheftall. I knew of no one else beyond them, and *that* was frustrating. I have a whole PhD in rhetoric and composition, a master's of English education, and a bachelor's degree in journalism, yet my limited knowledge of Black feminism made me feel like an imposter. I'm Black. I'm female. I'm a woman. Yet, I have no idea what it means to be a Black feminist. Do my race and gender automatically render me an identified participant of the Black feminist movement? Do my academic credentials, coupled with my race and gender, imply my Black feminist thought? Should I have come across Black feminist discourse with all the access to information technology now affords us? I wasn't sure I could pull off this essay—that it was within my creative reach—until I recalled Alice Walker's *In Search Of Our Mothers' Gardens*.[1]

Walker's 1983 text has been sitting on my shelves since my eighth-grade teacher gifted it to me. (And, of course, I felt even more inadequate regarding my ignorance of Black feminism. I *owned* Alice Walker's collection of womanist prose since 1993, and here I am—almost a quarter into the twenty-first century, and I'm ignorant about Black feminism.) Even so, I read Walker's front matter where she introduces and defines *womanism*—and just to be clear: I had already read Walker's text, and years prior, had even developed and taught a first-year composition curriculum themed on Alice Walker's works, but I did not *consciously* instruct from a Black feminist (or womanist) perspective. And *that* negligence bewilders me. And so, I *reread* Walker's four-part *womanist* definition, and as I pondered it—savoring especially the part about "lov[ing] other women, sexually and/or nonsexually"[2]—I remembered what I read about Walker during my initial research in Collins' brief acknowledgment of womanist theory: "Alice Walker's preference for the term *womanist* addresses the notion of the solidarity of humanity," Collins says [author's emphasis],[3] before explicating Walker's definitions of *womanist*, particularly part two wherein Walker defines a *womanist* as one "committed to the survival and wholeness of entire people."[4] Collins continues: "By redefining all people as 'people of color,' Walker universalizes what are typically seen as individual struggles while simultaneously allowing space for autonomous movements of self-determination."[5] Collins then refers to the social politics of Pauli Murray—Black woman civil rights activist, lawyer, Episcopal priest (who probably would identify as a trans man in this century)—who wrote in her 1970 "The Liberation of Black Women":

> A built-in hazard of an aggressive ethnocentric movement which disregards the interests of other disadvantaged groups is that it will become parochial and ultimately self-defeating in the face of hostile reactions, dwindling allies, and mounting frustrations . . . Only a broad movement for human rights can prevent the Black Revolution from becoming isolated and can ensure ultimate success.[6]

"Without a commitment to human solidarity and social justice," writes Collins, "any political movement—whether Black nationalist, feminist, or anti-elitist—may be doomed to ultimate failure."[7] And boom! The light bulb finally illuminated my dark spaces: I don't know that to which I don't identify. I am not a Black feminist. I am Alice Walker's *womanist*.

If this is true, if I am a womanist, then why didn't womanism first register to me when Lemons queried me about my feminist approaches to teaching composition? Why hasn't womanism grounded my instruction? *Has* womanism grounded my instruction? Does it matter if my womanism was unconsciously delivered? Herein began my research into myself—a self who feels more like a womanist than a feminist, but who realized my composition courses reflected a Black nationalist agenda—that "backward" movement, centered on Black male masculinity. How did that happen?

SAY IT LOUD! I'M BLACK AND I'M PROUD!

In *The Courage to Teach: Exploring the Inner Landscape of a Teacher's Life*, Parker J. Palmer asserts that . . . "seldom, if ever, do we ask the 'who' question—who is the self that teaches? How does the quality of my self-hood form—or deform—the way I relate to my students, my subject, my colleagues, my world?"[8] Before Alice Walker coined the term *womanist*, she, undoubtedly, was a civil rights activist quite aware of the race and class differences that rendered her merely "Negro." As expressed in her 1967 "The Civil Rights Movement: What Good Was It?" and later reiterated in reports by Walker biographer Evelyn White,[9] Walker's waking up to herself was caused by her watching on television Martin Luther King being arrested for his involvement in Alabama protests. According to Walker, she saw in King "the hero for whom [she] had waited so long,"[10] for King insisted on nonviolence, love, and brotherhood despite an often-muted reception. Nonetheless, "[b]ecause of the Movement," writes a twenty-three-year-old Walker, "because of an awakened faith in the newness and imagination of the human spirit, because of 'black and white together' . . . I have fought harder for my life and for a chance to be myself, to be something more than a shadow or a number."[11] I share Walker's sentiments. Although I was not born a year before World War II in rural Georgia to sharecropping parents, nor did I live inside the 1960s Civil Rights Movement, the "faith in the newness and imagination of the human spirit, because of 'black and white together'" has centered the self to which I most identify—a racialized Black self with whom I've been (un)consciously acquainted since middle school, since the early 1990s.

As a middle schooler, I began my civil rights movement. I believed I was Blackity Black with purpose, although my daddy reminded me that I was a revolutionary with no cause—and he did not necessarily, or at least, not blatantly, provide me with one to which I needed to bear arms. As a middle schooler, I knew nothing about Bill Clinton's "three strikes" crime bill. I had no idea Rodney King was part of a long legacy of police brutality against Black bodies. And I was unaware of the mammy figure portrayed in *Good*

Times; the white savior archetype in *Different Strokes*; and the jezebel figure placed on Anita Hill (while Clarence Thomas was a real-life Uncle Tom). Reflecting on those missteps, as well as the more mainstream happenings of the 1990s, I really was just suckin' and jivin'—and maybe as a middle schooler my parents wanted to give me the freedom to do just that: to be "foot loose and fancy free," uninhibited by hegemonic structures intended to maintain my subjugation.

Nonetheless, with popular phrases such as, "the blacker the berry, the sweeter the juice" and "the blacker the college, the sweeter the knowledge," floating around the early 1990s—detached from critical thought—the notion of systemic racism and sexist oppression, didn't penetrate my consciousness. Sure, Queen Latifah[12] was rapping "ladies first," and Public Enemy[13] was telling us to "fight the power," but besides jamming to those songs—alongside the 2 Live Crew's[14] "Pop that Coochie"—I was not *listening* to lyrics more than I was just hearing the music and mindlessly repeating the chorus. It was a mimicry mirroring my response to Spike Lee's 1992 *Malcolm X* biopic, which premiered two years after Queen Latifah and Public Enemy's albums dropped.

Nobody could tell me my Baptist-born self wasn't a born-again Muslim after watching Denzel Washington play Malcolm X. I think most of Black America wanted to be Muslim after witnessing the Black power Malcolm X seemed to carry and express in his street activism. I found myself begging my mother to buy me an African medallion necklace from Hassan, the Muslim brother who sold them and *The Final Call* on the corner of 27th Avenue and 183rd street—the intersection that led us to our house. I wanted to be suited up like him, too—with bow tie and all. Muslims—these Black men dressed in suits, standing in Malcolm X's unrivaled genius and courage, spittin' a rhetorical swagger that called me to their attention—was what the revolution looked like to me. And I wanted to be *that*, down to changing my name, which never sounded Black enuf to me (and for others to mispronounce). But unlike Alice Walker's Dee,[15] I did not change my name; instead, I led "revolutions" through extracurricular school activities.

I was the president of the middle school's Afro-American Heritage Club, where I participated in Theodore Gibson Oratory Contests and Afro-American Heritage Bowls; traveled out of town to Atlanta and Washington, exploring the city's Black history; and engaged in volunteer weekend clean ups of Black-owned grave sites in Overtown Miami. I also participated in the school's Black History Month activities, and throughout the school year, made sure every project my teachers assigned me reflected my Black history: From constructing a replica of Garret A. Morgan's first traffic signal to writing a myth with African characters, creating a newspaper I called *The*

African Gazette and memorizing Abiodun Oyewole's[16] "A Protest Poem for Rosa Parks," I *was* Black history. I mean, I was wearing dashikis *before* they were in vogue—long *after* Black History Month ended. But what I did not realize about the Black nationalist movement I was mimicking was the sexism that was prohibiting it from being a *universalist* movement. According to Walker, the Black nationalist movement was "a movement *backward* from the equalitarian goals of the sixties" [author's emphasis].[17]

In her 1973 essay, "Choosing to Stay at Home: Ten Years after the March on Washington," Walker explains why she decided to stay in the South to counter racism, and thus responds to northern news regarding "'nationalist wom[e]n [who] cannot create or initiate.'"[18] Black nationalist women's oppression by Black nationalist men "is heartbreaking," she says. "Not just for black women who have struggled so equally against the forces of oppression, but for all who believe subservience of any kind is death to the spirit."[19] Walker then recalls Sojourner Truth, Harriet Tubman, and Fannie Lou Hamer—Black women activists, none of whom had even marginalized my composition curriculum. These Black women, who I had known, I shelved, just like I did Walker's *In Search of Our Mothers' Gardens*—which, now that I think of it, my eighth-grade teacher probably gifted me so I might be acquainted with the womanist self I had yet to discover.

Unlike hooks and many other Black women who profess to having experienced "varying degrees of patriarchal tyranny"[20] in their households, which thus acquainted them to the feminist struggle, "[m]y awareness of feminist struggle was [*not*] stimulated by social circumstance [emphasis mine]."[21] I was reared in a middle-class household where my father and grandfathers were more maternal than my mother and grandmothers were expected to be. Even my childhood best friend's father was more "nourishing" than her mother, and in neither of our households did our parents assume traditional husband/wife, female/male roles. Those binaries and ultimate hierarchies just weren't visible in my childhood household, neither were they in the other middle-class households I visited. As such, sexism never quite occurred to my young self, which is the most impressionable self, thus making race that more visible to me.

Race, this very visible thing I wore, was as persuasive as the Black Panther's militant black attire, and so, it led my relationship with myself sans sexuality, gender, and class. As a result, my "movement" failed to address the intersectionality implicit in creating overlapping social identities that thus produce "compounding experiences of discrimination."[22] In other words, my movement mirrored the "parochial" approach Murray articulated was doomed to failure. Obviously, I was unaware of Kimberlé Crenshaw's intersectionality theory, conceptualized in her 1989 "Demarginalizing the Intersection of

Race and Sex"—although theorized years prior in Anna Julia Cooper's 1892 *A Voice from the South*; Frances Beal's 1969 "double jeopardy"; and the Combahee River Collective's 1977 Black feminist statement. Nonetheless, I was only ten years old in 1989. I am still trying to wrap my head around my into-adulthood-ignorance, especially considering I am Black, I am a woman, *and* I'm lesbian. bell hooks offers some clarity.

THIS IS A MAN'S WORLD

In a line from a dialogue in Wendell B. Harris' 1989 film, *Chameleon Street*, this statement is made: "I'm a victim of four hundred years of conditioning. The man has programmed my conditioning. Even my conditioning has been conditioned."[23] In the introduction to her 1981 *Ain't I a Woman?* hooks explains:

> Contemporary black women could not join together to fight for women's rights because we did not see 'womanhood' as an important aspect of our identity. Racists, sexist socialization had conditioned us to devalue our femaleness and to regard race as the only relevant label of identification. In other words, we were asked to deny a part of ourselves—and we did. . . . We clung to the hope that liberation from racial oppression would be all that was necessary for us to be free. We were a new generation of black women who had been taught to submit, to accept sexual inferiority, and to be silent.[24]

Those "new generation of black women who had been taught to be silent" include my mother, my grandmothers, my grade-school teachers, my aunts. They were quiet about sexuality, gender, class—which doesn't suggest their personal submission or feelings of sexual inferiority, per se; but may be more about the success of the meta narrative—the political agenda pushed through and reinforced by the hegemonic structures that ensure white privilege and superiority, that subdue working class folks into consenting to capitalistic behaviors and neoliberalist ideals of individualism.

Inarguably, the way we talk about race matters (or not), as well as all the other isms, including feminism, is so ingrained inside white male heteronormativity, we blindly consent and submit to practices that maintain what hooks calls "white supremacist capitalist patriarchy."[25] So, of course I could undergo over twenty years of formal education and be none the wiser about Black feminism, which insists on the intersectionality Crenshaw may have formally conceptualized, but has been theorized since Sojourner Truth's 1851 "Ain't I a Woman?" School, after all, is a hegemonic structure. And although some academic programs (not mine) offer students courses in critical race theory, social justice, and women's and gender studies, school is structured just as myopically as my middle school "movements." In other words, students accumulate subjects like they do their identities, and rarely, if ever, are students taught or encouraged to consider the intersectionality of the subjects they've consumed. Without critical thinking skills grounded in synthesizing practices, how do students learn to read across texts, across subjects, across histories?

How do students learn about and garner appreciation for the genius and courage of the Harlem Renaissance without conversations regarding the post-Reconstruction era and the Great Migration? How do they understand Amiri Baraka's Black Arts Movement if they don't discuss the racism, classism, and sexism generating from the Beat Generation? How do students consciously practice composition skills without some discussion on Aristotle, Cicero, and Plato—of Egyptian hieroglyphs?

Additionally, rarely, if at all, are students—or in my case, English doctoral students—provided with the language and theories by which to understand systemic racism, classism, and sexism beyond our materialized experiences of them—especially when "88 percent of all teachers in schools are [w]hite women,"[26] who often fall inside the "teacher education gap"[27] that almost trapped me. While I absolutely value real life experience and understand the pitfalls of intellectualizing race+ matters, *I* require an instruction—even if it's just a nudging toward—that invites me into a deeper thinking about, a queered reading,[28] if you will, of myself in relationship to others so I might be less ethnocentric in my being. For, it was an ethnocentric[29] self, grounded in race matters alone that entered my classroom instruction, thus further marginalizing (via erasure) the queered[30] person. As such, I was complicit in maintaining the hegemonic order.

With that said, for the first ten years I taught first-year composition—from FAMU to University of North Georgia to Florida International University—I have grounded my writing assignments on the rhetorical genius of Martin Luther King Jr. Unfortunately, because I neither grasped the concept of Black feminism nor consciously identified as womanist, "human rights" translated into eradicating racial oppression—sans classism and sexism. Furthermore, as hooks explains, because I am the product of twentieth-century Black communities who revered and respected Black men of the civil rights movement—an attitude that is reinforced via American education and mass media—my King curriculum further promoted "the establishment of black male patriarchy."[31] While I definitely believe King's rhetoric belongs in the composition classroom, my failure to juxtapose his voice with Black women like Fannie Lou Hamer, June Jordan, and even Coretta Scott King, actually prohibited me from providing my composition students a writing practice that explored Walker's notion regarding "survival and wholeness of people, male *and* female."

Therefore, I entered the composition classroom as a Black woman whose pedagogical practices were constructed within a Black male patriarchy that muted the polyvocalism of Black women—at least three with whom I identify: I am Black. I am a Woman. I am a Lesbian—the latter two of which I didn't consider in my heteronormative Black male constructed classroom. As such, I have summoned writing students to social activism via Black male, heterosexist speech, which further advanced the white male patriarchy—to which, I am convinced, I was coerced when I consented to being trained in rhetoric and composition solely through the Greco-Roman lens upon which Western education is grounded. Nevertheless, although the Black male orators I've brought into my writing classrooms inevitably encouraged students to exercise their humane selves, I was not aware of my omitting the Black female voice from participating in such liberatory classroom practices until editor Gary Lemons invited me to contribute to this collection.

The truth of the matter is, "We [classroom teachers] teach who we are,"[32] and when Lemons asked me to contribute to this collection, I neither identified with nor knew much about Black feminism, nor did I consciously associate myself with womanism. I had not purposely constructed my writing classroom within an aggregated womanist framework. I had neither assigned nor created reading and writing tasks with the intention of engaging my composition students in writing exercises that purposely explored womanist thought and practice. Instead, I've occupied my composition students in reading and writing practices that are *"traditionally* universalist" [emphasis mine], for assignments, as well as my communicated instruction, insisted on freedom via racial harmony between country*men* who praise a male God. Thus, by channeling my "commitment to survival and wholeness of entire people" through a myopic ethnocentric lens reflecting a Black self, committed to human rights, I used the writing classroom as a social activist space that explored race matters by privileging the male voice.

Undoubtedly, as Wendell B. Harris claims in his 1989 independent film, *Chameleon Street,* "My conditioning has been conditioned." As a result, I, too, believed "that problems black women faced were [solely] caused by racism—not sexism."[33] And I carried that racial belief about the problems Black women faced into every facet of my life, including my burgeoning career as a writing teacher. I privileged King over Sojourner Truth, heterosexuality over homosexuality, and status quo over authenticity. My writing classroom wasn't a brave space, but a safe space.[34]

While race matters, and the heteronormative male voices I shared with my writing students still inspirited their social activism, my students were not invited to know neither Black woman's genius nor their humanity. Even when

I permitted students to write rhetorical analyses of a speech and orator of their choice, the very few students who did choose a woman's voice either chose Mary Fisher's 1992 "Republican National Convention Address" or Hillary Clinton's 1995 "Women's Rights Are Human Rights"—to which those students still didn't realize the inequities Black women encounter which urged the inception of Black feminist theory. No student chose speeches by Barbara Jordan, Shirley Chisholm, or Anita Hill—all of whom were included in the speech archive from which I directed students to choose their reading assignments. And so, albeit subconsciously, my writing students moved through my classroom the way I was moving through the world, and thus, they mirrored my preferences regarding reputable speech, which did not include the Black female orator.

And to be clear, my male-centered curriculum wasn't *bad.* Students were inspirited. Students did self-reflect. They learned about activism and social justice. Their reading and writing improved. We achieved all state, university, and department mandates. But the Black woman was still the most denigrated person on the planet, and my course did nothing to awaken students to that grave injustice. And if, says hooks, the Black female's struggle for liberation "has significance only if it takes place within a feminist movement that has as its fundamental goal the liberation of all people,"[35] then my humanitarian efforts in the writing classroom were curtailed by my failure to invite the Black woman's *whole* experience, including my *whole* self, into my assigned writing instruction. So, when Lemons inquired about my Black feminist approach to teaching writing, not only did he invite me into another publication, which my tenure-track self really needed, but he also invited me to wake up to the womanist my Black self also needed.

WHEN YOU KNOW BETTER, YOU DO BETTER

In *Words of Fire: An Anthology of African American Feminist Thought,* Beverly Guy-Sheftall employs Nellie McKay's Black feminist standpoint as an epigraph to introduce chapter 6 of the book. McKay says, "I consider every course I teach a course in black feminism. Whether I am teaching William Faulkner or Henry James, by speaking out on my position as a black woman, the course becomes a black feminism course."[36] Her words underscore Guy-Sheftall's "Reading the Academy."[37] While I agree with McKay's assertion—considering my failure to know my womanist self—I believe constructing a womanist classroom relies more on than just *being* a Black woman. Within this post-postmodern society whose technological advancements—coupled with the residuals of a narcissistic, sociopathic presidential administration, a global pandemic, and a modern civil war, spurred from

George Floyd's murder—we are further distanced from ourselves and each other. And so, if I aim—in this twenty-first century "cancel culture" wherein politicians are attempting to reverse *Roe vs. Wade*, prohibit openly trans-gendered persons from military service, and remove critical social theory from the academy—to provide my predominantly Black composition students a social activist writing experience that offers them a chance at being "[c]ommitted to survival and wholeness of entire people, male *and* female,"[38] then I must fully enter the classroom and teach from a holistically authentic place—a brave space.

What follows are my three initial attempts at integrating Black women's voices into my composition classrooms. I am clear, however, that supplementing Black women's text with other readings doesn't make my courses *womanist*, per se, especially if those women's voices are situated at the curriculum's margins. My attempts, therefore, are to illustrate my initial efforts. I have since enrolled in the Women's, Gender, & Sexuality Studies Master's Program at University of North Carolina-Greensboro where I am concentrating on the sociology of education. Needless to say, I have come a long way and have consciously been working to construct an Afriwomanist pedagogy about which I've written.[39]

BELL HOOKS AND ACADEMIC DISCOURSE (2017)

Undoubtedly, my being formally disciplined in rhetoric and composition at a predominantly white university whose teachers told me they could not comprehend my Black vernacular and my cultural references were not universal, have contributed to my negligence regarding the Black woman's voice in traditional writing classrooms. Rhetoric and composition is a white male-dominated discipline, and with voices like Peter Elbow, Ken Macrorie, and David Bartholomae dominating discourse, one must dig to find female voices. *I had to dig to find female voices.* And even after the digging, white female scholars like Andrea Lunsford, Sondra Perl, and Anne Ruggles Gere surface first. (I have since acquainted myself with Geneva Smitherman, Jacqueline Jones Royster, and Elaine Richardson.)

Nonetheless, when I taught *Techniques of Research in the Field of Writing Studies* at Barry University where I adjunct for a year, I consciously added bell hooks to my reading list, which already included Gloria Anzaldúa and Andrea Lunsford's 2004 "Toward a Mestiza Rhetoric: Gloria Anzaldúa on Composition and Post Coloniality" and Patrick Bruch and Richard Marback's 2002 "Race, Literacy, and the Value of Rights Rhetoric in Composition Studies." With groundbreaking work such as *Ain't I a Woman?* 1981; *Feminist Theory* 1984; *Sisters of the Yam*, 1993; and *Feminism is for Everybody* 2000, bell hooks is often associated with Black feminist politics and practice. However, her work on composition studies, which is grounded in Paulo Freire and Thich Nhất Hanh's theories regarding radical pedagogy and mindfulness, respectively, invites composition scholars to consider race, class, and gender within an academic space that operates inside the white patriarchy. And so, for the first time in my teaching career, I integrated bell hooks into my reading and writing instruction, more specifically, Gary Olson's 1994 "bell hooks and the Politics of Literacy: A Conversation."

Admittedly, teaching this interview/essay proved challenging, for Barry's course objective is to teach students how to critically read within the writing studies discipline. While hooks' interview invites readers to consider the politics of literacy (*Who has access?*) on feminist theory and practice, my students could not quite comprehend the relationship between feminism and the white male structured academy, and they were not at all interested in writing studies. Therefore, as I am often challenged to do in the writing classroom, I had to help my students unpack hooks' arguments so they could begin thinking critically about them, while helping students to understand rhetoric and composition as a discipline.

In this multilayered space, many of my composition students did not see feminism at all, but focused on the politics of literacy, which was grounded on their preconceived notions of race. Like me, my Black (and Latinx) classroom body identified themselves primarily and solely through a racial lens. Since we were reading about a Black bell hooks whose interview also discusses the multicultural writing classroom, my students could not attach themselves to feminist politics. And, unfortunately, my limited knowledge of feminism at the time, along with the time constraints of the writing classroom, maintained their limitations. But I persisted with truth.

SOJOURNER TRUTH AND THE RHETORICAL ANALYSIS ESSAY (2018)

Critically analyzing speech for its rhetorical appeals and elements is a task with which most first-year composition instructors are required to teach. Since I began teaching on the collegiate level as a doctoral student, I have grounded my rhetorical analysis essay assignment on Martin Luther King Jr.'s rhetorical genius, specifically, his 1963 "I Have a Dream" speech. While I use King's work to help students understand rhetorical elements, I began integrating Sojourner Truth's 1851 "Ain't I a Woman?" speech[40] as a point of departure for in-class writing practice and discussion regarding the rhetorical analysis essay. Usually, my writing courses are fifty minutes long; therefore, using Truth's short work was not only appropriate for the time limit with which I must work in class, but it was just as rhetorically rich as King's "I Have a Dream" speech and allowed my writing students to hear a Black woman's voice that precedes King's.

Because I had only fifty minutes to teach—which was more like forty minutes after the students and I settle into the classroom—I read Truth's speech out loud to the class, which I projected onto a white board. I also read Truth's speech out loud because her Black English often slowed students' reading thus curtailing their comprehension of it. Once I read her speech out loud, students and I then engaged in a fifteen- to twenty-minute discussion about Truth's text: *How does Truth's speech appeal to a reader's sense of ethos, logos, and pathos? Identify a rhetorical or literary element Truth employs in her speech. What is Truth's main argument? Explain the effect of Truth's rhetorical question, "Ain't I a Woman?"*

By the time we completed our discussion, circa twenty minutes of class time remains, which allowed me ten minutes to explain students' written assignment and the remaining ten minutes to answer student questions about their assignment. Students' first writing task was to compose a rhetorical precis paragraph—which they were given a sample of prior to their writing assignment—that reflected their understanding of Truth's argument, the development of it, and the rhetorical appeal most reflected in it. This initial paragraph writing assignment prepared students for the reading, writing, researching, and critical analysis that are required of them to write an extended essay on a speech of their choosing. It also introduced them to a Black woman's voice—and for many of my twenty-first-century students—it was the first time they were being acquainted with Sojourner Truth and the fact that Black women were not given the same rights as their white counterparts, despite the women's rights movement.

Unfortunately, because I teach writing courses *supplemented* by readings, I cannot spend as much time as I'd like discussing the assigned literature. In a writing classroom, composition teachers must be mindful of how much time they spend on reading practices versus ones on composing exercises—even though reading informs and improves writing. Therefore, during our Truth discussions, while Black women's rights did surface, I had to make a concerted effort to move students beyond a narrowed conversation on race and/or slavery and invite them to consider the intersectionality of race, class, and gender Truth implies. Alas, the time I allotted to complete the rhetorical analysis unit so my students had enough space to complete the other department requirements prohibited me from taking a deep dive into intersectionality and critical race theory; however, I planted the seed, and while I may not witness its blossom, I trust my students will emerge like lotus flowering in their awakening.

HELENE JOHNSON AND THE SONNET (2019)

While integrating poetry into the traditional composition classroom is not a usual occurrence—because "poetry belongs in a creative writing classroom"—I have included a poetry unit in my writing courses for two main reasons: 1. to give my right-brained students a creative reading assignment that hopefully encourages them to write a critical analysis about which they can feel successful; and 2. to help students understand and develop their own concise writing skills including purposed word choice, thoughtful sentence structure, and intentional punctuation. Because I am working within an academic structure that requires students to be more mechanical than we teachers like to admit, I tend to teach poetic forms such as the sonnet, so students receive continued practice in stylistic, formulaic writing as well as in following directions.

I learned to write the traditional Shakespearean sonnet in eighth grade, and since then, it has been one of my favorite poetic forms to practice. But not until I was introduced to Claude McKay's 1919 "If We Must Die" sonnet as a practice in writing back to the empire did the sonnet as a social protest poem become my preferred poetic form and style to teach in my social activist composition classroom. So, for the past ten years I've integrated poetry into my writing classrooms, I've relied on Claude McKay as my prototype for sonnet writing. Not until recently, however, did I stumble upon Helene Johnson's 1927 sonnet, "Sonnet to a Negro in Harlem."

I came upon Johnson's work while teaching African American literature at University of North Georgia (UNG). I never taught a literature course before, so I had to do some digging for African American anthologies that were accessible to the undergraduate students I was assigned to teach. (The popular Norton Anthologies African American literature courses often require felt way too daunting.) As I explored various textbooks, I settled upon the 2016 *Wiley Blackwell Anthology of African American Literature, Volume 2: 1920-Present.* Edited by Gene Andrew Jarrett, it is an accessible collection that, based on my limited research in African American literature anthologies, includes more unfamiliar voices than I can recall reading in other texts. Thus, enter Helene Johnson. Prior to teaching African American literature, I had not known any female sonnet writers, let alone Black women sonnet writers—and truthfully, I had never sought them.

While my UNG students read Johnson's work for literary discussion, I included her sonnet as required reading in the *Advanced Grammar and Rhetoric* course I was assigned to teach years later at North Carolina A&T. These students, most of whom were graduating seniors, were required to critically read her work and to compose a comparative critical analysis of it and McKay's "If We Must Die."

Like McKay's sonnet, Helene Johnson's sonnet is written in a protesting voice that sets the Black body against his oppressive other. With lines such as: "Your dark eyes are flashing solemnly with hate, / Small wonder that you are incompetent / To imitate those whom you so despise,"[41] Johnson conveys a disgust for the racist other whose narrator cannot mirror an oppressor who expects him (the Black narrator) to assimilate to his (the oppressor's) white patriarchal culture. As such, both McKay and Johnson speak back to the empire, writing in a poetic form specific to European literary culture, while inciting Black folks to openly oppose a denigrating system. Helene Johnson's Black female voice also talks back to a white male dominated poetic form. In this vein, Johnson's sonnet operates within the social activist/womanist framework with which I began constructing my writing classrooms—which my senior level students eventually realized, because I juxtaposed Johnson's work with McKay's, while having already incorporated just as many female voices as I do male into their semester's reading and writing requirements.

Since integrating Helene Johnson into my reading and writing instruction, I have become aware of my failure to include a Black female spoken word artist into my poetry writing unit. In that space, I rely on The Last Poets to showcase spoken word writing and performance, and I have not considered any other example of spoken word artists, particularly Black female performers. Sonia Sanchez's haikus, however, have always grounded my instruction regarding haiku writing. Embarrassingly, however, although Sanchez is a Black woman of the Black Arts Movement using a Japanese poetic style to write about her Black female experience, when I've shared her "Haiku": "I want to make you / roar with laughter as I ride / you into morning,"[42] I never invited my students to explore the Black woman's sexuality and her freedom of self-expression. Instead, I've instructed them to count syllables and consider Sanchez's word choices.

I AM DOING BETTER.

As a classroom teacher who is still uncovering and accepting her whole authentic self and becoming more aware of the political coercing, media brainwashing, and academic conditioning that effect how I move through the world, much rides on me to ensure I'm not downloading such preconceived notions into my writing students. Therefore, as I become more "woke," I will be more able to awaken my students to the oppressions white patriarchy maintains and to offer them a universalist writing classroom where their academic practices ensure "survival and wholeness of entire people, male *and* female."[43] However, my awakening won't happen if I fail to question, as Parker Palmer dares: *"Who is the self that teaches?"*[44]

Undoubtedly, I am a longtime member of "the great majority of black women [who] allied themselves with the black patriarchy they believed would protect their interests."[45] But how can a Black patriarchy mirroring white patriarchal values avoid being sexist oppressors? This is a question I've asked myself since being invited to write this chapter. According to bell hooks, "Black activists defined freedom as gaining the right to participate as full citizens in American culture; they were not rejecting the value system of that culture. Consequently, they did not question the rightness of patriarchy."[46] As a result, white male patriarchy progresses long after the 1960s Civil Rights Movement, moves throughout the current #metoo[47] movement, and persists inside Kamala Harris' vice presidency.

Thankfully, although patriarchy's oppressive politics seem more prevalent, this is, as Charles Dickens writes in his 1859 *A Tale of Two Cities* and Alice Walker echoes in her 2006 *We Are the Ones We Have Been Waiting For*, "the best of times and the worst of times."[48] For more of us are waking up, thus helping to foster a more conscious nation predisposed to tools with which to ensure our humanity (and to assure we don't suffer from insomnia, which then will do our awakening no good).

Indeed, our task as human beings is to live fully in our awareness, and my challenge as a Black, female lesbian teacher is to enter the classroom as a *whole* person courageously and mindfully so my composition students can see themselves in me and write themselves into their own authentic being. Yes, I am visibly Black. I am also a woman, and lesbian, too. Those identities, along with my spirituality and middle-class privilege, affect how I move through the world, how I am seen (or not) in the world, and how I treat others with whom I come in contact as I traverse the world. I feel free in this clarity—in this awareness of my position as a Black woman. It's a freedom that invites me into "a wider struggle for human dignity, empowerment, and social justice"[49]—of which Black women's struggles are a part. My students deserve to be awakened to themselves, too—to know that freedom.

According to Alice Walker, "[Wo]man only truly lives by knowing; . . . When we are children, growing up in our parents' care, we await the spark from the outside world. Sometimes our parents provide it—if we are lucky—sometimes it comes from another source far from home."[50] I am a possible source. But to give my students "a knowledge of living that will save [them] from [their] innocuous lives that resemble death,"[51] I must have the courage to consciously "know myself as I am known."[52] And if I bring *that* womanist into the classroom space, then I help to foster a brave space wherein (Black) "feminism is for everybody."[53]

BIBLIOGRAPHY

Clinton, Hillary. "Women's Rights Are Human Rights." United Nations Fourth World Conference on Women, Beijing, 5 Sept. 1995.

Collins, Patricia Hill. *Black Feminist Thought: Knowledge, Consciousness, and the Politics of Empowerment, Second Edition*, Routledge, 2000.

Combahee River Collective. "Combahee River Collective Statement," in *All the Women Are White, All the Blacks Are Men, But Some of Us Are Brave: Black Women Studies*, edited by Gloria T. Hull, Patricia Bell Scott, and Barbara Smith, Feminist Press, 1982, pp. 13–22.

Cooper, Anna Julia. *A Voice from the South*, The Aldine Printing House, 1892.

Crenshaw, Kimberlé. "Demarginalizing the Intersection of Race and Sex: A Black Feminist Critique of Antidiscrimination Doctrine, Feminist Theory and Antiracist Politics," *University of Chicago Legal Forum*, vol. 140, 1989, pp. 139–68.

Dickens, Charles. *A Tale of Two Cities*, Chapman & Hall, 1859.

Different Strokes. Created by Jeff Harris and Bernie Kukoff, NBC, 1978–1985.

Fisher, Mary. "Republican National Convention Address." Houston, Texas, 19 Aug. 1992.

Good Times. Created by Eric Monte and Mike Evans, CBS, 1974–1979.

Guy-Sheftall, Beverly. "Reading the Academy" in *Words of Fire: An Anthology of African American Feminist Thought*, The New Press, 1995, p. 451.

hooks, bell. *Ain't I a Woman? Black Women and Feminism*, South End Press, 1981.

———. *Feminism Is for Everybody: Passionate Politics*, South End Press, 2000.

———. *Feminist Theory: From Margin to Center*, South End Press, 1984.

———. *Sisters of the Yam: Black Women and Self-Recovery*, South End Press, 1993.

Johnson, Helene. "A Sonnet for a Negro in Harlem," in *The Wiley Blackwell Anthology of African American Literature*, edited by Gene Andrew Jarrett, John Wiley & Sons, 2014, p. 194.

King, Martin Luther. "I Have a Dream." March on Washington for Jobs and Freedom, Washington, D.C., 28 Aug. 1963.

Lee, Spike, director. *Malcolm X.* Warner Bros, 1992.

McKay, Claude. "If We Must Die," in *The Wiley Blackwell Anthology of African American Literature*, edited by Gene Andrew Jarrett, John Wiley & Sons, 2014, p. 15.

Oyewole, Abiodun. "A Protest Poem for Rosa Parks," in *Make a Joyful Sound: Poems for Children by African-American Poets*, edited by Deborah Slier, Checkerboard Press, 1991.

Olson, Gary. "bell hooks and the Politics of Literacy: A Conversation." *Journal of Advanced Composition*, vol. 14, no. 1, 1994, pp. 1–19.

Sanchez, Sonia. "haiku," in *Under a Soprano Sky*. Africa World Press, Inc., 1987, p 72.

The 2 Live Crew. "Pop That Coochie." *Sports Weekend: As Nasty As They Wanna Be, Pt 2.*, Luke Records, 1992.

Truth, Sojourner. "Ain't I a Woman?" Women's Convention, Akron, OH, 1851.

Walker, Alice. "Choosing to Stay at Home: Ten Years after the March on Washington," in *In Search of Our Mothers' Gardens: Womanist Prose*, Harcourt Brace Jovanovich, 1982, pp. 158–70.

———. *In Search of Our Mothers' Gardens: Womanist Prose*. Harcourt, 1983.

———. "The Civil Rights Movement: What Good Was It?" in *In Search of Our Mothers' Gardens: Womanist Prose*, Harcourt, 1982, pp. 119–29.

———. *We Are the Ones We Have Been Waiting For: Inner Light in a Time of Darkness*. The New Press, 2000.

NOTES

1. Alice Walker, *In Search of Our Mothers' Gardens: Womanist Prose* (New York, NY: Harcourt, Inc., 1983), xii.

2. Ibid., xi.

3. Patricia Collins, *Black Feminist Thought* (New York, NY: Routledge, 2000), 42.

4. Walker, *In Search*, xi.

5. Collins, *Black Feminist Thought*, 42.

6. Ibid., 42.

7. Ibid., 42.

8. Parker J. Palmer, *The Courage to Teach: Exploring the Inner Landscape of a Teacher's Life* (San Francisco, CA, John Wiley & Sons, Inc., 1998), 4.

9. See Evelyn White, *Alice Walker: A Life* (New York, NY: W.W. Norton, 2004).

10. Walker, "The Civil Rights Movement: What Good Was It?" in *In Search*, 124.

11. Ibid., 125.

12. Queen Latifah, whose birth name is Dana Owens, is an African American rapper, among many other things, who, in 1989, signed with Tommy Boy Records, during which time she debuted *All Hail the Queen*, which features her hit single, "Ladies First."

13. Public Enemy is an African American rap group formed in 1986 in Long Island, New York. Consisting of members: Chuck D, Flavor Flav, et al., Public Enemy is known for its politically charged rap, usually about African American concerns.

14. The 2 Live Crew is a 1980s–early 1990s Miami rap group who was notorious for their profane lyrics, most of which sexualized women's bodies.

15. Character in Walker's 1973 short story "Everyday Use" who changes her name to a more African-sounding one after moving away from the deep South to go to college.

16. Abiodun Oyewole is a founding member of the 1960s spoken word group The Last Poets, considered to have laid the groundwork for the hip-hop movement.

17. Walker, "Choosing to Stay at Home: Ten Years after the March on Washington," in *In Search*, 169.

18. Ibid., 169.

19. Ibid., 169

20. bell hooks, *Feminist Theory: From Margin to Center* (Boston, MA: South End Press, 1984), 1

21. Ibid., 10.

22. "Intersectional Feminism: What It Means and Why It Matters Right Now" (*unwomen.org*, 2020), https://www.unwomen.org/en/news/stories/2020/6/explainer -intersectional-feminism-what-it-means-and-why-it-matters.

23. Line from a dialogue in Wendell B. Harris' 1989 film, *Chameleon Street.*

24. bell hooks, *Ain't I a Woman? Black Women and Feminism* (Boston, MA: South End Press, 1981), 1–2.

25. Ibid., "Cultural Criticism and Transformation" from Media Education Foundation (Northampton, MA, 1997), 7, https://www.mediaed.org/transcripts/Bell-Hooks -Transcript.pdf.

26. Bettina Love, *We Want to Do More Than Survive: Abolitionist Teaching and the Pursuit of Educational Freedom* (Boston, MA, 2019), 131.

27. According to Bettina Love, "the teacher education gap" describes "education programs [that] perpetuate the stereotyping and myth-making targeted at dark children and their communities" (131). Although I am far from being comparable to the white teachers Love discusses in her *We Want to Do More* text, like them, I have participated in teacher workshops as well as education courses that offer lessons that do more to reproduce inequities than they do to irradicate them via a curriculum of refusal; or in other words, a radical liberatory pedagogy—which most recently is referred to as an "abolitionist pedagogy."

28. See Deborah P. Britzman's "Is There a Queer Pedagogy? Or, Stop Reading Straight" in *Educational Theory*, vol. 45 no. 2, 1995, wherein Britzman invites readers to engage in a nonheteronormative reading practice so they might read beyond what they have been trained to think about a text, and therefore, open their minds to new ways of thinking, and ultimately, being.

29. Here, and throughout my essay, I use "ethnocentricity" to refer to my having privileged my race self, which thus made me more conscious of my race than my other identities. I am not using "ethnocentricity" to infer a superiority over any other person.

30. In Eric Stanley's "Near Life, Queer Death: Overkill and Ontological Capture" in *Social Text* 107, vol. 29, no. 2, 2011, he defines "queer" as "the collision of *difference* and violence" [author's emphasis], 3.

31. hooks, *Ain't I a Woman?* 4–5.

32. Palmer, *The Courage to Teach*, 1.

33. hooks, *Ain't I a Woman?* 12.

34. While "safe spaces" are intended to "provide a format for people of color and whites to come together and discuss issues of race in a matter that is not dangerous as well as inclusive," explain Zeus Leonardo and Ronald K. Porter in their "Pedagogy of Fear: Toward a Fanonian Theory of 'Safety' in Race Dialogue," in *Race Ethnicity and Education*, vol. 13, no. 2, 2010, 147, in my classroom, "safe spaces" were void of discussions regarding gender, sexuality, class, and the like. Thus, although I didn't create a classroom that was "safe" for the white students Leonardo and Porter argue are the students' "safe spaces" guard, I did create one that safeguarded nonheteronormative Black students.

35. bell hooks, *Ain't I a Woman?* 13.

36. Beverly Guy-Sheftall, *Words of Fire: An Anthology of African American Feminist Thought* (New York, NY: The New Press, 1995), 451.

37. Ibid., 451.

38. Walker, *In Search*, xi.

39. See Kendra N. Bryant, *"Democracy Matters* in the 21st Century HBCU Writing Classroom: AfriWomanism as a Political, Pedagogical Tool," in *Reimagining Historically Black Colleges and Universities: Survival Beyond 2021*, edited by Gary B. Crosby, et al. (Emerald Publishing, 2021), 135–47.

40. Although the often-anthologized 1851"Ain't I a Woman?" speech has been attributed to Sojourner Truth, it is actually a heavily revised version of Truth's original speech, which was written and published in 1863. Princeton University historian Nell Irvin Painter uncovered this historical faux pas, more of which can be read at the sojournertruthproject.org.

41. Helene Johnson, "A Sonnet for a Negro in Harlem," in *The Wiley Blackwell Anthology of African American Literature*, ed. Gene Andrew Jarrett (New York, NY: John Wiley & Sons, 2014), 194.

42. Sanchez, *Under a Soprano Sky* (Trenton, NJ: Africa World Press, Inc., 1987), 72.

43. Walker, *In Search*, xi.

44. Palmer, *The Courage to Teach*, 1.

45. hooks, *Ain't I a Woman?* 9.

46. Ibid., 4–5.

47. #metoo is a *Twitter* hashtag movement that began in 2007 with Tarana Burke, a black community organizer who began the *Me Too Campaign* for rural black girls who needed a safe space from sexist, racist, classist oppression. It has since been attributed to white celebrity actress Alyssa Milano who used the hashtag in 2017 to encourage women to speak out against sexual assault and harassment.

48. Charles Dickens, *A Tale of Two Cities* (London: Chapman & Hall, 1859), and Alice Walker, *We Are the Ones We Have Been Waiting For: Inner Light in a Time of Darkness* (New York, NY: The New Press, 2006).

49. Collins, *Black Feminist Thought,* 41.

50. Walker, "The Civil Rights Movement: What Good Was It?" in *In Search*, 123.

51. Ibid., 123.

52. Title of Palmer's *To Know As We Are Known: Education as a Spiritual Journey* (San Francisco, CA: Harper & Row, 1983).

53. Quote is taken from bell hooks' 2000 title work, *Feminism Is for Everybody: Passionate Politics* (Cambridge, MA: South End Press, 2000).

PART II

Education "as the Practice of Freedom"

Holding on to bell hooks' Pedagogical Legacy

Chapter Five

Still Becoming Me

My Journey through bell hooks'
Vision of "Engaged Pedagogy"

La-Toya Scott

In the evolution of my self-identification as a Black feminist-womanist scholar and teacher, I have been profoundly influenced by the radical peda-gogical legacy of bell hooks—especially related to her vision of "education that is healing to the uninformed, unknowing spirit . . . [and] knowledge that is meaningful"[1] to one's personal life experiences. I open this chapter with these liberating words to represent the liberating power of hooks voice throughout her commentary in *Teaching to Transgress: Education as the Practice of Freedom.*

In this contemporary moment, I have found that the most difficult part about becoming who I profess to be was actually starting my journey to self-hood in academia. Academia was never something I personally planned to be a part of nor was it a location in which I typically saw people who looked like me. My parents, immigrants from Jamaica, wanted me to be a medical doctor. For Blacks in general that hope is not unique. Having a career in the field of science or math is seen as "respectable." Thus, with the hopes of making my family proud, I worked hard and entered college as a first-generation student. I registered as a biological science major with no real love or passion for math or science. The lack of interest quickly reflected in my grades. Eventually, in the latter part of my studies, my academic advisor nearly begged me to switch majors while I was still "marketable" to other departments. With that I switched my studies to English. I always had a love for literature, and the art of truth-telling. However, I did not graduate as an English major to become a professor. I graduated as an English major to go to law school. I still yearned to be "respectable." My time at law school was short-lived as I was still seeking a profession that would provide the validation that I sought from my parents and not one that made me happy. I became unsure of my purpose, felt like a failure, and ultimately a disappointment. The only consistent aspect of my life was my love of literature. In need of work, I soon took a job at a community college while also becoming inspired by a "Black Lives Matter" course I started to sit in on a weekly basis at a university nearby. These two experiences heavily impacted my life because it led me back to school and created an opportunity for me to reflect on who I was as a Black woman within these spaces. The lessons that I learned and continue to learn now as a Black female educator are ones that challenge not only the way I learn but the way I teach.

Employing Black feminist womanist theory and framework throughout this autocritographical[2] chapter, I argue that it is necessary for Black feminist-womanist epistemology to be integrated in academia to foster a liberating vision of pedagogical reciprocity in the college classroom—between students and teachers. This is vital because it produces a symbiotic relationship that ultimately benefits students and teachers. In addition, it creates an opportunity to dismantle white supremacist thinking within institutions of higher learning that dictates whose stories should and should not be told. Black feminist-womanist theory, epistemology, and pedagogy normalizes the presence of Black thought and bodies in colleges and universities (both public and private). In her pedagogical trilogy—*Teaching to Transgress: Education as the Practice of Freedom*; *Teaching Community: A Pedagogy of Hope*; and *Teaching Critical Thinking: Practical Wisdom*—bell hooks shows that community building within the college classroom allows for the intersection of culture, literature, and critical thinking. This approach to teaching subverts the normalized, one directional way of learning where students are only seen as bodies in the classroom where teachers lecture as opposed to dialoguing with students to create a learning environment for self-transformation. In this chapter, I will outline my experiences as a student *and* as a teacher to foreground my argument for a liberating vision of black feminist womanist pedagogy, providing a critical context for my narrative of critical self-consciousness—toward *becoming* me.

HAD I INTERNALIZED WHITE SUPREMACY?

"Welcome to FAMU . . . I mean FSU (insert laughing emoji) #monkeyseverywhere #FSU #MarketWednesday." This was the text, created by Mandy Thurston, a white female student at Florida State University, that sub-headed the widely circulated screenshot of Black students enjoying market Wednesday, in September of 2013. Market Wednesdays at Florida State University have become a traditional gathering that pulls Black college students together from FSU, Florida Agricultural and Mechanical University (FAMU), and Tallahassee Community College to share the multitude of Black cultural experiences. This may take the form of music, dance, and crafts. The outrage over her comment did not take long to get to local news outlets, such as the *Huffington Post*, and even *New York Daily News*. Unfortunately, during my time as an FSU undergraduate student, the views and thoughts of Mandy Thurston were not isolated. Thurston was merely representative of the under-lying racism that had frequently reared its ugly head at this PWI. When your institution still has statues honoring slave owners posted at pristine corners of the university, only has a handful of Black professors in the entire university hired as faculty, and keeps a mangled and tattered Black Student Union house right next to the police department—racist ideology is not only systemic but normalized. My reflection, related to this incident, coincides with bell hooks' thoughts concerning her experience as a Black female student navigating through the racist and sexist world of academia.

In reference to her graduate study years at a PWI hooks states: "While these racist and sexist opinions were rarely directly stated, the message was conveyed through various humiliations that were aimed at shaming students, at breaking our spirit."[3] Although I never experienced overt racism during my undergrad years at FSU, the racial atmosphere on that campus was cre-ated to target "minorities." For Black students, the implications of these daily assaults were heavy and discouraging. I knew I was Black. I was cognizant of my Blackness. I knew I was in a white space. I had white peers who did not want to address the racial tension and "did not see color" all the while I lived it. I had peers that did come to me and would ask, "Well, what can I do?" Often, questions like that were frustrating because I felt no responsibil-ity in helping someone understand my humanity. Thus, when hooks says in *Talking Back*: "We must show the way,"[4] in reference to aiding white people in understanding the circumstances of oppressed marginalized groups, I believed that to be problematic. On the other hand, hooks does make me contemplate my apprehension by drawing upon a valid point: "If as a black person I say to a white person who shows a willingness to commit herself or himself to the struggle to end white supremacy that I refuse to affirm, or help in that endeavor is a gesture that undermines my commitment to that struggle."[5] hooks expounds on this position by saying that the mediating and empowering force that is needed to confront these issues of gender, race, and class is love.[6] And while this may be true, I can't help but side more with James Baldwin's critique of racism in *Notes of a Native Son* when it comes to the power of love. Although love is needed, "this does not mean . . . that love comes easily: the white world is too powerful, too complacent, too ready with gratuitous humiliation, and above all, too ignorant, and too innocent for that."[7] To automatically love a people that have historically worked to subjugate others on the basis of race and continue to be privileged by racial constructs is a hefty request.

What was even more conflicting for me was being a Black female student at a PWI that sits right across from FAMU, a very well-known HBCU. Its main campus literally and figuratively sits on the other side of the train tracks from Florida State University. This in itself alluded to the racial divide in the U.S. academic system. Often, I would cross those tracks to connect with a community of Black students even though I already had a small community of fellow Black students at FSU. However, it was different being in an atmosphere where, as a Black student, one was not the *minority*. I was welcomed, but often I did get confronted by Black students that called my *blackness* into question—having internalized white supremacy interconnected to my class status—as a student attending a PWI. I would be taunted and told, "Oh, you go to that rich school over there with the money." I was asked, "Why didn't you just attend the Black school?"

Had I, too, internalized white supremacy? In truth, I did not attend FAMU for my undergraduate degree because I thought FSU was the better school because it was predominantly *white*. In reality—considering ways historically white established institutions have been educationally normative *and* economically accredited—FSU was more appealing. Indeed, it offered a wider, more varying range of disciplinary studies, more scholarships, and access to more possible employment opportunities. In this racialized, classist context—the politics at hand that contributed to the demarcation between resources amongst the Black and white institutions was clearly evident. For example, FAMU, during my time of attendance there, had not had a new dorm built in about a decade, while FSU had built one every year during the time of my enrollment. Moreover, it continually received million-dollar donations to build state of the art learning facilities for their students. Also, as told to me by a FAMU professor, the school had to cancel classes on Fridays at one point for economic efficiency that could maintain the school's existence. This was only part of an already muddled history of heated trials and battles for survival FAMU had to endure because it was "the Black school."

In my educational journey to self-consciousness—experientially crossing "tracks" between an HBCU and a PWI—I have come to conclude that what must happen is that "we"—people of all races and ethnicities—all need to acknowledge the power of white supremacist colonization, rooted in privileges associated with the "American Dream." For those of us who have *bought* into this nationalist, capitalist, heterosexist ideology—we must personally reflect upon ways we (and "I") perpetuate its exclusionary politics, particularly related to the price we *all* pay for the privilege(s) of "inclusion."

In my journey toward critical consciousness as a Black feminist student and college instructor, I must admit my own privilege enabling me to promote neoliberal notions of "diversity and inclusion"—even as I have *not* often academically benefited from them.

Like author and professor Roxane Gay points out in her book *Bad Feminist*, "the acknowledgement of my privilege is not a denial of the ways I have been and am marginalized, the ways I have suffered."[8] As for my white peers that have asked me and continue to ask me "What can I do?" My answer is, "You need to first understand the extent of your privilege." Gay says, "[acknowledge] the consequences of your privilege, and remain aware that people who are different from you move and experience the world in ways you might never know anything about."[9] Next, actual action is needed to tear down these institutionalized, reductive forms of "higher" education.

EXPERIENCING A RADICAL WHITE MALE PROFESSOR "TEACHING TO TRANSGRESS"

In *Teaching to Transgress*, bell hooks credits "the passion of experience"[10] as a radical means for creating space for active self-reflection in the classroom. I will always remember sitting in one of my first college classes during my undergraduate years at Florida State University. I had already become accustomed to being one of only a few Black faces in the room. I also already expected my professor to be a white man. The odds of that had to be high when there were few Black professors in the school's faculty. My experience with white male instructors had been racially exclusionary ever since middle school. Back then I remember once being told by a white male teacher: "Use your sweater to blow you runny little nose because your mother's and father's taxes don't pay me to let you use the bathroom." What he *taught* me really set the tone of what I thought to expect in the future from any white male teacher allocated such power in the classroom.

Many years later, seated and ready to take my first English literature course in college at FSU, I looked at the clock and took in the blur of white faces surrounding me. Right on time, in walks a white man with a scrubby face, messy hair, and a suit a little too big for him. He tells us his name and that he'll be our instructor for the semester. I have to say that his approach to teaching the course reminds me of bell hooks' idea of "[e]ngaged [p]edagogy" in *Teaching to Transgress*.[11] She asserts time and time again that teachers should envision the classroom as a strategic site for self-liberation for themselves and their students.[12] hooks' approach and mode of teaching, inspired by fellow teachers Paulo Freire and Thich Nhat Hanh, critically decenters the traditional one-sidedness of the teacher-student relationship.

During the first day of the class, the professor told us to call him by his first name. He said, "Doctor was too formal." He told us to move our desks out of the rows because it freaked him out, and that he would be sitting with us. He began to tell us about his life experiences and struggles to survive. He even told us that he did not agree with the grading system (required by the English department) for the course, but he would have to enforce it to keep his job. Throughout the course of the semester, he shared with us that growing up he was bullied, bashed, and picked on because he was just too feminine. He also told us that he loved songs by Beyonce and Nicki Minaj, and that he had a deep understanding of Tupac Shakur's music. In addition, he also had an affinity for episodes of the TV show *Say Yes to the Dress*. To say the least, I was impressed by this white professor's willingness to share so openly his life stories with our class. He was like an open book. I include here a discussion of my transformative experience in his class to demonstrate the critical importance of teacher-student self-reflections in the classroom. In *Teaching to Transgress*, bell hooks underscores the transformative power of teachers sharing their life-experiences with their students.[13]

I confess that it wasn't only the fact that this professor had shared a lot of strange and peculiar personal things in our class that I would have back then readily labeled as "some white people shit" (that actually intrigued me), but it was the fact that he so readily gave up his white male privilege in a space in which he could have exercised it with ease. Once again, his professorial openness not only intrigued me, but it also kept me (over the course of three years) enrolling in more of the literature classes he taught.

As I recall, at the end of the first course I took with him, he admitted that he did not teach the class as it was outlined by the department. We were part of his experiment. Oddly enough, he also let us pick our own grade for the class at the end of the course (based on what each of us felt we had accomplished in it). Yes, truthfully, I thought this white man was crazy, but in actuality I really liked the way he taught. In hindsight, he represented what I thought "engaged pedagogy" should be. The most impressive thing that I ever experienced related to his style of teaching occurred during my last undergraduate literature course with him before I graduated. This moment came during a time that there had been much media attention surrounding the slaying of Black boys by police officers and the growing "Black Lives Matter" movement. During that particular August class session, this professor was always consciously "woke"—particularly about issues of social justice and human rights—stood at the front of the class and announced, "I know I have privilege. I am a white man that gets to walk around in a suit and be respected, and I know that I won't be stopped by the cops, and that I will get to go home, and see my wife, and child. And that is not okay and that is not right. So, let's talk."

Through his "transgressive" pedagogical standpoint, I learned that in conventional ideas of "higher" education, professors and students are expected to intellectually and emotionally compartmentalize themselves—upholding the systemic structure known as "the Ivory Tower." In its construction, this is an institutional facade rooted in exclusionary wall-building. In such an environment, professors and students are pressured and pushed to become its brick and mortar—unimpressionable, unbiased, individualistic, and ultimately inhumane. In the conventional college classroom, teachers and students are structurally molded to keep our feelings and personal stories of survival to ourselves. While this method appears to enhance our professional pursuits, this way of being in the classroom actually creates an atmosphere that ultimately does more harm than good for all of us.

That white male professor who taught the literature courses I took with him never tried to claim or appropriate "the Black experience." However, he was sagacious enough to openly call out his white privilege, call out the injustice of white supremacy, and then listen to the stories of those who experienced it (across racial and ethnic differences). He never spoke for me nor anyone else in the class. He taught life-lessons. He purposely grounded them in liberatory knowledge that emerged from stories of folks suffering and surviving varying forms of oppression. His practices of "engaged pedagogy" and his commitment to self-transformational knowledge was strategically evident in each course. He knew when it came to certain issues that he was a guest at the table ("of color") never making demands for a seat at it. As this professor possessed a critical understanding of the politics of racism *and* racism, he was a strong self-identified, white male feminist. As his pedagogy was informed by this positionality, it not only transgressed heteronormative, patriarchal ideas of manhood and masculinity. As I have intentionally revealed in this section, my experiences in this white man's courses promoting social justice significantly impacted my journey as Black student in literary studies at a PWI.

Ultimately, as a Black woman coming to know bell hooks' stories of her struggles as a Black female student and professor in institutions of higher education, I would realize the life-transforming power of a teacher-student learning environment conceptually grounded in her concept of "engaged pedagogy."

MY LABOR TOWARD BECOMING A RADICAL BLACK FEMINIST TEACHER AND *THE HELP*

The Help, a 2011 Academy award–nominated film, based on the 2009 novel by the same title written by Kathryn Stockett, introduces the viewers to the plight of Black female domestic workers during the Civil Rights Era of the

1960s. The main characters, Aibileen Clark (played by Viola Davis), Minnie Jackson (played by Octavia Spencer), and Constantine Jefferson (played by Cicely Tyson), portray a life as in-house maids that attend to every need of the white families for whom they work. These black women cook, clean, rear the children, and even act as companions to the white women of the house-hold. This life of servitude is acted out while they are dually being subjected to cruel acts of racism, and sexual assault carried out by the white male head of the household. *The Help*, although a fiction-based movie, is grounded in the real-life experiences of Black women. In this representation domesti-cized Black female labor, bell hooks points out that, "Black women were the servants, and white women were the served."[14] I argue that the history of Black female domestic servanthood to elite white families foregrounds the ideology of white supremacy and continues in an economic "servant-served" relationship between Black and white women in the United States. I contend that even in the realm of academia, it has hindered the possibility of more authentic cross-racial "sisterhood." Walls of racism and heterosexism still need to be torn down.

Growing up as a Black female, I have always realized the friction and competitive nature among women across racial *and* class differences. In her book, *Black Feminist Thought,* Patricia Hill-Collins states:

> According to the cult of true womanhood that accompanied the traditional fam-ily ideal, "true" women possessed four cardinal virtues: piety, purity, submis-siveness, and domesticity. Propertied White women and those of the emerging middle class were encouraged to aspire to these virtues. African American women encountered a different set of controlling images.[15]

The historic servant-served reality of Black female domestic workers not only functioned within a gendered and "propertied" economic context, but it also created mythic foundation for the sexualized racist objectification of Black women. bell hooks also addresses this systemic injustice in *Teaching to Transgress.*[16] In this context, the idea of "true" womanhood would become a critical issue within the (her)stories of feminist movement(s) in the United States. hooks underscores this issue by quoting Hill Collins, who further states that—"Maintaining images of US Black women as the Other provides ideological justification for race, gender, and class oppression."[17] Historically, it is certainly ironic that the same Black women domestics that elite white women "othered" were the same women that they trusted to wash their clothes, cook their dinners, and breastfeed their children. What I find inter-esting is the perpetual conflict that arises in this servant-served relationship. In my academic experiences toward embracing the liberatory (her)stories of Black feminist activists, I have found it disheartening that many liberal white women who claim the *universalism* of womanist collective inclusion across racial lines, still perpetuate a politics of individualism. "Race" in a *politically correct* feminist context becomes a form of utility, only picked up by white women who consider it when beneficial for the promotion of *diversity* as racial progressiveness. As I have experienced, potentially progressive *necessary* dialogue in pro-feminist classrooms about the perpetuation of racism within U.S. feminist-based movements is placed in the back of the classroom. Talking about race becomes really problematic—especially when Black/women of color call out "white" privilege(s).

In and outside academia, there are white women who *employ* Black culture to their advantage while still not feeling the urgency to fight for the liberation of their Black/women of color sisters. Conceptually, when the Combahee River Collective was founded in 1974, comprised of radical Black feminist activists, it emphasized that, "The sanctions in the Black and white communities against Black women thinkers are comparatively much higher than those against white women, particularly ones from the educated middle and upper classes."[18] To this day, when Black women speak about their multilayered oppressions, the backlash is more severe than the responses white women would experience. In reading *Talking Back: Thinking Feminist, Thinking Black*, I learned from hooks that—

> The contemporary feminist call for sisterhood, the radical white woman's appeal to black women and all women of color to join the feminist movement, is seen by many black women as yet another expression of white female denial of the reality of racist domination, of their complicity in the exploitation and oppression of black women and black people.[19]

In my experience—when I have attempted to converse with white women about the history of racism within US feminist movements, calling out in them the perpetuation of ignorance related to white privilege(s)—that re-enforced the oppression of Black women—I have often had to confront the forcefulness of silence. However, there are those among them who readily become defensive. Some often say as a defense mechanism: "I don't see race." And therein lies the problem. If one does not see race, then one does not see me. One does not see what I have to experience and have to survive as a Black woman . . . still going through. In this form of racial blindness, one cannot be my ally, nor my "sister."

I know that I must *pay a price* for calling into question "politically correct" visions of cross-racial sisterhood. What is the price I must pay for calling out white female privilege(s) in the context of what hooks calls "white supremacist capitalist patriarchy"—stated throughout more than three decades of her published works. As a Black feminist pedagogue, scholar, and cultural activist, she boldly stands against the servant-served paradigm. In this contemporary moment, hooks contends that this inscripted, historically racist model of "true" womanhood must continually be called into question. Otherwise, it re-enforces the misguided notion that Black women must feel responsible to enlightened whites about the dehumanizing effects of white supremacy—at the expense of our own lives. This is a form of systemic oppression that creates a cycle of constantly revisiting sites of trauma that benefits white people at the expense of Black female self-care and preservation.

In truth, my experience with white female colleagues in academia as "sisters" in the struggle against racism has been problematic. In classes I have had with them, I often sense that when they feel they have mastered the subject of anti-racist struggle—via feminist thinking—it is used as a means to justify them becoming its mouthpiece. Without having shared any personal stories of their own knowledge of the power of white privilege(s) or any analysis of their own internalization of racism—"feminism" becomes the justifiable way to address the disparities of Black women as a path to cross-racial "sisterhood." In my dialogues with white women who desire to steer what they perceive as a feminist-oriented conversation about race and racism—without addressing their complicity in the problem—I suggest the need to focus on it in a Black/women of color feminist, intersectional framework that may not always feel comfortable for everyone, as hooks clarifies in *Teaching to Transgress*.[20]

Furthermore, in my academic experience, white teachers and students often become threatened by the perspectives of Black/students of color who speak up about the myth of feminist studies classrooms as "safe haven" spaces. As an undergraduate college instructor, I actually had a student of mine (a Black woman) share with me that she tried to speak about the March for Women's Rights Movement in one of her other classes in reference to it not being inclusive of Black women and women of color in general. My student recalled being shut down by a white woman peer and told that what she was saying was "too radical." I felt compelled to say to that Black female student:

What you speak of is not radical at all. It is the confidence that you exude while being grounded in telling the truth that becomes threatening, and the fact that you dare to speak and have called out shortcomings in the face of prevailing beliefs of racial inclusiveness and diversity—THAT is what is radical. Don't stop.

If speaking up in reference to varying forms of injustice, marginalization, and inequality is radical, then maybe all people should strive to be just "that"— *Radical*. In reflecting on occurrences like the one my Black female student had in her class, it reminds me that ideas of womanist *inclusiveness, diversity,* and *universality* in a racialized, capitalist culture may be viewed, according to hooks, as a "bourgeois" ideal as she points out in *Teaching to Transgress*.[21]

This classist point of view may cause Black students (calling into question meanings of terminology related to the promotion of racial and ethnic diversity) to feel that what they have to say transforms the college classroom into an *un*-"safe haven." Often, in this space, Black female students in particular are put in a position where they have to choose a standpoint based on either race or gender. Depending on what Black females (both students and teachers) decide to do within the classroom, as hooks points out once again, we are "rewarded if we [choose] to assimilate, estranged if we [choose] to maintain those aspects of who we [are] . . . all too often [we're] seen as outsiders."[22] This idea of *free speech* in the classroom is limited if it makes the classroom uncomfortable for the dominant identity group as the prevailing force of vocal authority.

In this context, open discussions of race are shutdown if they cannot fully *serve* the purposes of the white hegemonic setting. Again Black/women of color most often have to choose between racial or gendered identification.[23] Which are we first "Black" or "women"? As a Black feminist graduate student and undergraduate college instructor if I only talk about gender plights, am I denying my Blackness, and if I talk about race in parallel to my struggle in a feminist context, am I overlooking my woman-ness? This *servant-served* paradigm again gets enacted over and over again in this internalized struggle as hooks recalls in *Teaching to Transgress*.[24] Many feminist-identified Black/women of color teachers *and* scholars are seriously concerned about having their pedagogical practice(s) and scholarship viewed as ONLY racially biased. Thus, some of us choose to remain silent about our own racial realities and struggles for voice in order *to serve* colonized, neo-liberal ideas of universality and perpetuated *politically correct* ideas of what feminism should be defined as.

To create a liberating learning community where feminism can be employed to *transgress* racial, gender, and sexual boundaries—teachers and students need to enact a liberating vision of it, rather than it being reductively appropriated. An inclusive, diverse, and universal learning community must be seen as a necessity—not as a safe haven for political correctness. The historical *servant-served* myth-laden relationships between white and Black/women of color must be eradicated. Black/women of color should not be expected to separate their mind from their body and womanist "Spirit" in academia in order to have their concerns understood as valid. We must confront oppression at the intersection of class, race, gender, sexuality, *and* ability to promote critical consciousness in the way students view each other and the world. Those of us who identify as *radical* teachers of "engaged pedagogy" must envision the classroom as a strategic location for self-transformation. Only then can we manifest a radical vision of pedagogical practices rooted in love and being as *woke* teachers—for ourselves and for our students in and outside of the college classroom.

TEACHING FOR "CRITICAL THINKING [*AND*] PRACTICAL WISDOM": BUILDING COMMUNITY AND MY INSTRUCTIONAL EXPERIENCE WITH THE EXCEEDINGLY ABLED

In this final section, I conclude with a personal reflection focused on my first experience teaching at Miami Dade College North Campus in Florida. This chapter in my academic career journey was the beginning of becoming an "educator that changes the world." In hindsight, however, I remember living in Miami was always scary for me. As someone that grew up in South Florida, Miami became known, through media, for its high crime rates or extreme poverty in places such as Liberty City, Overtown, or Little Haiti. I was hired as a tutor for the Access Services for Students with Disabilities Department at Miami Dade College. Due to the fact that the students that were assigned to me had particular challenges that impeded their learning process, I had to "re-teach" them in the form of tutoring. I had on average 10 students that I met with per day. I was their teacher for the entire academic year. Two of them would become my favorite students—Roberta and Ebony.[25] I was not to "favor" any student over another, but I did. For me, these two students exemplified bell hooks' concepts of the life-transformative power of personal storytelling she promotes in *Teaching Critical Thinking: Practical Wisdom*. My personal experiences with these two students as their teacher/tutor taught me critical lessons that would transform me into the transgressive educator I am now and will continue to be.

Starting my teaching career at this Miami Dade College, I remember being told in a tutorial training session that I was supposed to be understanding but firm in reference to how I interacted with students with "disabilities." I supposed the idea was that maybe they would take advantage of me by using their (dis)ability to their advantage. When I began my first teaching/tutoring semester, my students appeared very curious to know how the new instructor (tutor) would respond to them. To them I became, "Ms. Scott." Initially, my students were reserved, and they struggled in what I thought were basic concepts of communication. Yet, I remained enthusiastic about the work we would accomplish together. My student Roberta, a mixed-race young woman, was in her early twenties and always had a smile on her face each time we met. She outwardly let me know, "Ms. Scott I am excited to work with you. I needed a new tutor. The last one didn't understand me. I learn at a 'sloooower' pace. My doctor says that I'm like a thirteen-year-old in a grown-up's body." I never knew what Roberta's "disability" was classified as, but she sure had the ability to speak whatever was on her mind whenever it came to her mind—a lot of it was *personal*. She just could not help it, and I did not perceive this as an inability but rather a standpoint full of possibility.

I soon learned that for Roberta to be able to learn her lessons—be it math, writing, or reading—she needed to be able to tell personal life stories in between. In *Teaching Critical Thinking,* hooks pointedly remarks: "Telling stories is one of the ways that we can begin the process of building community, whether inside or outside the classroom."[26] Thus, I was not only Roberta's teacher, but I had to be an avid listener to all her stories no matter how painful I thought her sharing them with me to be. I learned in the first couple weeks that as a toddler, Roberta lost her mother to a chronic disease. She was also being raised by a sickly father and his new wife. I learned that her stepmother used to beat her, leaving bruises on her body because Roberta looked like her mother, the woman her father still loved. I learned that Roberta used to be starved. Soon, I learned by watching the way she spoke and grabbed her mother's necklace (that she wore around her neck every day) that she hungered for safety and her mother's embrace. One day when Roberta arrived for her tutorial session with me, she was walking around barefoot. "Where're your shoes?" I asked. Roberta admitted that her sandal straps had broken. It hurt me to see her trying to staple those old dirty sandals back together. At this point, I told her to come with me. We went to Payless (an inexpensive shoe store) down the street, and I bought her some new shoes. She loved them. On the drive back to campus, Roberta looked at me and said, "You know, Ms. Scott, sometimes I got all these feelings inside and I don't know what to do about them. I care about people, and I can't help the way I feel." I told Roberta, "That is not a bad thing. I know what it's like to care and feel hurt because you care too much, especially with people you love."

In my experience with Roberta, I learned the power of sharing stories even if an academic setting did not condone it. hooks in *Teaching Critical Thinking* reflects about her own teaching practices. She says, "I am continually awed by our power as teachers to help or hurt our students, to bolster their spirits or break them."[27] I greatly share in that feeling as I think about the relationship Roberta and I fostered during our time together. That semester Roberta passed *all* her classes.

My other student, Ebony, was a young, Black Haitian female with a thick dialect and a quite obvious behavioral attitude. For a blind young woman, she had a very clear way of "seeing" things. I was Ebony's tutor/teacher for her class "Introduction to Computers." I was scared at first, unsure as to how was

I going to teach a blind female how to use Microsoft Word and PowerPoint. I absolutely agree with hooks' pedagogical standpoint employing creative learning strategies for "self-recovery" in the classroom.[28] I remember asking Ebony if she had ever "seen" the internet. She told me, "No." Surprised, it was then that I learned that Ebony had been blind for most of her life. Sitting in front of the computer, I activated the program JAWS, a technological application for blind students that speaks to the user. I had to use my imagination. I told Ebony to imagine the internet as a house. I told her, "You have a front door that you walk into. Each turn you make leads you to a different door and into a new room where you can find new things. That is the internet." "Oooooh," Ebony said with a smile appearing on her face. Ebony often had moments of frustration. Sometimes I did not think that I could explain something the way it needed to be. Often, I was terrified of messing up. Often, I was uncomfortable, but soon Ebony grew comfortable with me. She allowed me to use my imagination to best guide her through these lessons.

Ebony and I had to develop a relationship of trust in which we had to talk and converse often with each other—on a *personal* level. Underscoring the critical importance of the "personal" in academic learning environments, hooks posits that, "The future of learning lies with the cultivation of conversations, of dialogue."[29] Looking back, I reflect upon the real truth of this statement. Students, especially ones that have been deemed by society to be "disabled," rely on more than just a teacher's ability to recite information. They question who you are as a person and need to be able to form and rely on this *form* of an authentic interdependent relationship—between student *and* teacher. Comprehending this conceptually means that one is not only a teacher, but this *instructor* also becomes a student as well. Ebony—although visually blind—gave me the opportunity to *see* the academic world with new open, imaginary eyes. Ebony passed her computer class that semester.

Too often we, as teachers trained in conventional ideas of higher education, are taught that "engaged pedagogy"—in which students and teachers share our personal life stories in the classroom—serves no useful, practical learning purpose. However, in my tutorial experiences with Roberta and Ebony, I learned many self-transformative lessons from things. Most importantly, their willingness to share their feelings with me about the classes they were taking added a level of self-liberating emotional depth to our interactive engagement. According to hooks, teaching that links the "personal"—not only with the political but with the analytical—represents a powerful, strategic tool for a *student-teacher* learning-centered environment. Moreover, she maintains that "emotional intelligence" is a critical principle that teachers should be taught as a strategic pedagogical tool.[30] Had it not been for Roberta and Ebony's willingness to feel and speak, *and* my "ability" to receive their feelings and *talk back* to them, I do not think they or I would have gotten all that we accomplished *together* in our sessions. I am forever grateful to have been able to work with both these *exceedingly abled* young women. They taught me a lot about what it means to self-identify as a Black feminist *and* womanist teacher.

At the end of the day, I am secure in the fact that I know that I committed to practicing "engaged pedagogy" ("*Regardless*" as a womanist would boldly assert). As a radical form of teaching it reaches, touches, and transforms the lives of *all* people in and outside academic institutions. It is critically important that those of us who teach "education as the practice of freedom"—across differences of gender, race, ethnicity, class, sexuality, *and* abilities—remember that we are much more than intellectual figures in the classroom. We not only possess the power to become bridges for sharing a wealth of knowledge, but we—teachers and students—can be facilitators of life-changing conversations focused on what it means to be human beings. This is a vision of the classroom that we need to foster in order to move forward—promoting social justice and human rights for our students and for ourselves—particularly reflecting on what it means to enact Black feminist and womanist pedagogy in the college classroom. Heartfully considering this standpoint, I am still *becoming me*.

BIBLIOGRAPHY

Awkward, Michael. *Scenes of Instruction: A Memoir.* Durham: Duke University Press, 1999.

Baldwin, James. *Notes of a Native Son.* New York: Penguin Books, 2016.

Du Bois, W.E.B. *Souls of Black Folk: Essays and Sketches.* Chicago, A.G. McClurg, 1903. New York: Johnson Reprint Corp., 1968.

Hill Collins, Patricia. *Black Feminist Thought: Knowledge, Consciousness, and the Politics of Empowerment.* Boston: Unwin Hyman, 1990.

Gay, Roxane. *Bad Feminist: Essays.* London: Corsair. 2017.

hooks, bell. *Talking Back: Thinking Feminist, Thinking Black.* Boston: South End Press, 1989.

—*Teaching to Transgress: Education as the Practice of Freedom.* New York: Routledge, 1994.

—*Teaching Community: A Pedagogy of Hope.* New York: Routledge, 2003.

—*Teaching Critical Thinking: Practical Wisdom.* New York: Routledge, 2010.

Morrison, Toni. *The Origin of Others.* Cambridge, MA: Harvard University Press, 2017.

Hull, Gloria T., Patricia Bell Scott, and Barbara Smith, eds., *All the Women Are White, All the Blacks Are Men, But Some of Us Are Brave: Black Women's Studies.* Old Westbury, NY: Feminist Press, 1982.

NOTES

1. bell hooks, *Teaching to Transgress: Education as the Practice of Freedom* (New York: Routledge,1994), 19.

2. In *Scenes of Instruction: A Memoir,* Michael Awkward defines "autocritography" (7).

3. bell hooks, *Talking Back: Thinking Feminist, Thinking Black* (Boston: South End Press, 1989), 56.

4. Ibid., 118.

5. Ibid., 118.

6. Ibid., 26.

7. James Baldwin, *Notes of a Native Son* (New York: Penguin Books, 2016), 603.

8. Roxane Gay, *Bad Feminist: Essays* (London: Corsair, 2017), 17.

9. Ibid., 17.

10. hooks, *Teaching to Transgress*, 91.

11. Ibid., 13.

12. Ibid., 13.

13. Ibid., 21.

14. Ibid., 94.

15. Patricia Hill Collins, *Black Feminist Thought: Knowledge, Consciousness, and the Politics of Empowerment* (Boston: Unwin Hyman, 1990), 89.

16. hooks, *Teaching to Transgress*, 95.

17. Patricia Hill Collins, *Black Feminist Thought,* 87.

18. Hull, Gloria T., Patricia Bell Scott, and Barbara Smith, eds. 1982. *All the Women Are White, All the Blacks Are Men, But Some of Us Are Brave: Black Women's Studies* (New York: Feminist Press, 1982), 17.

19. hooks, *Talking Back: Thinking Feminist, Thinking Black,* 102.

20. hooks, *Teaching to Transgress,* 113.

21. Ibid., 180.

22. Ibid., 182.

23. Ibid., 122.

24. Ibid., 122.

25. To maintain the privacy of the two students I tutored at Miami Dade College, I created the names "Roberta" and "Ebony."

26. bell hooks, *Teaching Critical Thinking* (New York: Routledge, 2010), 49.

27. Ibid., 27.

28. hooks, *Teaching to Transgress*, 61.

29. hooks, *Teaching Critical Thinking,* 44.

30. Ibid., 81.

Chapter Six

I Ain't No Damned Pedagogue

Reevaluating my Stance in the Classroom from a Black Feminist Perspective and Reclaiming my Mother Tongue

Maggie Romigh

In *Teaching to Transgress: Education as the Practice of Freedom* bell hooks boldly states, "Teachers are not performers in the traditional sense of the word in that our work is not mean to be a spectacle."[1] In the evolution of my "learning" and teaching practice, I have strategically linked hooks' concept of "education as the practice of freedom" with the Black feminist standpoint Gary L. Lemons articulates in his book *Black Male Outsider: Teaching as a Pro-feminist Man: A Memoir*. He writes, "Whether a black man should be allowed to call himself a feminist is a bone of contention for many black women feminists and for black male detractors of feminism."[2] This leads to my own question: Can a white woman raised in a racist community in the Deep South, when schools were still legally segregated, evolve enough to become an advocate for Black feminist thought and claim Black feminist concepts as the basis of her own pedagogy? Would bell hooks or Patricia Hill Collins accept this white woman as a practitioner of Black feminist thought or would this be another "bone of contention"?[3] Hill Collins states that the term *Black feminist* has sometimes been used to label all Black women, even those who did not identify as feminist.[4] But Hill Collins points out that the "term *Black feminist* has also been used to apply to selected African-Americans—primarily women—who possess some version of a feminist consciousness"[5] To further the discussion about who can be called a black feminist, Hill-Collins cited Beverly Guy Sheftall who "contends that both men and women can be 'Black feminists' and names Frederick Douglass and W. E. B. Du Bois as prominent examples of Black male feminists."[6] Hill Collins goes on to point out, "Though the term Black feminist could also be used to describe any individual who embraces Black feminist ideas," she sees this as problematic.[7] In *Black Male Outsider*, Lemons writes, "Black feminist focus on the interrelation of domination serves as the foundation for the pedagogy I practice—precisely because it links a critique of patriarchy not only to female oppression, but also to the experience of heterosexism and homophobia in the lives of gay, lesbian, and transgender persons."[8] These are precisely the reasons that I have embraced Black feminist pedagogy. While Lemons can label himself a Black feminist with support from at least some female Black feminists, it becomes more problematic if I, a white woman, use that term, so I will not. However, my pedagogy has distinctly been influenced by reading Black feminist theory, and by witnessing, in Lemons' classroom, the impact Black feminist pedagogy can have in the classroom.

Like Lemons, my feminist awakening came through reading the works of bells hooks. Lemons writes, in *Black Male Outsider*, "As a black feminist theorist, critic, and teacher, bell hooks has been the single most important influence in my development as a professor of feminism. Her memoir-writing style was the catalyst for my vision of teaching autobiographical composition as a strategy for self-recovery. Her work *Feminist Theory: From Margin to Center* compelled my rejection of patriarchal thinking."[9]

My introduction to hooks came through taking a class with Lemons, but my awakening to the evils of racism and classism began early in my childhood, when I witnessed both of them first-hand in my small Southern hometown. But for most of my life, I lived far away from the ivory tower of academia. I was a working-class, white woman, waiting tables, working behind department store counters, and even working as an electrical technician after studying electricity at a technical school. Still, I always recognized that, despite my lower status as a working-class lesbian, I held privilege when compared to the Black women of my hometown. As a working-class woman, I never dreamed that I would one day become a university instructor, so my ideas about teaching have sprung up and slowly evolved only over the last twenty years.

When, as a forty-something-year-old, white, working-class, lesbian, I finally found a way to return to my own education and began working toward a BA, I instantly felt at home at Eckerd College in St. Petersburg, Florida, where many of my instructors and professors used methods of teaching based on Quaker thought. Educational practices rooted in Quaker principles emphasize community learning, service learning, personal responsibility both in the classroom and in the community, and social action.[10] But a Quaker education is not based solely on Christian teachings. In classes at Eckerd, I was required to read texts about Islam and Judaism and texts written by people of all races and religious persuasions. My classrooms at Eckerd were often set up in circles; instructors and students alike were referred to by their first names, and students were expected to bring as much to the class discussions as the instructors and learn as much from each other as they did from the instructors. At Eckerd, students learned to "hear each other (the sound of different voices), to listen to one another, [and that was] an exercise in recognition."[11] Though I did not realize it at the time, I was learning then ideas about teaching that are similar to those of hooks about inclusivity in the classroom[12] At Eckerd College, learning was a communal experience; it was as hooks says, "education as the practice of freedom."[13] At Eckerd, education was not about receiving a degree; it was about self-actualization, learning to understand the world from many perspectives, and gaining the tools needed to become a responsible citizen in the world.

A few years after graduating from Eckerd College, I went on to pursue an MA at New Mexico Highlands University in Las Vegas, New Mexico. In that small-town northern New Mexico university, over 80 percent of the students were Latina/o, approximately 80 percent of the staff were Latina/o, but approximately 80 percent of the professors were white. In *Teaching to Transgress,* hooks discusses how Black and people of color who are members of the staff of a university often remain unseen by white professors.[14] I would argue that the opposite is true as well. When the privileged identity for college professors is white, few of them notice the lack of people of color teaching in their university, even when most of the students at the university are people of color. In *Teaching Community: A Pedagogy of Hope*, hooks writes, "Teachers are often among the group most reluctant to acknowledge the extent to which white-supremacist thinking informs every aspect of our culture including the way we learn, the content of what we learn, and the manner in which we are taught."[15] But I think college instructors are often completely *unaware* of the way their own ideas about education and teaching have been shaped by a culture built on a white supremacist foundation. They simply don't *see.* Marshall Gregory states, "conventions of social rhetoric often mask large subterranean structures of value and belief, the power of which goes unchallenged as long as the structures lie mostly unseen."[16] Part of that "structure of value and belief" is erected upon Eurocentric foundations. Namulundah Florence states, "Not only are most textbooks Eurocentric but educational policies and practices also reinforce racial and ethnic stereotypes."[17] Those textbooks, policies, and practices are often also sexist, classist, and homophobic. But for most university-trained professors, those structures, because of their very subterranean nature, "lie mostly unseen."[18]

Because my MA program classes were juxtaposed with the liberating educational experiences I had at Eckerd College, I was able to recognize the insidiousness of white supremacist thought in textbooks and in teaching practices that placed the instructor in the position of autocratic ruler of the classroom, with some instructors who relished having that power over students and abused that power. I feel sure NMHU is far less hierarchical than most of the larger and more prestigious universities in the United States, but hierarchy still exists there, as it does in most universities. Though I had some wonderful professors at NMHU, it was clear that most of them had been taught and trained to be instructors in universities where the hierarchy of white male supremacy and the hierarchy of the classroom had never been challenged, much less explored. I quickly realized that if I chose to continue teaching in college classrooms, I did not want to become *that* kind of instructor, though I did not, at the time, have the words to define what *that* was. In the classes I was required to teach as a graduate teaching assistant, I began testing ideas and practices, with some successes and some failures, in an attempt to free myself and my students from the strict hierarchy of the academy. After completing my MA at NMHU, I worked for almost ten years in New Mexico, with three different non-profit organizations, but I continued to teach one class per semester, as an adjunct, simply because I loved teaching.

As an adjunct, I was continually working, during those years, to find ways to resist racist, sexist, homophobic, hegemonic teaching practices, though I still had not acquired the vocabulary to put those thoughts into the words I have used here. Gregory argues, "Knowledge that gets absorbed shows up not as knowledge but as features of mind and character that are much more valuable than mere information . . . when a thing gets absorbed it turns into ideas and skills, and it turns into forms of socialization and cognition that shape [our] powers of language, imagination, judgment, and reasoning."[19] This is how I came to my philosophy of teaching, with absorbed knowledge that I could not articulate, but that I used in my classrooms to empower my students. One idea I did fully understand was the power of language, and I taught my students about that power. I taught students why it was racist to label those who were different from ourselves by color or ethnicity or religion or sexuality without labeling ourselves and those who were like us as well. I taught my students how even unconsciously used sexist language demeaned women, placed women in the category of second-class citizens, and even subtly influenced how much money women made in their careers. In their daily writing assignments, I taught my students to express themselves in ways that would undermine a racist, sexist, classist, homophobic society. But I still had no theoretical framework for my classroom stance.

My embrace of Black feminist theory came to full fruition only when I was in my early sixties, when I came to the University of South Florida to pursue a PhD In my second semester, I enrolled in a class titled "bell hooks and Autocritography," which was taught by Gary L. Lemons. His exemplification of the practice of Black feminist pedagogy in his classroom and the in-class discussions of hooks' Black feminist theory finally gave me the theoretical language I needed to identify my own classroom stance. It also motivated me to continue to reshape my own feminist, anti-racist, anti-classist, anti-homophobic ideas into a unified theoretical pedagogical concept I could use in the classroom. In many ways, hooks named for me what I was unable to name, my own teaching philosophy.

To fully place myself within the conversation about black feminist pedagogy requires more personal information. I am a white lesbian of the Baby Boomer generation, born into a sharecropping family in the South, raised by an abusive stepmother and a neglectful father struggling to become upwardly mobile with only a ninth-grade education. Though I loved learning and found my source of support in school during my early childhood education, because of lack of support emotionally and financially from my family, I struggled to reach my own educational goals, with years passing between each level of college and university education I achieved. At age sixty-seven, I am currently working to attain a PhD in literature, focusing my dissertation specifically on the link between power and naming in African American literature.

In his article, "'Young Man, Tell the Stories of How We Made it Over': Beyond the Politics of Identity," Lemons discusses pedagogical questions he raises in his classroom, questions related to the identity of the professor: "Should white professors teach black, Native American, Asian or Chicano/a studies. . . . Should heterosexuals teach gay and/or lesbian studies?"[20] He points out that in discussing the "politics of identity," sometimes "the teacher's body/identity stands at the center of contestation."[21] Some well-intentioned people, concerned about the misappropriation of African American culture, might argue that I, as a white lesbian, have no right to teach or to write about African American literature, but I have discovered that I absolutely *must* write about naming and power in African American literature because naming is an instrument that has been used by white people to maintain white supremacy, and, as an older, Southern white woman, I have been a witness to racial injustices perpetuated by white people against Black people. As Lemons says:

> We have arrived at a moment of crucial urgency in the academy for those of us who educate as the practice of freedom. We know that crossing borders has been a question of life and death. In the stories of black women / women of color, the voices of the oppressed tell me that I have a political obligation to teach about them—their struggle, the battles they wage for liberation.[22]

Just as Lemons says he has "a political obligation" to teach the literature written by women of color, I feel I have "a political obligation" to "cross borders," to speak out, to write about the way people embedded in white supremacist culture have used naming as a tool to suppress Black people and how the historical trauma related to naming continues to express itself in African American literature. I am weighted down by the injustice I have witnessed during my life, and, in reading African American literature, I hear multiple voices speaking out about the injustices perpetuated by those who have been inculcated into white supremacist thought. The voices of our African American brothers and sisters need to be heard; their truths need to be shared. I write to share those truths, to draw attention to the voices of Black authors that many professors would leave out of the canon. I put ink on paper in writing my dissertation, to be a witness to racial injustice and to be an ally to black people in the United States.

I grew up in South Georgia, the daughter of a peanut sharecropper, and my family would have been labeled by upper-class whites as "poor white trash" because of my family's lack of education and low-income status. In my family, racism and bigotry were taught to me before my ABCs. But two experiences early in my life "woke" me and made me begin to question the ingrained racism of my family and my community. I want to talk about the second event first, which was listening, in a classroom in my white segregated school, to a speech by Dr. Martin Luther King Jr. when I was nine years old. My parents had taught me that black people were not as smart and capable as white people, but, listening to Dr. King, it was immediately clear to me that he was smarter than any adult I knew, far smarter than my white parents, smarter than my white teachers, even smarter than our college-educated white preacher. For me, that knowledge knocked down the already shaky foundations of racism and prejudice in me. But the first moment of my awakening was even more powerful, and I have carried it like a stone in my heart, with horror, with shame, with sadness, and with anger, for over fifty years.

When I was seven years old, I was on a rare excursion downtown with my dad, walking along a sidewalk. An old Black man approached my dad with his hand extended, but, when he opened his mouth, only a horrible jumble of grunting and mumbling emerged. My dad ignored the man and kept walking. I looked up at my dad and said, "Daddy, what's wrong with that old colored man?" Without breaking stride, my dad said, "He doesn't have a tongue." Puzzled, I asked, "What happened to his tongue?" In the same tone he would have used to say the man fell and skinned his knee, my dad said, "The Ku Klux Klan caught him talking to a white woman, so they cut out his tongue."

My father kept walking, while I stood stunned, eyes wide and mouth agape, in the middle of the sidewalk, unable to express the roiling emotions that overwhelmed me in that moment. I was shocked; I was horrified; I was ashamed; I was angry. I wanted to go back and comfort that old Black man; I wanted to hammer my white father with my small white fists for the nonchalant tone in which he delivered this inconceivable story. It was in that moment that I was awakened to the reality that I swam as a small fish in an ugly ocean of white supremacy that was rife with violence against Black people.

After that experience, I saw my community with open eyes; I paid attention to interactions between white people and Black people. I saw the discrimination and humiliation black people faced every day, and I was ashamed of my racist white family and my racist community. I made the decision to speak out about racism whenever I could, even before I knew the word "racism," and though I received quite a few beatings from my dad and my stepmother when I tried to tell them how wrong they were to disrespect Black people, I continued to feel compelled to speak up against racism.

In *Teaching Community*, bell hooks clearly intersects her critique of racism with the perpetuation of classism in the United States.[23] In my own small way, I have always worked to overcome undemocratic discrimination, to speak out about racism and injustice. In writing about naming in African American literature, I use my white privilege to draw attention to the powerful, but sometimes neglected, voices of African American authors. By writing about the link between power and naming in African American literature, I do not want to appropriate or commodify the work of Black people. I want to awaken other white readers to the way naming continues to be used to exert authority over Black people. Janaé E. Bonsu writes, "Black feminists and allies cannot fight against racism without that addressing sexism, classism, ableism, or any -ism that is rooted in the lived experiences of Black women without fighting them all."[24] In my writing, I position myself as an ally to Black people, especially Black women, adding my voice to their collective voices, speaking truth to power. Writing about the way naming has been used to stereotype and oppress Black people gives me an entry into the conversation to talk about issues of sexism, classism, homophobia, and other -isms as well.

In 2003, I graduated with an MA in English and have spent most years, since graduating, teaching English classes as an adjunct in the English departments of several colleges and universities. Gregory points out, "typically teachers are profoundly averse to modeling for students the messy, ragged parts of learning,"[25] but this is a method I employ in all my classes. In fact, my work on naming and its link to power sprang out of a research project I set for myself when I was modeling for my students how to write a research paper in a literature class. I went back to an essay I had written as a junior at Eckerd College about the significance of naming in Maya Angelou's *I Know Why the Caged Bird Sings*, with curiosity about whether naming was used in similar ways by other African American authors, and I used that question as the starting point for my research. The iceberg nature of that research project is what eventually brought me back to graduate school. I share this to put into context the fact that I had been teaching at the college level for over fifteen years when I enrolled as a PhD student, first came into Dr. Lemons' class, and, in that class, discovered the works of bell hooks.

All of the hooks' texts about feminist theory and about teaching that we read in Lemons' class helped me to reexamine my own pedagogy in different ways, but in reading hooks' *Teaching to Transgress: Education as the Practice of Freedom,*[26] I was compelled to reevaluate my own teaching practices, especially to reconceptualize the value of vernacular and reconsider the ways that my working-class background makes me feel marginalized even while it offers me a platform for empowerment in the hallowed halls of academia.

I have always considered myself to be a good teacher. Prior to beginning my doctoral work, I have taught mostly at community colleges and small universities where most of my students have come from working-class families, and the student bodies have been quite diverse, with each class containing mostly students of color, older students, and high-school dropouts who had earned their GEDs. In the composition classes I have taught, I have always been open with my students about my own broken path to a college degree, and I encouraged them to think of education as a tool that could be used to empower them in their own lives. I pointed out to my students the sense of accomplishment and pride to be found "in grappling with difficult material."[27] In *Teaching to Transgress,* hooks writes autocritographically about the critical importance of pedagogical practice grounded in the intersectionality of race, gender, and class.[28]

I have learned the same thing about teaching my students difficult concepts. In the composition and literature classes I've taught, when explaining assignments, I read the academic terms usually required by the institution but then repeat the assignment guidelines using more easily accessible language, providing an entry point for students who felt shut out by the very language that was supposed to help them understand the assignment. I also used examples related to my students' own lives, based on information gleaned from the personal narratives I assigned at the start of the semester, to explain complex ideas that arise in class discussions. To empower students who had been disempowered or to educate those students who had been blind to injustice, I pointed out to students the many ways that race, class, and gender impacted their lives, and I discussed with students how I had faced discrimination as a woman and as a lesbian. I brought up political issues with students, and I acknowledged the discrimination that many of them had experienced because of their color, their ethnicity, their religion, their sexuality, their differences. I have cried with my students when they felt threatened by our current political realities, and I have written, on the whiteboards of my classrooms, statements of support for students of color, for female students, for immigrant students, for Muslim students, for LGBTQ students. I believed I was "woke." But reading the works of hooks made me realize that I needed to be even more aware of how I approached teaching my students.

Before enrolling in Lemons' class, I had never studied feminism as theory or joined feminist groups, though I have essentially lived my adult life as a feminist, refusing to accept the patriarchal boundaries for what is considered appropriate behavior for women or what was considered appropriate "women's work." I have talked my way into jobs at factories and businesses, jobs that no woman had ever held, and I have proved to employers that sometimes women can do the work better and faster than men. But I had not considered ways to bring the practice of feminism into the classroom. My own working-class childhood, my female gender, my sexual identity, and the fact that I've often been the oldest student in any class often make me feel like a marginalized member of the academic community, but I also realize that in academia I have a position of privilege because I am a white person. Stephanie A. Shields, who is, like me, a white woman of the Baby Boomer generation with working-class roots, writes about intersectionality and white privilege. She says:

> The white privilege that I focus on here, for example, offers more than avoiding disadvantage or oppression by actually opening up access to rewards, status, and opportunities unavailable to other intersections. While I experience a set of intersections as my individual social identity, those intersections also reflect a complex operation of power relationships among social groups. In other words, intersectionality not only defines who I am as a social individual but also reflects my relative position of power and status because of the social groups that define my identity.[29]

My own intersectional identity defines my lower status because I am female and because I am a lesbian and because I come from uneducated parents, but my white skin still gives me privilege within a complex society whose very foundations spring from white supremacy. Though I fight against elitism in academia, nevertheless, I must acknowledge that I benefit from some its hierarchal structures. Therefore, I struggle to make sure my praxis reflects my philosophy.

In *Teaching to Transgress,* bell hooks writes about teachers like me who work to undercut the elitism of academia, but fail to recognize that their words may not match their deeds—"perpetuat[ing] those very hierarchies and biases they are critiquing."[30] However, in reevaluating my pedagogical praxis, I knew I was not teaching "to reinforce domination."[31] And I am sure that I have never set myself up as the all-knowing authority. I frequently talk to my students about the shaky foundation of my own education, and I tell them that I often learn as much from them as they learn from me. I also feel sure that my word choices have not perpetuated biases, since that is something of which I am acutely aware and on which I base many of my teaching practices. But in reading hooks' critique of traditional, dominating ideas of professorship, I realized that my body posture, my position at the front of the class, my tone of authority might be negating the message I've been trying to send to my students.

After reading *Teaching to Transgress*, I spent several weeks considering ways to decentralize the power in my classrooms to create a more open, feminist environment that would encourage growth and self-actualization for both myself and my students. I remembered my years at Eckerd College and the circle of the classroom, and I made plans to adopt that format for myself, but I kept putting it off, telling myself, "I need to wait until the start of a new semester," or "I need to wait until I'm teaching a literature class instead of a composition class. As Florence points out, "There seems to be in most of us an inherent resistance to change,"[32] and I came to realize I was afraid of change, terrified to step outside the teaching style I had created for myself over the past fifteen years. Fighting to overcome my own resistance to change, I began to implement ideas gleaned from hooks' works, and I have grown excited as I find that bringing a more progressive persona into the classroom has reenergized me as an instructor and has begun to empower my students. My voice is no longer the only voice heard or heeded in the classroom. My students are beginning to recognize the value of working together and learning from each other. The Black feminist approach to teaching that I've adopted, learned from hooks' texts and from Lemons' example, has brought a powerful new energy into my classrooms.

Notice that in the previous paragraphs I refer to myself as an "instructor" or a "teacher" before I earned my PhD in 2021. Before then, I refused to allow my students to call me "professor," though I secretly love the sound of that title, and I have gladly adopted that title once I earned it. However, the one title I will always refuse is "pedagogue." In one of my MA level classes, I was required to write about my teaching philosophy and to define my own pedagogical style. I wrote about my teaching philosophy, but I assiduously avoided the words "pedagogue" and "pedagogy." My resistance to those terms springs out of the negative connotation of the term "pedagogue" I have absorbed as a member of the working class. When I hear the word "pedagogue," I picture the dull, boring, pedantic teacher almost all students have had at one time or another; in my vision, he is always a frowning, older, white male. Part of the negative connotations of the word "pedagogue" for me is related to professors who use complex, difficult terminology and obscure references that set them up as superior and force students to look up words used in class before they can even begin to understand the basics of the class discussion. That kind of language, especially as I found it in research I conducted while working on my MA degree, was what kept me from pursuing a PhD immediately after completing my MA I did not want to use language in ways that obscured meaning, shutting out all readers except those who were equally educated in my field. hooks argues that "one of the many uses of theory in academic locations is the production of an intellectual class hierarchy."[33] I believed doctoral level work would require me to learn to write like that, but I did not want to read such work, teach such work, or write such work. hooks maintains that the theoretical jargon of higher education has become a tool used to reinforce classism.[34] Moreover, she contends that until teachers begin to question the disconcerting power of academic intellectual abstractionism—particularly related to issues of racism, sexism, homophobia, and other forms of systemic domination—we all become complicit in the perpetuation of them.[35]

As a graduate student I resisted "highly abstract, jargonistic" writing, and I continue to resist it now. For me language is about communication, and the more obscure and abstract my writing becomes the more I know that many people will be shut out of that communication. As a working-class white woman with a sporadic educational background, I have often felt shut out of academic conversations by such jargonistic language, and I do not ever want to be the writer or instructor who leaves people feeling like they are on the outside looking in. I want to empower people who want to learn, want to understand, want to join the conversation. So, my teaching practices become acts of resistance to the classist hegemony of academic discourse; I practice activism for democracy in education. John Dewey famously stated, "democracy has to be born anew in each generation, and education is its midwife."[36] If there is no democracy in education, there will be no democracy in any other aspect of life. As hooks points out in *Teaching Critical Thinking*: "educators [are] deemed crucial conveyers of democratic ideas."[37] I truly believe that when democracy in education dies, democracy dies, and only educators can keep democracy alive.

Though I have strong ideas about avoiding academic jargon, hooks' discussion of language in *Teaching to Transgress* made me realize that I, nevertheless, had internalized academic views of my own mother tongue, the white Southern working-class vernacular of my childhood.[38] Throughout my life, I have consciously worked to suppress my Southern accent; I have worked to scrub distinctive "white trash" phrases from my vocabulary, and I have often felt embarrassed by the vernacular of my family members. While I have refused to adopt the multisyllabic, jargonistic vocabulary of academia, I have moved into the liminal space between the language of my youth and the language of academia. I acknowledge that learning standard English has helped me to achieve my own goals, to succeed in college and in graduate school;

I, therefore, understand, on a personal and academic level, the usefulness of standard English as a tool needed achieve success in American life. But hooks' discussion of "the link between language and domination" in *Teaching to Transgress* was eye-opening,[39] especially when she says, "the rupture of standard English enabled and enables rebellion and resistance."[40] In writing about the use of vernacular, hooks speaks for herself and other Black people about its potential healing, discursive power.[41] Contemplating this standpoint was another moment of awakening for me. Before reading hooks' pedagogical works, I had never considered "the power" of the vernacular used by many African Americans, as a way to resist white culture or as a way to forge "a space for alternative cultural production and alternative epistemologies."[42] Through hooks, I have gained a new respect for Black vernacular.

In *Teaching to Transgress,* bell hooks also addresses the language situation of working-class students enabling them to "avoid feelings of estrangement" regarding how they speak and sound in a vernacular context.[43] I was that kind of student. I had assimilated to some degree, and I had so readily accepted the negative judgment of my own Southern vernacular by classist and elitist white academics that I never appreciated the power of that vernacular, just as I never recognized the strength and integrity that Black people must use to maintain the vernacular of their various communities in the face of elitist judgment. hooks' ode to the vernacular made me want to reclaim at least a little of my own mother tongue. So, I need to state this clearly: "I ain't no damned pedagogue, and cain't none of y'all make me act like one."

Despite the internalized shame I have carried about the vernacular of my childhood, I have had moments when I stood up to the elitist, classist assumptions of academia. One such instance occurred while I was working on my MA degree. In a creative, non-fiction class, one of the assigned readings was a book by Annie Dillard, *An American Childhood.*[44] The book is a collection of stand-alone essays each of which begins as a lovely moment of contemplation and then moves into a memory of Dillard's experiences as a child. The book is beautifully written, with lovely, though unemotional, tales about Dillard's privileged childhood, in which she experienced dance lessons, music lessons, debutante balls, and adoring parents. The book made me furious. To be more specific, the title made me furious. To tell such stories of privilege and then name the collection *An American Childhood,* as if Dillard's experiences were common to most American children, made me so angry I ranted for days to the lovely professor who was teaching the class, a white woman whose childhood, no doubt, was similar to Dillard's. Her response was perfect. She said, "So write your own memoir." And I did.

That memoir, *Flashing Lights in my Review Mirror,* was fueled by anger, and it became my MA thesis in my creative writing program. That lovely, privileged, white professor who first assigned Dillard's memoir, became the chair of my thesis committee. The memoir was my response to an academic assumption that MA level students studying English and creative writing must all came from upper-class, wealthy homes. I wrote of my "white-trash" childhood. I wrote of my uneducated, ignorant, abusive parents. I wrote of poverty and racism, and I wrote the dialogue of my family in the vernacular, which I then had to explain and justify to my thesis chair. I wrote my thesis as a way to *transgress* and to confront issues of class that are often embedded in conservative ideas of higher education, as hooks contends.[45] She also argues that students and teachers who enter academia from working class backgrounds must share our stories of intellectual survival as a demonstration of solidarity and support for each other.[46] I will always remember that my thesis was read by perhaps a dozen professors and graduate students at the university. It was a small audience, but I hope "the assumption that we share a common class background and perspective [was] disrupted" by writing that sprung up out of my frustration with elitist assumptions.[47]

In *Black Male Outsider*, Lemons shares a list of things he learned from teaching in a white majority college. The first two of the things on that list struck a chord with me because they mesh with the classroom experience that I want to create for my own students. Lemons says that he learned:

> that pedagogy founded upon black feminist thought about race and gender poses a liberatory challenge to the ideology of white supremacy for white students and students of color.

> that black feminist pedagogy as a specific response to racism and sexism offers a more complex critique of white supremacy than a race-only approach (which may or may not address the institutional and systemic nature of racism predicated upon the myth of white racial superiority).[48]

While it is clearly not appropriate for me, as a white woman, to call myself a Black feminist, Lemons and hooks have taught me that Black feminist theory is crucial to challenging sexism, racism, classism, and homophobia in the classroom, and embracing Black feminist thought has given me the tools I need to liberate and empower my students—considering the intersectionality of their race, ethnicity, gender, class, sexuality, ability, as well as all other forms of difference. Beyond the classroom, Black feminist thought, as expressed by bell hooks, has liberated me and my Southern vernacular from the judgment of elitist academic culture. Black feminist thought continues to embolden me to empower myself and to empower my students "to embrace diversities of experience, standpoint, behavior, or style," at least in my classrooms.[49]

BIBLIOGRAPHY

Bonsu, Janaé E. "Black Queer Feminism as Praxis: Building an Organization and a Movement." *Black Women's Liberatory Pedagogies: Resistance, Transformation, and Healing Within and Beyond the Academy*, eds. Olivia N. Perlow, Durene I. Wheeler, Sharon L. Bethea, and BarBara M. Scott. Palgrave McMillan, 2018.

Dillard, Annie. *An American Childhood.* New York: Harper Perennial, 1987.

Florence, Namulundah. *bell hooks' Engaged Pedagogy: A Transgressive Education for Critical Consciousness.* ed. Henry A. Giroux. Westport, Connecticut: Bergin & Garvey, 1998.

Gregory, Marshall W. "Do We Teach Disciplines or Do We Teach Students? What Difference Does It Make? *Profession,* 2008: 117–29. https://www.jstor.org/stable /25595889.

Hill Collins, Patricia. *Black Feminist Thought: Knowledge, Consciousness, and the Politics of Empowerment.* New York: Routledge, 1990.

hooks, bell. *Teaching Community: A Pedagogy of Hope.* New York: Routledge, 2003.

———. *Teaching Critical Thinking: Practical Wisdom.* New York: Routledge, 2010.

———. *Teaching to Transgress: Education as the Practice of Freedom.* New York: Rutledge, 1994.

Kennedy, Robert. "Quaker Education: What's Different About a Friends School?" Jul. 26, 2017. *Boarding School Review.* https://www.boardingschoolreview.com/blog/ quaker-education-whats-different-about-a-friends-school.

Lemons, Gary L. *Black Male Outsider: Teaching as a Pro-Feminist Man: A Memoir.* New York: State U. of New York P., 2008.

———. "'Young Man, Tell the Stories of How We Made It Over': Beyond the Politics of Identity." *Teaching What You're Not: Identity Politics in Higher Education.* Ed. Katherine J. Mayberry. New York: New York University Press, 1996.

Romigh, Maggie. *Flashing Lights in My Rearview Mirror.* Thesis. New Mexico Highlands University College of Arts and Sciences, Las Vegas, NM. May 2003.

Stephanie. A. Shields. "Waking Up to Privilege: Intersectionality and Opportunity." *Presumed Incompetent: The Intersections of Race and Class for Women in Academia.* Eds. y Muhs, Gabriella Gutiérrez, et al. Utah State U.P., 2012. *ProQuest Ebook Central,* http://ebookcentral.proquest.com/lib/usf/detail.action ?docID=1031958.

NOTES

1. bell hooks, Introduction, *Teaching to Transgress: Education as the Practice of Freedom* (New York: Routledge, 1994), 11.

2. Gary L. Lemons. *Black Male Outsider: Teaching as a Pro-Feminist Man: A Memoir* (New York: State U. of New York P., 2008), 14–15.

3. Ibid., 15.

4. Patricia Hill Collins. *Black Feminist Thought: Knowledge, Consciousness, and the Politics of Empowerment.* (New York: Routledge, 1990), 19.

5. Ibid., 19.

6. Ibid., 19.

7. Ibid., 20.

8. Lemons, *Black Male Outsider*, 33.

9. Ibid., 31.

10. Robert Kennedy. "Quaker Education: What's Different About a Friend's School? *Boarding School Review.* July 26, 2017, https://www.boardingschoolreview.com/blog/quaker-education-whats-different-about-a-friends-school.

11. bell hooks. *Teaching to Transgress: Education as the Practice of Freedom* (New York: Routledge, 1994), 41.

12. Ibid., 8.

13. Ibid., 4.

14. bell hooks, *Teaching Community: A Pedagogy of Hope* (New York: Routledge, 2003), 37.

15. Ibid., 25.

16. Marshall W. Gregory. "Do We Teach Disciplines or Do We Teach Students? What Difference Does It Make?" *Profession,* 2008, 122. https://www.jstor.org/stable/25595889.

17. Namulundah Florence. *bell hooks' Engaged Pedagogy: A Transgressive Education for Critical Consciousness.* ed. Henry A. Giroux (Westport, Connecticut: Bergin & Garvey, 1998), 28.

18. Gregory, Marshall. "Do We Teach Disciplines," 122.

19. Ibid., 120.

20. Gary L. Lemons. "'Young Man, Tell the Stories of How We Made It Over': Beyond the Politics of Identity." *Teaching What You're Not: Identity Politics in Higher Education.* Ed. Katherine J. Mayberry (New York: New York U. P., 1996), 277.

21. Ibid., 277.

22. Ibid., 282.

23. bell hooks, *Teaching Community*, 32.

24. Janaé E. Bonsu. "Black Queer Feminism as Praxis: Building an Organization and a Movement." *Black Women's Liberatory Pedagogies: Resistance, Transformation, and Healing Within and Beyond the Academy.* Eds. Olivia N. Perlow, Durene I. Wheeler, Sharon L. Bethea, and BarBara M. Scott (Palgrave McMillan, 2018), 214.

25. Gregory, Marshall. "Do We Teach Disciplines," 126.

26. As I point out, studying bell hooks' *Teaching to Transgress* really compelled me to write about my pedagogical standpoint from an autocritographical approach, merging the personal with the professional.

27. Ibid., 154.

28. Ibid., 51.

29. Stephanie. A. Shields. "Waking Up to Privilege: Intersectionality and Opportunity." *Presumed Incompetent: The Intersections of Race and Class for Women in Academia.* Eds. y Muhs, Gabriella Gutiérrez, et al., (Utah State U.P., 2012.), 30.

30. bell hooks, *Teaching to Transgress*, 141.

31. Ibid., 4.

32. Namulundah Florence. *bell hooks' Engaged Pedagogy*, 139.

33. bell hooks, *Teaching to Transgress*, 64.

34. bell hooks, *Teaching Critical Thinking: Practical Wisdom*, 30.

35. Ibid., 32.

36. John Dewey. Source unknown. Quoted in bell hooks. *Teaching Critical Thinking: Practical Wisdom*. (New York: Routledge, 2010), 14.

37. bell hooks, *Teaching Critical Thinking*, 14.

38. bell hooks, *Teaching to Transgress*, 167–76.

39. Ibid., 168.

40. Ibid., 171.

41. Ibid., 175.

42. Ibid., 171.

43. Ibid., 181.

44. Annie Dillard, *An American Childhood* (New York: Harper Perennial, 1987).

45. bell hooks, *Teaching to Transgress*, 183.

46. Ibid., 185.

47. Ibid., 186.

48. Gary L. Lemons, *Black Male Outsider*, 5.

49. bell hooks, *Teaching to Transgress*, 187.

Chapter Seven

You Poured Your Soul into This Work

A Dialogue in the Spirit of Self-Transformation

Paul T. Corrigan

In 2012, as a doctoral student in English at the University of South Florida, I (Paul) took Gary's course on Literature by Women of Color. We read This Bridge Called My Back: Radical Writings by Women of Color, *edited by Cherríe Moraga and Gloria Anzaldúa, along with several other anthologies of feminist and womanist writing. Each week, in addition to reading a selection of texts, we also wrote short essays in which we were to engage critically not only with what we had read but with the relation between what we had read and our own lives. During class, we would share and discuss both the readings and our work. The discussions were often heavy and sometimes heated. We engaged the whole range of crucial topics the writers wrote about, including the ways categories of identity (gender, race, class, sexuality, and more) shape people's lives and what we could do about that to help being about a more just world. The course proved a transformative experience for many of the students, including for me, which attribute to a number of factors: the power of the texts we read, the power of the analytical and personal mode of writing Gary asked of us, the willingness many of us demonstrated to engage at a deep level with the work and with each other, and the words and presence of Gary himself as a teacher.*

One more factor that contributed to my own transformative experience of the course was that before the course ever began, I read Gary's book Black Male Outsider, a Memoir: Teaching as a Pro-Feminist Man *(State University of New York Press, 2008). Reading this book helped me develop not only a greater theoretical understanding of Gary's purposes and practices for the course but also a greater investment in and commitment to the work and relationships at hand in the course. So, for instance, while our weekly response assignments only needed to be four or five pages long, I threw myself so fully into the process that I ended up writing over two hundred pages for the course that single semester, my way of engaging with the work(s) as seriously as I could. It is little wonder, then, that the experience of the course helped me deepen my understanding and commitment to literature and to social justice, particularly with respect to the words and lives of women of color.*

It is also little wonder that, seven years later now, as I write my own book on the teaching of literature and have decided to reread those pedagogical works that have meant the most to me—so that they will be fresh and "alive" within me as I write—that Black Male Outsider *is on a short list of key volumes I am returning to, alongside books by bell hooks, Parker Palmer, Sheridan Blau, and a few others. It is this occasion of rereading* Black Male Outsider *that prompted me to ask Gary to have this interview/conversation with me. Afterward, Taylor Lyon transcribed the audio recording, and I edited the transcript for length and clarity.*

Although this dialogue emerges from questions I ask Gary about Black Male Outsider, *readers who have not yet read that book should still find our discussion of interest, we unpack unpacks a number of issues of broad significance: the purpose of higher education; the integration of the personal and the academic; the mode of writing called "autocritography"; what it means for men to read and teach the writings of feminist and womanists of color; the way some students resist this work while others find it liberatory; the value of reading physical books; what the #MeToo movement reveals about how not even straight white men actually live up to the exclusionary standards of white supremacist heterosexist patriarchy; how challenging white supremacy is potentially dangerous; the relationship between teaching and activism; and how hope can be found in building alliances across ethnicities, genders, and other categories of identity. Additionally, our exchange begins and ends with what it means to be a teacher, what it means to be a student, and how that relationship can last far beyond the classroom.*

> GARY: I'll call you "Dr. Corrigan" and "Paul" at the same time. We're scholars but also colleagues. It's certainly a pleasure for me to have this conversation, this dialogue, with you.
>
> PAUL: We should add to the record that I'm your student as well.
>
> GARY: It's interesting you would say, "I'm your student." You have gotten your PhD and so you're now, I would say, a former student. But if you want to

continue to use the term "student of mine," that's absolutely fine. It's a kind of honor.

PAUL: I mean it that way. I think there are times you have somebody who *was* your teacher But other times the impact is so significant that it continues, that they *are* your teacher.

GARY: I absolutely agree with you. I think you know this really well in terms of our relationship, that the professor isn't the only one who teaches in the classroom. Students have the capacity to teach as well, particularly when we begin to engage the stories of our lives in relationship to the literature that we're reading. So, I would say it's about a concept of reciprocity, a pedagogical standpoint where there's a dialogue. I know, now that you are Dr. Corrigan, you are teaching your students how to work within a literary framework. But one of the things I think is critically important, in the way that you're addressing me as a continued professor in your life, is that learning works on the number of levels. As I just said on the personal level, I would also say on the social level, on the political level (particularly in this time we're living in), but also on the spiritual level.

So much of what we experience when we study literature has to be within the context of the pedagogical foundation of literary studies. Here we have the thematics, the literary terminology, and so on and so forth. But when we move our students into a place where we ask, "So what does this mean to you? What does this have to do with you?" we move them into a framework of critical self-consciousness where they have to begin to think about, "Oh, it's not only what I think of this work or that I know that there are a number of literary strategies that the author has used to create this work, but when I began to think about this work in relationship to my life and what I'm taking away from the composition, I have to start self-reflecting." So, for me—in the context of Michael Awkward's concept of "autocritography"—it's not enough to be a literary scholar in terms of your employment of secondary sources; you have to really integrate the impact of the work on your person. It has a deeper impact when you talk about why this work impacted you in the way that you chose to write about it. So, autocritography has been a strategic way for me to position myself in a feminist, womanist context.

I'm always concerned about whether I'm perceived as appropriating feminism and womanism when as a man I say I identify as a pro-feminist, womanist man. Is this ground-breaking or is this appropriation? I would want to say, given my work in *Black Male Outsider* and the way I talk about the evolution of my teaching, that so much of what I teach is not just about, "Oh, I'm an ally for women's rights and social justice." I've had to go beyond that. I've had to write about life-altering changes and liberatory transformation in studying the literature, particularly by Black women, women of color feminists, and womanists to the point to where it's like, "Oh. I've been reading this to the extent that I've had to question my whole concept of manhood and masculinity."

You saying "I still think of you as a teacher" has such an impact on me given that your work—as you produced it when we were working together in the graduate course on women of color writers and feminist writers—was outstanding such that I wanted to make sure it didn't remain in the classroom but took a journey into the world. So, your chapter in—*Building Womanist Coalitions: Writing and Teaching in the Spirit of Love* (Ed. Lemons, 2019)—says that what we did together in that course is a testament to the power of a pedagogy rooted in student-centered learning.

> PAUL: Amen. It's been some years now since we did this course together. It was obvious to me even then that we were doing important work. But as several years have passed, I think the extent of the impact has become clearer in my own teaching and my own writing. I can see what the writers you introduced me to have meant to me over this time, how the commitments you've helped me strengthen and bring more sophistication to have continued to unfold in my life—in terms of desiring and teaching toward justice for everyone, inclusion for everyone, hearing everyone's voices.

> GARY: When we're in these pedagogical moments of self-reflection, hindsight becomes a strategy to really reassess what we were doing in the moment, because we may not in the moment realize its full significance. We might be having a discussion, "Wow, these texts are really moving," all while thinking about these issues and what have you. It's like that in the moment. But several years later: "Wow. Looking back, now I really understand why I was supposed to be doing that. Now I want to talk about it. Now I want to write about it because it had an impact on me that was so moving and too transformative to not go back and actually write about it when I own the experience." For me, hindsight is always about reclamation because you get to look back, retrace, recapture those memories of the impact of the writers on your life not only as a scholar but as a person. It's not just about your expertise but it's about your transformation toward commitment to social justice from a feminist, womanist standpoint. So, you get to be a testament. You say, "Well, wait, a testament is actually a document." Well, when we write from an autocritographical standpoint, merging the personal with the professional, as Michael Awkward would say, we become metaphorically testaments of the power of speaking and writing about our lives and about how, in the context of our work, feminists of color transform the way we think about ourselves as men, men who are not into this patriarchal, masculine-ness idea of what manhood is.

> PAUL: I want to take a step back to get a bird's-eye view of the vision behind *Black Male Outsider* of what education is. You ask a lot from people. Many people remain on a surface level: "Education is so you can get trained so you

can get a job." Some people go a little deeper: "Education is so you can learn to think critically and develop a life of the mind." Then we get to your book. You talk about survival and liberation and transformation, which are even deeper than just a life of the mind. For you, what is education for?

GARY: When I think about education, particularly higher education, it really is about critical consciousness. You and I have gone through PhD programs in literary studies where we had to cross every *t* and dot every *i* in terms of our knowledge of primary and secondary sources. But for me higher education is this idea that you really have to move to a place where it's not just about your academic expertise but about questioning your identity politics: Who are you in relationship to what you're doing, what you're studying, what you're teaching as a professor?

PAUL: That phrase "Who are you?" stands out. I've rarely, if ever, seen somebody talking about teaching literature who puts as much on the line as you do in this book. On page 6 you use a phrase quoted from some of your earlier work. You talk about teaching "what I am"—and, if I might paraphrase "*who* I am"— teaching your *self* so that your self as the teacher is integrally part of the teaching that's happening. You poured your self into this book and into your teaching. It's not just some replaceable person at the front of the room doing some set of methods. It's you as the teacher, present and unfolding.

GARY: It's interesting you would use that phrase, "You poured your soul into this work." We can't even talk about my vision of higher education without centering the work of bell hooks because the whole idea for me of higher education, in relationship to who I am, is really about my having been transformed by reading the works of bell hooks. That course I'm discussing on that page you quote from, "Redefining Womanhood: Rewriting the Black Female Self," I taught as an advocate of a feminist movement in which people *including* men unite across race, class, and sexuality struggle to end sexist oppression. I really am not who I am without my commitment to the vision of ending sexist, racist, classist oppression and domination.

I would really want to add—although I do not discuss this much in this book—ending oppression of individuals who are not "able" in terms of their abilities. We use this term "disability," which I don't really care much for because "dis" means "not." Not able. I started to think who I am in relationship to what I teach really comes from a history of being African American and understanding the history of oppression through that lens in this United States, enabling me to say if you really understand the history of survival for African Americans in this country, that should enable you to align your commitment to justice with anyone who has been historically on the margin. That is intersected with race, class, gender, sexuality, abilities, generation, and it goes on and on and on. Anyone who has been marginalized because of their identity, once I understand your movement to survive, I should be able to say,

"Oh." Chinua Achebe uses this phrase: "empathetic imagination." I should be able to step into your shoes—and you may not even have any shoes because your butt may be so poor that you may not even have the money to afford shoes—but I should be able to step into your footprint and say, "Dang. Wow. You really are going through it. But you know what? I'm going to stand with you and help you to go through."

So that's who I am. Survival for me is what higher education ought to be about: bring everyone, teacher and students, into this framework of critical self-consciousness where who I am has to be related to not only disciplinary expertise but also to social justice and human rights.

> PAUL: On that same note, on page 4 of *Black Male Outsider*, you write, "I tell [students] that a purely analytical response to oppression, an approach solely through the intellect and exempt of emotional investment in human devaluation, is void of humanity, spiritually bankrupt, and ultimately not self-sustaining. Students acknowledging inner wounds of race and sex oppression begin a journey of self-transformation from silence to voice." I love the way you have written that. Poetic. There are a couple things I want to ask you about it. First, since we often think of higher education in terms of the purely analytic, I appreciate you saying that this is inadequate, so maybe you'll speak to that a little more. Second, I want to hear more about that wounding, the inner wounds of race and sex oppression. One of the things I'm learning from you and from reading your book, among others, is that in this society you get wounded merely by existing. Nothing specific even has to happen. If something specific does happen, it can be even more traumatic, but just existing in a society set up like our seems wounding to many, if not everyone.

> GARY: If I'm only teaching you about the canonical structure of literary studies, then I'm perpetuating what has been and continues to be the misnomer of what the ivory tower is all about. The more you know, the more you become an expert. I don't have an issue with acquiring expertise in your field, specialization, because that's exactly what I know is so much at the core of what we do as professors. It's to enable our students to become empowered through their intellectual growth. But, simultaneously, that intellectual growth has to prompt the student into this place of critical consciousness where it's like, "What does this have to do with who I am in the world?" So many people are wounded by how or what we say. There is a wording that says, "Death and life is in the power of the tongue." So, what we speak and what we write has the power to enable people to live or to die.

We have to really be careful in academia, because you've got a hell of a lot of smart folks and professors. I can say, "Oh, now I'm a full professor," and they'll say, "Oh, let me bow down to you." I'm like, "Wait just a minute." When we start to give credence to this notion of "I've jumped over every hoop in the ivory tower and so I'm at the top of the ivory tower," now we have to be really careful about that. In a biblical context people got together and said, "We want to build a tower! We want to be up there. We want to be up there with that One because, you know, we're really smart!" So, they started building a tower and working together and then they're like, "Hmm. Wait just a moment. You and I are not the same." You think you know everything, but that's all in the intellect where you think your knowledge has to be. But there's a deeper place. And because you don't know anything about it, that tower you all are building is going to be torn down, so you can understand. You're not everywhere, you're not all powerful, and you don't know everything. That's not to take anything away from you, but it's to give you a sense of humility. When you start to understand that you're not the best because you are rationalistic, you see, you hear, you taste, you smell, you touch.

I question the preeminence of intellectuality. There are many things that you don't see that you need to see. So that really brings me back to this idea of integrating and intersecting the spiritual with intellectual. That means we have to go inside and write from the inside out. That goes back to the power of the personal, the power of storytelling—which is really, when you think about it, the way that so many marginalized people, people of color in particular, have survived, telling a story of how we made it over is, which gets passed from generation to generation and becomes a strategic device for survival. Again, I don't have problems with analytic power but analytic power in and of itself is not your savior.

PAUL: On page xviii, speaking about writing *Black Male Outsider* and embracing black feminist thought, you write, "I have learned that it is better to love justice than to love manhood." I love that. Although I don't want to give too short attention to manhood specifically, it seems like there's so many things you could plug in there. It is better to love justice than to love all of these categories we have as a society have invested with some sort of value, as somehow better than justice—to love whiteness, to love money, to love patriotism—

GARY: Or heterosexist ideas of manhood. . . . Yeah. Here's the part that I didn't want to do but had to do: unpack. Peggy McIntosh wrote this essay, "Unpacking the White Knapsack." She started it not from a critique of whiteness and white privilege but by conceptually critiquing heterosexual male identity politics. But that led her into this, "Well, hey, wait just a moment. That's not just separate from 'I'm a white woman,' as a feminist, talking about the politics of patriarchy and sexism." Then she moves into this place which Kimberle Crenshaw really has solidified: intersectionality. Sexism is interrelated to white privilege, white supremacy, heterosexism—all the ways that we normalize a politics of identity that says, "If you're not this, if you don't meet all of the criteria I have dictated to you, then you're not normal." For me, unpacking my privilege as a man had to be tied to the ways that I experienced white supremacy within the context of my Black identity, and even more profoundly within the context of my experience growing up in a household where domestic violence was normalized.

If we're just talking about the composition of the literary text and the theme, the plot, the conflict, the resolution, the antagonist, the protagonist, and, you know, metaphor, simile, I'm not impressed. That's a way for us to distance ourselves. You say, "Oh, it's just fiction!" But there's this cliché that fiction is often more real than life itself, which has some truth to it. One of the things as men—and you know this as a pro-feminist man—that you can't simply say is, "Oh, these texts by these women are so interesting and so challenging." I'm like, "To whom? To whom? What about, perhaps, you as the critic?" "What? I have to talk about myself in relationship to this stuff?" "Yeah. Go back. Unpack." Writing this book, I said, "An adult man having embraced Black feminist thinking as a radical form of male recovery, I have learned that it is better to love justice than to love manhood." That meant putting all of the stuff that I didn't want to talk about out of the bag.

Now Zora Neale Hurston has this essay, "How It Feels to Be Colored Me." The whole premise of the essay is, "I'm not ashamed of being black. And to be a Black woman, I love it. And so y'all might have some issues with it, but I don't." At the end of the essay, metaphorically, she thinks of herself as a bag of miscellany. She says that the creator put all of these things in this bag that composes her. She pours out the bag of all these different things and describes them, and it makes her seem so complex, and so I see that. That's exactly what bell hooks does over and over in all of these forty-something books she's written. She's always going back to childhood and talking about the implications of that in terms of who she would become as an adult black woman. Unpacking one's herstory or history or his story is about telling the stories.

And this is not just about writing it in a book but about making it a part of your pedagogy, where if you want your students to be critically self-conscious in relationship to what they're studying in your courses from an autocritographical standpoint, then you've got to give them a model and that model has to be you. It's unfair to say to students, "Oh, you need to be talking about yourself in relationship to this and what you learned from it," and I'm listening to you talk about all the pain and different struggles that you've gone through—"Oh, that's just wonderful. You get an A+"—but I've never said anything about myself as a professor. bell hooks would say you've cheated your students. If anybody should have gotten an F in a course like that, it should have been the professor, because she would say self-actualization is at the center of pedagogy, rooted in education for the practice of freedom.

PAUL: This phrase that you've just used and that you use throughout the book—"autocritography" as well as "memoir writing"—you're talking about memoir writing in relation to the texts being read. Can you help me see what that looks like concretely? You've been talking about the theory. What's the method? For instance, on page 140, you describe a specific assignment where you have each student pull a crayon out of a box and then metaphorically talk about what that color could mean and tie it back to their life. You quote from a really interesting essay where the student describes how he picked red, trying to avoid talking about race, but then found he couldn't avoid it anyway. So, what are some of the practical ways, maybe like this assignment or different than this, that you've helped students do autocritography?

GARY: As you well know, in my classes, you're writing all the time about whatever you're reading. You're writing about it critically, certainly analytically, but also from a standpoint of self-reflection. Well, this past semester and two semesters ago, teaching the course I teach called "The Bible as Literature," I conceptualized a final paper that I called "A Field Work Interview" where the students had to go back to any reading she or he or they had done and had written about during the semester and take that out of the classroom and have someone else (a friend, a family member, whoever) read it. Then I created seven questions, with the option for students to add their own, and I told students, "You've got to interview that individual based upon their reading of the work you chose for them to read. By the time you set up the interview, they should have read the piece so that they will be able to respond to the questions you're going to pose to them. Then you have to write it out, you have to document the interview. That's your final paper." It had to be 2,500 words or something like that. When I conceived it, I wondered, "Uh, is this going to work?" Because some student may really, *really* not like this assignment. But let me tell you, now that the semester's over and I've graded all of the student interviews, most of them were absolutely excellent.

PAUL: That's such a creative assignment. As for the quality it produced, I'm not surprised. In this book, you quote a good bit from student writing, and I was just struck by how good the writing is for student writing. For instance, on page 148, a student writes about her childhood in relation to the text and recalls the different kinds of black she has been. The rhythm of her writing really works. If you had not told me this was student writing, I wouldn't have assumed or thought so. This is really good work they're doing. Is it because you're focusing on the true meaning—what does this all mean for our lives—that that just naturally spills over in better quality work, maybe because students care about it more? Do you have any guesses on why the work is so good?

GARY: Remember when we were in high school? It was the personal essay. Kids will write about "What did you do last summer?" and "Did you travel somewhere?" and "What was travel like?" and "What would you like to eat? Write about that." It got kind of played, like that's just fun, the personal essay. So, we really didn't think of that as anything serious. Sometimes people are like,

"I've never heard the term autocritography." "Okay. You never heard it. But let me explain it." So, I explain it. These are people who are in literary studies, whether undergraduate or graduate students or professors, actually. "You know reader-response theory and criticism?" "Oh yeah." "Well, actually, there's a link between autocritography and reader-response criticism." So, we started talking about that. Well, let's move the personal essay from this fun place to put it in the context of reader-response criticism, which has a history and was and still is considered to be serious by some, although maybe not by a whole lot of literary professors, because I think this idea of talking about yourself in relationship to what you're teaching your students is still risk-taking. When we give preeminence to the personal within the context of the analytical, it moves the personal into a ground-breaking place where it's like, "I really am somebody in relationship to the text that I am reading."

You say, "Gary, why is it that the excerpts from these students' writings that you used in *Black Male Outsider* are so well written?" When we start to reflect, there's a whole lot of really profound stuff in us that we need to get out, and the evidence of that is in the quality of the writing about our personal stories in relationship to the analytic. It says something about the rootedness of soul work that is profound. "You mean I'm somebody?" "Yes."

So, the quality of the student writing in *Black Male Outsider* had everything to do with the interior, the internal, as a critical source. See, I'm always working from a subversive standpoint in teaching. We're teaching literary studies, and you've got to teach your students how to analyze texts. Okay, I don't have a problem with that. But here's my subversive intention: I want my students to know, "You've included ten to fifteen sources. Okay, so, great. So, you've met the requirement. But before you leave this classroom, I want you to understand the power of this work and its potential in your everyday lives to transform you so that you can say, 'Oh, I read all of these books, all of these authors.' And what did that experience do for you? Then when you go home, 'Oh. I've got to start writing this.' Write it out." That's where writers who are coming from a feminist, womanist standpoint, aimed at issues of social justice and human rights, have the power to give voice to individuals who think they have no voice. If there's anything that *Black Male Outsider* represents for me, it is the commitment to move students from silence to voice through their own self-transformation in relationship to what they've learned from the text they've read.

PAUL: On page 128, I was surprised to hear you describe how, historically, not many white men have taken your classes. I may have to unpack this a bit myself to see where my surprise comes from. You describe how some white men sign up for your class but then drop out in the first week or stay in the class but don't talk. "Few possess the courage to openly disclose their feelings about being white and male." This work has been so manifestly valuable to me—this work of reading womanist writers has been so liberating to *me*—that on one hand I'm just confused. Where are my white brothers? Why aren't they *all* here? Then I also wonder, to start questioning myself, maybe I just felt welcome in your classroom because I've been socialized to feel welcome everywhere. Why wouldn't I be welcome here as a white man?

GARY: As a heterosexual white man, you're normal. So, why wouldn't you be welcome?

PAUL: Why wouldn't I, in this literature class, at this university? So, on one hand I feel like my sense of comfort in a class focused on womanist writing is radical, and then on the other hand maybe it is privilege. Maybe there's not just one explanation.

GARY: Yeah, I would say it's not a *maybe*. It *is*. As a white heterosexual male, why wouldn't you always feel comfortable? Because you're at the top.

PAUL: So then what's wrong with my—maybe that's not exactly the right way to put it, let me rephrase it—why are more white men not reading these writers? At the very beginning of your book, talking about your concern that you might be appropriating feminism or feminist writers as a man, you used the term "ally" to describe your relationship to feminism. Maybe you will disagree with me and can help me see this from a different perspective, but I'm a little uncomfortable sometimes with the language of *ally*, as if I'm here to help.

GARY: "I'm going to *save* you." [laughs]

PAUL: I'm here to survive, *myself*. I do want to help, too. Let's all help one another. But I find this as the work that everybody needs to do: soul work. I have been so blessed by women of color writers. I can't even imagine my life without Gloria Anzaldúa, Toni Morrison, Naomi Shihab Nye, Lucille Clifton, and Alice Walker. They've transformed me. I think part of that answer is on pages 130–132. You use this phrase "finding the other in oneself." You say even someone who is white can be marginalized within whiteness. "I argue that even the whitest of white students cannot bear the mantle of perfection white supremacist ideology demands." You could apply that to patriarchy, heterosexism, all the categories. Everybody is outside. Some people haven't realized that yet. Which is not to equate everyone's experience, as if all outsideness were the same. But everybody is outside in some way, and that is a starting point to connect. If more of us could realize the ways in which we were so, that would be good.

GARY: Yeah, because even if you're white, male, did you grow up middle class or upper class?

PAUL: We fluctuated a little bit between middle and working class.

GARY: This is a point I really tried to clarify in this book. If we actually sit down and reflect on everyone, human beings, no one is at the center. I'm going to tell you the truth about it. This is why in this country right now heterosexual white men are really, really angry, especially middle-class and aristocratic white men. Because the #MeToo movement is like, "You know something wrong with your butt because you've been sexually harassing these females, all the way back, even when you were in college and probably before that." "Oh, I don't remember that. Yeah, and at that party I was probably drunk and, you know, I don't remember that and so why are you bringing that up now?" Because the truth of the matter is even in white supremacist heterosexist patriarchy, there are still white men who have issues that they don't want to talk about and now it's all coming out in the #MeToo movement. It has something to do with sexuality, and we live in a society where if you're heterosexual you've got to prove it, especially if you're a man. You've got to prove it. And the way you prove it is to objectify women and to sexually objectify women. But do you really want to talk about that? Heterosexism? No, no. Because what it would start to show is that perhaps you're not as perfect as you want to portray.

You said, "Where are the white men in the classes?" I would add, "Where are the men of color?" Where are they? How many men of color English majors are there in this program? Black men, undergraduate and graduate level? Now, this is something we probably don't want to have to talk about, literary studies, for men and for white men, straight men, reading dead white men. Why else would I want to major in English? This opens up a bag of issues not just for white heterosexual middle-class men but for all men. When I finished high school, I wanted to major in art. When I told my parents, they were like, "Art? What is that?" because I came from a working-class black background. I was like, "Oh, you know, I like to draw and paint and all that." "You won't make any money off that." So, I faked it and went, "Okay, so, um." And then I like writing too. I was the first black male editor of the newspaper at the high school I graduated from. I like writing, too. So I thought, "Okay, maybe I can major in teaching or something like that," because, you know, black people if anything historically—as bell hooks had said—if we would become professionals, it would be in the area of teaching. So my parents understood. So I said, "Oh, okay. I want to be a teacher." They said, "Okay." They were okay with that. So, I kind of combined this notion: double major of studio art and English. But again, in terms of colleagues, I was often the only male in my literature classes, undergraduate school in particular, always the only black male, and usually the only black person.

So, we have to challenge our students. "Do you ever feel like you have issues where you don't fit in?" Whatever text you're reading, "Okay, you see this character has some issues here and perhaps this character doesn't feel united or part of the family. Have you ever felt that way?" It becomes a strategic entrance into getting everybody to understand nobody's perfect and everybody's on the margin. So even for heterosexual white middle-class men, "Have you ever been sad? Have you ever cried about something? Have you ever felt insecure? Oh, yeah? Well, let's talk about it." That decenters every-one, even the ones were considered to be in a heteronormative framework. Push everybody out of the center because in reality there is no center. You think money might save you just because you're a white man who has money and who is heterosexual, but look at the president right now. They're talking about impeaching his butt. We still don't have a tax report from him. I actu-ally met someone who was an executive in a bank where he had money and he had all of these bankruptcies. So even white male heterosexual privilege doesn't save you because you're covering up something. The whole point of the matter is to get your students to uncover, and that means going on the inside and having feelings.

PAUL: My next question is meta in that we're having this dialogue. *Dialogue* is very important in your book and in your teaching, the students dialoguing with themselves, with the texts, with each other and with you. I love the way you put it on page 185: "Commitment to dialogue is a course requirement." Of course, I'm reading that as slightly tongue-in-cheek. Practically speaking, in terms of assessment, that would be hard to do, although you could certainly make partici-pation a requirement. But *commitment* to dialogue being the goal and process, tell me a little bit about that. Also, how do you facilitate dialogue? What is the role of dialogue in your teaching?

GARY: It starts by reconceptualizing the classroom, visually, structurally. Why in all the classrooms are the chairs in rows? I situate all the chairs in a circle. That way everybody sees everybody, rather than having it where you can't see the person behind you, can't see the person in front of you, where you might look to the side but it's not personal. Rows are actually very impersonal because it's just about you and you're not connected with anyone else in the classroom, except looking at the professor who's lecturing the whole time, and you're prob-ably on your cell phone and all that. Also, I don't stand up. I sit in the circle because first and foremost the professor is not the center of the class. This comes from bell hooks and Paulo Freire, this whole idea of education as the practice of freedom. It's student-learning centered such that the movement in the class-room, in terms of how the texts are interpreted, is based upon collectivity rather than individuality.

Then, as you know, every class you have to come having already written a paper, so there's no reason why you couldn't report, no reason to say, "I don't know what we're talking about." "Well, read your paper." I always require my undergraduate students to speak. It's in the syllabus, ten percent of the grade in this class. You can make A's on all of the writing, on the quizzes, and so on and so forth, but if you don't speak in the class, you will evidently get a B. If you're fine with that, okay. But if you're not, then you need to drop the class because I'm not going to be doing all of the talking. It's got to be interactive, really requiring students to speak. "Oh, I'm shy." Well, then this is not the course for you, because you will actually have to speak and represent your work in this class. That's risky because you might have everybody saying, "Well, I don't like talking, and I'm dropping the class." But it's usually only one or two people and sometimes not even one person will drop.

I also say, "I'm not going to prompt you to speak. You already have your work there, and all you have to do is to represent it." Or one student can say to another, "I didn't really get what you were saying in your paper. Could you speak a little bit more about that?" While people are interacting, I put a red mark by each person's name on the sign in sheet when they participate. You may not be presenting your paper but you're asking a question: "Could you speak more about that?" I'm checking your name because you have spoken. I say in my classes, "This class is about voice empowerment." You actually have to be consistent in your speaking. So, I record grades for weekly participation. I want to give students a compelling sense of what the course is centered around: not professor. It's centered around *you*. You're at the center of this course, and that's what student learning center radical pedagogy is all about. You don't have the option not to speak. You have to speak.

> PAUL: I may be reading between the lines in the book. You don't talk a lot at least directly about reading. But reading is important in your teaching. In a sense, the class is all about reading. People are reading every day. It seems you are teaching a particular way of reading, which I want to try to summarize. You want to teach students to (a) read voices on the margins, especially black feminist and womanist writers; (b) read with an openness to reimagine one's stereotypes and assumptions about all of the identity categories and to rebuild more critical theories (so, read to theorize); (c) read to have one's own life interrogated, and (d) read to write back. I hope you will talk back to this summary of how I'm imagining you teaching students to read.

> GARY: I think all the ones you named are quite accurate because the sum total of the points that you just made is that I want to move the student into a place of activism. It's simply not enough to have graduated with a 4.5-GPA-whatever-A+. Are you thinking about people's lives in terms of the way people are being treated or not treated as human beings? It's not enough for you to say, "Oh, I had such a high grade point average and everything that I got this great job where I'm making all of this money." What you've done is to simply perpetuate the system of objectification of human life, and we *cannot* continue to do that. So at the center of all of the points that you made about the way that I teach, the ultimate goal is to move the students into a position of activist thinking.

> PAUL: What about *reading* specifically? What's the role of reading versus singing or having conversation or just going out and thinking?

GARY: This is why literature became a place for me to live through or to survive challenging or traumatizing experiences, because, though my area is focused on fiction by feminists and womanists across gender and race and ethnicity, the whole idea is that texts contain words and words have meaning. "Okay, so you just like reading texts and that's why you have your students to read texts." I'm not into ebooks, where I can just be driving and just sitting and don't have to actually open a book and read words but can just hear somebody reading to me. I don't actually think that's a good place for us to be. You could say, "Gary, that's old school." Okay, I'll be old school. That's a paradox. You say you're radical but then you're old school because you want hands-on, you actually to read words, to actually see them, touch them, write around them, circle them, underline them.

PAUL: You can see how much I've marked up your book. [Flips through the pages.]

GARY: You're rewriting these texts from your standpoint. That becomes a documentation I need to be able to touch. [Reaches and touches several of the stacks of books nearby one by one.] Yes. This represents, I can look and see, this is my history of my work. But when it's just electronic, "Oh, I saw that film, you know. I didn't read the book. Yeah, I was on Facebook. Okay, so what difference does that make?" I'm always going to have issues with that because I want to touch that which I've read. I want to, as you've done, mark, put a stamp on the work that I've read. I want to be able to see it. "I read this book five years ago, and wow, I wrote this in there. I had this paper clip here. Oh! That's an important page." So, I'm going to go to that place with my students: "Hey. You may not want to do what I'm asking you to do in terms of holding onto these books. If you want to sell the books after you had the course, that's fine with me. But I know one thing: You will have touched, and you will have read, on paper, writing." So, reading for me, from the standpoint of tactile representation, is critically important to what I think is the radicalism of my teaching. It is about textual examination through tactile representation.

PAUL: On page 42, you say two things about how students often respond to your teaching. In some cases, students feel threatened by this examination of race, gender, orientation and the oppressions that attend those categories. On the other hand, further down on the page, you talk about how other students have found that it offers an "educational sanctuary." So, you get both of these responses from students. Some feel threatened. "Why does everything have to be about race?" or whatever other category, although on that page you refer race (or "race talk") in particular. Then other students are yearning and hungry and see the need for this and want to have these conversations. Might you speak to this dichotomy of responses? Do students sometimes move from the one sort of response to the other?

GARY: You'll read about this in *Teaching Womanist Liberation*, based on my work in teaching African American literature. In the general education requirements here at USF—although this has changed—African American literature is not only an elective for English majors at the undergraduate level but was also an option for the writing requirement for to graduate and obtain a bachelor's degree. Students from all of the university could take my African American literature course and it would count as one of the exiting writing requirements. So right away, the title African American Literature, "Oh, yeah, they're probably going to be talking about race." So that assumption is correct, and it gives me a kind of privilege to be able to say, "I know you didn't take this class thinking that we're not going to be talking about race when 'African American Literature' is all about race. But here is my approach: race is not the only thing that African American literary history is based on. We're going to approach the texts that we read from an intersectional standpoint." "What is intersectional? What does that mean?" "We're going to be talking about race in relationship to other forms of oppression and domination related to gender, sexuality, class, ability." So, we're not reducing the study of literature by African American writers only to racial identity politics. So that brings into this configuration the complexity of identity politics, where you're going to have to be thinking about a number of things in relationship to these Black writers and texts.

What that does is call into question all of the stereotypes. So, no, it's not going to be comfortable for you to have to be discussing these issues. But we have to create a space where no one is condemned by having an opinion or an observation that is not in coherence with a feminist, womanist perspective, because that's what I'm going to be teaching you: how to read these texts from a feminist, womanist standpoint. Now, is that going to be imposing a particular perspective on you? Yes. I think it's important to always say so in presenting the syllabus. You can say, "Well, if you tell students, 'Oh, you don't have to take this course if you don't want to study it this way,' then your course could possibly be canceled." But that's never actually happened to me.

One time I was teaching a collection of short stories by Langston Hughes called *The Ways of White Folks*. I had five white guys in the class, and they all walked out in that first class session. I was like, "Okay." I thought about it. That book title is pretty radical. All the short stories talk about ways white characters treat African American characters. And have I taught it since then?

PAUL: You'd think those students who walked out would want to learn a thing or two about themselves.

GARY: Of course, I still teach the perspective of interrogating white privilege and white supremacy. But I've stopped assigning that book. You can say, "Wow, Gary. Really?" Well, I've got a personal issue right now, and I have to be concerned about paranoia. "You're trying to cause trouble. You're going against white people teaching this stuff, with this book, and all that." You can say,

"Gary, man, you're taking things a little too personal." But now we have to put this in the context of media. Every doggone time I turn on the news, some doggone black person is being shot, beat up, kicked. As radical as I think I am and as I've represented my work to be, I also have to be careful *now* because this is this is a stand-your-ground state we live in. I can think I'm really trying to challenge students to come out and challenge certain things, but if I'm propagating something where it seems like I'm hating white people, I don't know, I could have somebody white come in and just, you know. As long as you have your gun packed in your bag nobody knows you have it. You could shoot me. You might say, "Is it really that bad for you in terms of the way you think things are going these days?" In my mind, it is.

PAUL: That's really heavy for a lot of reasons. One aspect is how senseless that is. Reading your work, having been in your class, the idea that you would be anti-white is just the most absurd thing. So is the whole idea that antiracist work is somehow against white people. This is liberating for white people.

GARY: This is where we are though. There are a lot of angry white people in this country right now because they're starting to understand they're not the majority anymore. People of color are actually the majority of people in this world. White men—heterosexual white men—start thinking, "They're taking this stuff away from us." Then this man as president is perpetuating hatred. I feel like this.

If anything, in my work what I'm trying to teach is the possibility of alliance. I've now been here over a decade now and in every class of African American literature I've taught here, both undergraduate and graduate, at the end of the course, there is a vision of alliance where I would say, "We're family now. This is what the world should look like. This is the United Nations." I always leave inspired, that we could get people to be like this, talking about ourselves with each other. I'm not talking about, "Oh I agree with everything you're saying." I'm not talking about that. We're talking about being complicated, complex, putting our stuff on the line, and believing that we respect each other and that we could stand up for each other. I said, "I couldn't be who I am without you. I wouldn't be able to teach if you weren't here. You are the evidence of what I've been given as my calling."

PAUL: One last thing, on page 195, there's a passage of yours where you are talking about Audre Lorde and commenting on a passage of hers, but I think what you say about her is just as much about the kind of teaching you practice and what this whole book is about. You write:

In the passage I understand Lorde as saying that teaching that transforms must emerge from a deep place in the teacher, a place connected to human need. I hear her saying that human need is about longing for connection in a deep place in us where the soul resides, a place full of calm passion. I feel her saying it is the place where body and intellect are superseded by our higher calling through the Spirit. I feel her saying it is a place where soul resides, a place of wholeness, not separation. There we long to release ourselves, to speak from a place of yearning, to express our greatest desires, to communicate a way of moving and being that surpasses the plane of the rational and the corporeal.

To me, that seems to capture so much of what you are doing, your vision of education and of teaching womanist and feminist writers. Would you agree? Would you like to comment on that or add to that?

GARY: Well, it's not even about agreement, because you just said it. Potentially, that is the vision of the work. I agree with the spirit—the spirit of the calling, of what I've done, what I'm doing, and what I will continue to do. The victory has been won because the soul will live, but it has to be given the imperative to the body and to the mind that your body is not going to last forever. Your intellect, no matter how profoundly intelligent you are, is not the sum total of who you are. But your soul in connection to the spirit of love will be the evidence of your life and the stories that you write about your life.

One of the things that I've committed myself to do is to publish the best writings of my students. For you as well as for Atika Chaudhary, who took that same course of mine with you, let me tell you, the book you are both in—*Building Womanist Coalitions Love*—will make some profound changes in people's lives. In hindsight, I wish I had had a professor like me in graduate school who affirmed my work so that I could believe that I could be a scholar. I didn't have that at all. So I get to be the professor I never had and you get to be the evidence of my calling.

This title of *Black Male Outsider* came from Audre Lorde's *Sister Outsider*. What I have come to realize in my teaching is that we have nothing to be ashamed about. Now, I tell my students that all the time. When you're writing in critical self-reflection of your interpretation of the texts that you're analyzing, there's nothing that you need to hold back that would make you feel ashamed of because you are a survivor, because what your writing does is to affirm someone who doesn't even believe she, he, they have a right to even be in a classroom of higher education. Your writing gives hope to the hopeless. So, if we have to go there and unpack the bag of miscellany and see all of the complicated stuff that we are composed of in order for somebody to believe they have a right to be, then give your life as a living sacrifice, acceptable, which ought to be a reasonable service.

You may not understand everything as to why the spirit is pushing you to write about yourself in relationship to what you're teaching, but you've been compelled to do it. You say, "I'm going to go back and ask my professor if we can sit down and talk because I have to write about myself in relationship to what I'm teaching so that people know the work that I'm doing has evidence of my knowing who I am." So, when you emailed me to ask about an interview, I was like, "Dang. Really? Really?" You're the evidence of my calling, so I have to always say yes because you're carrying forward the legacy of all of those who survived in spirit and in truth, even though some, physically, are no longer with us.

BIBLIOGRAPHY

Awkward, Michael. *Scenes of Instruction: a Memoir*. Durham, NC: Duke University Press, 1999.
Lemons, Gary L. *Black Male Outsider, a Memoir: Teaching as a Pro-Feminist Man.* NY: State University of New York Press. 2008.
———. Ed. *Building Womanist Coalitions: Writing and Teaching in the Spirit of Love.* Urbana, IL: University of Illinois Press. 2019.

Chapter Eight

Teaching to Progress

bell hooks, Radical Roots, and Branches

Scott Neumeister

I wish for this essay to embody a homage to and celebration of bell hooks' *Teaching to Transgress: Education as the Practice of Freedom*. Its liberatory message proceeded from its author to me during my time as a graduate student with Gary L. Lemons, who served as my "major" professor in my eight-year journey toward obtaining an MA and PhD in literary studies. Having immersed himself in hooksean ideas from the time he first read *Feminist Theory: From Margin to Center* (1984) in a graduate course at New York University in the late 1980s toward acquiring his doctorate, he would move on to teach and produce scholarship rooted in her publications. Moreover, as he has continually documented over time, *Teaching to Transgress* would become the fundamental ideological basis for his place for pedagogical praxis.

I first read hooks' life-changing work immediately after taking my first graduate feminist theory class with Lemons in 2009. At the time, I was five years into my career switch from the information technology industry into instructing English at the seventh-grade level. The transformative power of Lemons' course, empowered by hooks' ideal of "education as the practice of freedom," impelled me to become a pro-feminist/womanist man. Reading this book, I in turn devoted myself to implementing radical changes relating to this practice in my own classroom. Using Lemons' terminology, I took these ideas "from classroom to living room" and then into classroom again—as instructor, instead of student.

The narrative of my experimental work to bring critically conscious theory to a middle school environment became a major portion of my 2012 MA thesis, "Circling Back Home: My Lifelong Odyssey into Feminism." While

I did touch on hooks' pedagogical theories in the thesis, I have not until
now written about my teaching practices' direct link to her ideas and how I
encountered them. I will therefore highlight a few key concepts that found
their way from hooks' *Teaching* to my own teaching, and I will act as a
witness to the efficacy of her theory in the classroom. Ultimately, I wish to
acknowledge the roots of the life-transforming ideas that I have been so for-
tunate to embrace and teach as the practice of freedom.

AND SO . . . WHAT? TRANSGRESSING THE
NOTION OF KNOWLEDGE AS SILOED

The primary hooksean ideology that began to suffuse my classroom appears
early in *Teaching to Transgpress*.[1] I had witnessed this personally in Lemons'
2009 feminist theory class. He empowered his students to make these connections by prescribing autocritographical writing for us, the blend of personal
memoir with critically conscious theory that hooks herself employs throughout her work. Although I seemed to "get" the autocritographical mission early
on, many of my classmates' essays displayed *only* the marks of high quality,
rationalistic analysis. Appearing recalcitrant to integrating personal position-
ing and to connecting their siloed knowledge to their lived, historical realities, they did not put the "auto" into the "critography." I remember time and
again students reading these papers aloud, and then after a moment of silence,
Lemons asking, "AND?"—and as the semester went on without change,
"SO . . . ?" His unflagging drive to link classroom to living room flows out
of his deep roots in hooks' work. Her tireless advocacy of education as a
liberatory practice entails the fact that no solely left-brained, analytical, cere-
bral thinking, divorced from personal emotion and historical embodiment,
will ever help people achieve freedom. We must approach school as a place
for our entire being—our emotions, body, mind, and their history—not only
because we show up to class with these aspects intertwined but also because
so many "lessons" in life already enforce a false mind-on-top hierarchy that
throws our lives out of balance.

   I taught *The Iliad* and *The Odyssey* in my seventh-grade classroom from
2004 through 2014. Trying to even get a foothold in helping my students
relate to their broad themes—the horrors of ancient warfare and the perils
and uncertainties of ancient sea travel—seemed daunting to me. While I had
some success in doing so at first, encountering hooks' and Lemons' theoretical approach to reading about difference as an avenue to social self-critique
revolutionized my pedagogy. I stopped only teaching the stories as stimulat-
ing for the brain, because knowing them imparted cultural knowledge and
power, or because they might someday have an impact—although these are

honorable effects and aspirations. How women and men treated each other; how people of different races, cultures, and nation/states interacted; how varying classes operated in social dynamics; how heteronormative sexuality suffused the stories; all of these vistas of inquiry into the Greek epics opened to me once I understood how I could read, and help my students read in order to theorize and act "differently" as a critical means to transform daily life globally.[2] I gained a sense of urgency in teaching I had never known before, a feeling that, truly, lives were on the line. And when I devoted my energy to inspiring students to resonate with these ancient literary characters, and then to deconstruct that resonance as either complicity with or victimization by oppressive structures that still exist, suddenly that self-liberating viewpoint exploded into their view. I had found a teaching philosophy I could believe in, one that could carry me through the rest of my academic career. Whenever I teach, I am still asking the fundamental questions "Where are *you* in this literature?" and "What does that say about you, and about us, as humans?"

DISCIPLINE AND POSITION: ARRANGING MY CLASSROOM

The second most classroom-impacting approach I gained from bell hooks, theoretically, and Lemons, experientially, relates to the dynamics of power within the classroom itself. One of the biggest challenges I faced in entering middle school teaching after fifteen years of the adults-only information technology workplace was interacting with children. I had some previous background in athletic coaching, but it always occurred with nearby parental presence, as well as with other coaches assisting. Teaching for hours every day just with adolescent students in the enclosed classroom space had me defaulting to (quite white patriarchal) modes of control that I was accustomed to from my own youth—voice raising, threats of punishment, disapproving looks or words, and the like, as hooks critiques in *Teaching to Transgress*.[3] Although I never wanted to be or felt tyrannical in my classroom, I hoped to be given what Frederick Douglass called "the proud name of being a kind master,"[4] or as I referred to it in my master's thesis, a loving patriarch. Still, despite an inner attitude of love, the in-the-moment, external techniques were often knee-jerk, and the actual methods and processes of the classroom focused on me as the central arbiter of knowledge and dominance that left the students to be hierarchical underlings.

The main control I sought was preventing the students from off-topic socializing, although secondary physical concerns would arise like rough contact ("horseplay" and the like) or even the launching of harmless projectiles (such as paperclips or wads of paper). My traditional classroom design, with all the desks facing forward, assisted in this control. The double-desks in my room entailed that students sat in pairs, so to minimize chatting, I arranged boy/girl pairs as much as I could, trying to use gender difference as a regulating technique. Even this strategy was not foolproof, as flirtatious talk across genders also intensified as the seventh-grade year progressed. During tests, I would often sit in the back of the room so that students would not know at whom I was looking. Only years later when I read *Discipline and Punish* did I realize that Michel Foucault would have been proud of my classroom control strategies. I had learned and internalized well the tactics of controlling bodies—and mouths—in the academic institution.

Five years into arranging my room in this way, I arrived momentously at the opening evening of Lemons' Feminist Theory course. The university English department had assigned us a stepped, auditorium-like lecture hall. Lemons immediately expressed his disapproval of the physical setup, insisting that his class *must* be taught with all of us in a circle. He explained that *dialogue*, seeing and speaking to each other, constituted a lynchpin of his pedagogy. The following week we found our home in the physical education building, arranging the individual seats in a circular fashion before each meeting and returning them to their original spots afterwards. Only later when I read *Teaching to Transgress* did I find that hooks personally speaks of the same enthusiasm that I had gained for this arrangement.[5] Nowadays, Lemons also uses the term "conference mode" for his classroom style, and even that term *conference*, from the Latin roots meaning to "carry with," bears the etymology of sharing and supporting in a community. Every week of class, we would carry the weight of ideas, of analysis, and of personal and political histories with each other in a recognizing, dialogic, *awakening* space where we could not "sleepwalk."

I decided to implement my own room rearrangement only during the last quarter of every school year thereafter and during literature time, exploring how this might work with my seventh graders. I dubbed it "circle time." The students loved it. Although being in conference mode did not eliminate all their verbal and bodily control issues, it sharply reduced them. Moreover, something else happened. Students were so eager to share that they would often talk over each other, so I still had to exercise some influence in the classroom to avoid cacophony. In general, however, they were so engaged in listening and speaking that their desire for chit-chat and horseplay diminished. In *Teaching to Transgress*, hooks asserts the importance of the face-to-face community as well as the depth of communal sharing it fosters— "That moment of collective participation and dialogue" between students and teacher "engag[ing] in acts of recognition with one another."[6] Real connection, sharing real stories, and *especially* dialogue on subjects often silenced by white patriarchy (gender, class, race, sexual orientation) in relation to the literature we read kept my students' attention and organically fostered the "better behavior" found in both meanings of *respect*.

FORGIVE ME, STUDENTS, FOR I AM RACIST: CONFESSIONAL TEACHING

As the students began to articulate their stories in this atmosphere of respect, I found that getting especially female students to speak of the harms done to them by white patriarchy was relatively easy. Not so easy was successfully prompting them to tell when they themselves had inflicted suffering on others. Equally as important as a room arrangement that bespeaks an ideology of true seeing and sharing, bell hooks calls upon the teacher her/himself to model the openhearted, personal engagement that students need in order to obtain freedom: "When professors bring narratives of their experiences into classroom discussions it eliminates the possibility that we can function as all-knowing, silent interrogators."[7] Lemons had done so in his classroom, revealing many personal incidents in his life connected to our readings to inspire our own revelations. Hence, I once again took a cue from both hooks and Lemons—sharing my stories to not only encourage my class but also to deflate their imputed deference to me as not only teacher/authority but as the "kind master."

Once, I was teaching the portion of *The Odyssey* where Odysseus finds himself surrounded by foreigners on the island of Phaeacia. I chose to narrate a story to my students of how in high school I had boarded a city bus and found every rider and even the driver to be Black. Additionally, not a single seat was open that was not next to a Black person. Fearing both these unknown, somehow potentially "dangerous" Others and the thought of being labelled as racist myself, I stood dumbfounded and scared at the front of the bus until a rider arose at the next stop, opening a seat that was not next to anyone. I thus created a link to Odysseus and his own reaction to feeling completely out of place, in the "minority," and in fear. In *Teaching to Transgress,* bell hooks asserts the need for a teacher to interconnect her/his/their personal narrative(s) to support classroom discussion and interaction with students' comprehension of texts assigned for them to study.[8] My example of not being "all-knowing," of being a flawed, racist, and fearful person, opened an amazing dialogue in the classroom about their own encounters Otherness.

I did not stop here, though. After much discussion, I went deeper into my racist past in the name of personally revealing how silent, "non-malicious" bias can grow into overt racism by relating the following story. My majority white high school's sports field abutted what one might term "the projects," an area of low-income housing in Tampa. While no criminal incidents had ever happened on the field, we students were warned concerning "the facts" about the surrounding neighborhood and told to be vigilant. Having been well-indoctrinated into my white, middle-class constructions of poor blacks and their ties into crime, I took these warnings to heart, another reinscription of white supremacist thinking about race and class. In truth, I had repeated the classic joke "What do you call a black kid with a TV on a bicycle? Thief!" as a sort of mantra of my positionality. Two years after the bus incident I just narrated, my classmates and I were gathered during P.E. class at one end of the sports field. We noticed two Black youths scaling the fence on one side of the field and dashing across to the other side. Feeling "strength in numbers" with my multiple white male friends around me and wishing to elicit a laugh, I reworked the above joke and said in a faux-Southern black accent to the running youths, "Police after you boys?" Within seconds of obtaining the laughter I had desired, two policemen scaled the same fence in pursuit of the youths. Multiple police cars screeched into the adjacent parking lot, and the police apprehended the two young Black males. Finally, and most importantly to me at the time, my popularity skyrocketed, having verbally "confronted" and accused the young Black males without knowing the reality behind their running and then having my accusation turn out to be true. Apparently, it was somehow cool to be that gutsy and openly racist and then be justified by "the facts."

If I had let the narrative stand at that, I know what many of my students would have thought, because their minds were ruled by the tyranny of appearance and white supremacist logic. *Of course,* these young Black males (and probably all running Black males) were guilty. *Of course,* they were being apprehended justly and fairly. *Of course,* my friends and I were "superior" because of our race, class, and gender. *Of course,* compassion was not called for, because "justice" was being served. But by following my story with critically conscious approaches toward my attitudes and behaviors, I was able to reveal the nuances and empower my students to see the deeply inscribed racism and classism that led me as a young man, as much as them in the retelling, to arrive at white supremacist conclusions. To their minds, hearing the self-possessed confession of a white, male, middle class teacher *as a racist* but also as a human coming to conscientization about his racism stood as a subversive event. That subversion led to their speech acts that called out their own behavior and beliefs in the name of awakening them to social justice.

My story thus dethroned my "loving (white) patriarchal" role but also served as a model to follow. In my weakness, I became strong, but I used that strength to create the place of safety for students to confess, as bell hooks maintains "to show how experience can illuminate and enhance our understanding of academic material."[9] My own willingness to be open and, yes, "weak" in my classroom served both as an example of vulnerability for the students themselves to follow and as an example of a privileged authority figure casting off the power hegemonically "due" to him.

THE ROOTS GROW BRANCHES:
MOVING THEORY FORWARD

Although the power in bell hooks' ideas were self-evident just by my reading them, my witnessing them in pedagogical action, I believe, made all the difference in understanding their reasons and effectiveness. The influence of hooks and so many other women of color theorists gave me the critical, analytical tools to deconstruct my own past and beliefs in order to understand and revise them. Lemons provided me the space to "meet" these women and to feel safe to dialogue with them and my peers in speech and writing and heal myself of white patriarchy's wounding effects. I then could take what I had learned not only into my "living room" but also into my own classroom, to pay forward the beautiful gift of conscientization—moving toward critical consciousness—to younger minds. Both the classroom arrangement and the communal sharing of personal stories helped convert my teaching space to one of awakening and healing, just as I had encountered.

While bell hooks so often speaks of transgressive acts outside of the classroom, I assert that her aim in *Teaching to Transgress* is to awaken teachers into changing their operating milieu via radical pedagogy. Their teaching can in turn produce transformed and subversive students who can branch out into the world, carriers of this lineage. I am so privileged that I stand in a direct line of this ideology, via Lemons, to hooks herself. I sense bell hooks at the root of my transgressive teaching, and I feel the sap of her wisdom flowing as I facilitate the healing and emancipation of my students. In fact, since the word *radical* comes from the Latin meaning "root," in a sense this concept of transforming students at a "grass roots" level is the ultimate radical act which can foster the full self-actualization linked with liberatory justice needed to transform our society. We are both roots and branches of this feminist/womanist tree, an ever-growing and ever-changing tree of liberation and of life.

BIBLIOGRAPHY

Douglass, Frederick. *Narrative of the Life of Frederick Douglass, an American Slave.* Webb and Chapman, 1846.
hooks, bell. *Teaching to Transgress: Education as the Practice of Freedom.* New York: Routledge, 1994.

NOTES

1. bell hooks, *Teaching to Transgress: Education as the Practice of Freedom* (New York: Routledge, 1994), 19.

2. Ibid., 59–60

3. Ibid., 5.

4. Frederick Douglass, *Narrative of the Life of Frederick Douglass, an American Slave* (Webb and Chapman,1846), 3.

5. hooks, *Teaching to Transgress*, 146.

6. Ibid., 186.

7. Ibid., 21.

8. Ibid., 21.

9. Ibid., 21.

PART III

Black Male Radical (His)Stories

Teaching to Survive

Chapter Nine

Remembering *Intersectional* Interventions Teaching to Reclaim Human Rights Legacies

M. Thandabantu Iverson

Relating to the critical importance of pedagogical theory and practice grounded in strategies of support undergirding an intersectional approach toward the reclamation of human rights founded upon the revolutionary legacies of Black feminist and womanist activists, Margaret L. Andersen and Patricia Hill Collins, as co-editors of *Race, Class, and Gender: An Anthology* in "Shifting the Center," pose this question:

> How might we see the world differently if we were to shift our vision of society from one that is typically centered in the voices and experiences of dominant groups to the lives and thoughts of those who have been devalued, marginalized, and excluded? This shift is central to thinking . . . in ways that transform, rather than buttress, existing social arrangements.[1]

PREFACE: A FEW WORDS REGARDING
LOCATION AND ORIENTATION

The evolution of feminist agency and political struggles during the past several decades has challenged and encouraged U.S. agents of social transformation to situate themselves publicly to clarify their social locations and political commitments. This standpoint has become particularly important for feminist men. With this in mind, it is important to explicitly note that—as an African American heterosexual male, reared within the working class of Columbus, Ohio during the years from 1947 through 1965—I am neither an "expert" on (Black) women's lives, Black feminism, intersectionality, nor human rights. However, as one who earnestly believes that, as bell hooks has said, "Feminism is for everybody,"[2] I have been working and self-identifying as a Black male feminist for the past fifteen to twenty years. In situating myself, it is essential that I provide a word on my present class orientation.[3] While I have worked for the past two decades as a university educator, which some would readily regard as a "middle-class" occupation, I have consistently centered my life and work within the working class. This commitment to the working-class is a continuing rudder and compass for my feminist work. Becoming a feminist was the result of my personal and organizational experiences in (what we typically refer to as) The Civil Rights, Black Student, Black Power, African Liberation Support, New Left, and Human Rights Movements. The poem below speaks to both my social origins and my political moorings—

"AN EMAIL FOR TONI, CHERRIE, GLORIA, AND MOM"

(In commemoration of the 34th anniversary of *This Bridge Called My Back*)

here's a word of thanks
lettin' you know I heard
testifyin' that I ain't scared no longer
to say out loud that listenin' at the table and hearin' all those prayers
mixed in with all the truthtellin' makes sense to me now
remindin' me when momma made me sit and listen
that day after daddy busted her lip
she told me not to speak; it was time to listen then
said I should try to be somethin' better than a brute
told me I didn't have to be the center
if I could repossess and reposition my mind and my heart
if I could learn that I would always meet sisters like my own
and if I wanted goodness and love and peace and justice for her
I would need to plant a different kind of seed in the world
chart a different course speak in different tones raise my hands
to heal
and not deal hurt and heartache like daddy (she said he meant well
but his feet wasn't mates so he was walkin' backwards thru his life)
just want you to know that I heard you
and momma this is my word that I know
the backs of my sisters and brothers and no one else really
ain't no place for my feet
I can walk like a brother/man thru my life w/o that
I have left the plantations and i'm runnin' to make somethin' better

decided to be a bridge for love and justice on my own with others
don't want to walk on no one else (and ps)
I show my brothers 'cause i'm doin' what momma said[4]

INTRODUCTION

African Americans, other people of color, and working-class persons in the United States have a lot to talk about regarding the wrongs that shape our lives and the differences that human rights can make. This potent reality brought forty social justice activists to Highlander Center, in June 2015, for a weekend retreat organized by the U.S. Human Rights Network.[5] This FIHRE retreat (pronounced "F-I-R-E," Fighting Injustice through Human Rights Education) was held as the second yearly program designed to provide activists with opportunities for respite and reinvigoration. During the weekend change agents shared their experiences of injustice and resistance within the bucolic surroundings of the historic Highlander Research and Education Center. Throughout all the organized activities of the weekend, participants were encouraged to develop their capacities for radical change by claiming as their own the language and expectations of human rights.

INTERSECTIONALITY: SEEING A LENS
AND MODEL FOR HUMAN RIGHTS

Following my self-introduction and a brief statement regarding the objectives of the workshop, I began by offering participants a definition of Intersectionality, to briefly present "the basics" of a complex concept that has become almost a "buzzword"[6] in academic and social movement-building contexts. More specifically, my definition was intended as (1) a lens through which workshop participants could begin to assess the conscious and organized activities of Black women activists in addressing their oppressive economic, political, and social circumstances; and (2) a means of beginning to evaluate the contributions by Black feminist women to human rights in the United States prior to the post-WWII establishment of the international human rights system. Sharing with the workshop participants, I underscored the idea that with definitions of any complex concept, it must be considered an open-ended and evolving project, as my definition of "Intersectionality." It has been used by Black feminists (and some womanists) since the 1980s to name an approach largely developed by women of color to understand, explain, resist, and transform the unequal effects of principles and systems of oppression.

In the experiences of Afrodescendant peoples, Black women have been the originators of an intersectional, intellectual, spiritual, and political approach to personal and collective wholeness and empowerment. This approach constitutes a body of practice and thought by which oppressed women (and some men) have sought to oppose injustices and generate transformative social change. In its most rigorous and inclusive expressions, this approach to thinking and acting has confronted the effects of multiple forms of oppression, including (but not limited to) race, gender, sexuality, class, color, nation, ethnicity, and ability. Intersectionality challenges all unequal and structured relations of power within hierarchical systems. Moreover, this approach challenges us to recognize, examine, understand, and respond to the myriad effects that result when multiple systems of domination and privilege operate simultaneously and interdependently in the lives of groups and individuals 'othered' and marginalized in U.S. society. Intersectionality encourages us to be mindful of how discrete types of discrimination operate—within the same social spaces and in complex connections—to shape complicated experiences of groups and their individual members. An intersectional approach thus opposes every kind of discrimination and domination, resisting the notions that any form of oppression is more important than another or that any form of it is reducible to another.

Given the complexities and nuances theorized within this definition, several core ideas can be distilled and clarified to make the Black feminist offering more accessible and intelligible. The following may be understood as core, constitutive ideas of an intersectional framework: (1) Our social identities can never be understood apart from our positions (i.e., assignments to and struggles within) existing societal hierarchies of largely unequal and unjust power relations; (2) An intersectional approach acknowledges that multiple systems and principles of oppression exist, and continually intermesh, creating synergies of disadvantage in the lives of dominated, "inferior" groups in society; (3) Multiple forms of domination cannot be simply understood as *additive* (i.e., as independent disadvantaging factors, each resulting in a determinable impact).[7] Instead, the intersectional approach 'sees systems [and principles] of domination as *interdefining one another . . . each system of injustice defines and is defined by the others*'; (4) We should be mindful to analyze intersections within "various levels of institutional, cultural, and individual" activities "and in the dynamics between them"; (5) Intersectionality opposes any kind of reductionism, or primacy, of any single principle or system of oppression; (6) "Identities or (social) locations are not only sites of oppression but also sites of resistance; and . . . all individuals simultaneously occupy positions as oppressed and oppressor"; (7) "In a world of 'one identity to a movement,' the lived experience for those on the downside of multiple systems of oppression is fragmentation, erasure, partial denials, marginalization, and conflict."[8]

APPLYING INTERSECTIONALITY IN
ANALYSES AND DECISION-MAKING

Once we begin to understand how an intersectional approach can help us to think more carefully and inclusively about experiences of oppression, we must then learn to apply this conception in our personal and organizational behaviors. To help workshop participants address this challenge, I drew from the work of two scholars, Patricia Hill Collins and Sharon Kurtz (now deceased). Each of these theorists provided important guidelines for practicing intersectionality in our personal and collective lives.

In her chapter/essay, "Moving Beyond Gender: Intersectionality and Scientific Knowledge," Collins has offered the following insights:

> One approach to developing intersectional analyses consists of selecting a specific social location, social practice, group history, or topic, and subjecting it to an intersectional analysis. This . . . means *choosing a concrete topic that is already the subject of investigation and trying to find the combined effects of race, class, gender, sexuality, and nation, where before only one or two interpretive categories were used. . . . An intersectional approach grounded in the particular starts with specific locations as points of origin, and aims to build . . . not by pulling apart various pieces of social reality, but by investigating connections among what were deemed separate dimensions.*[9] (Emphasis added)

Anglo-American scholar Sharon Kurtz provides additional guidelines for how social-change agents can become more intentional in our organizing activities, our organizations, and movement-building generally. Focusing our attention on a concept of "identity practices," Kurtz encourages us all to follow new pathways to building working-class centered organization(s):

> Collective identity is not automatically determined by a movement's membership. Nor, as some activists argue, is it automatically shaped by demands. Identity is neither permanent not fixed. Rather, identity is socially produced, what we call a social construction. And as a social construction, it is a matter in which movements can intervene. [T]he concept of *identity practices* . . . is a tool for analyzing just *how* movements do this. The concept . . . allows activists and scholars to look at the arenas in which, and the extent to which, movements create single versus multi-identities. . . . Collective identity . . . is constituted in a range of *identity practices: demands, framing and ideology, culture, organizational structure and process, leadership and organizational power, and*

outside resources. These practices are a collection of specific social movement organization behaviors, each seemingly small, but which . . . together construct a movement's self-definition. However silently or unconsciously, this process of identity construction occurs among groups differently located in social systems of inequality, each situated with differing interests, power, and resources. . . . The demands a movement makes indicate the conditions of injustice—both material and cultural—a group seeks to change. Recall that multiple systems of domination shape different experiences of injustice for different groups within a movement.[10] (Emphasis in original)

It is important to note that our workshop discussion of this section on "Applying Intersectionality" was unduly brief, although the insights offered by Collins and Kurtz were shared with participants.[11] In an email message sent to participants following the close of the workshop, I underscored the importance of Kurtz's insights by recounting how the identity of social movement organizations, and social movements themselves, indicate and represent the human beings and social groups whose experiences, agency, and human rights are reflected, articulated, and (being) advanced by the organization(s) and/or movement. *If what we choose to do as we conceive and carry out our identity practices does not reflect the experiences, knowledge, democratic participation, and evolving vision of those most affected by the human rights violations we want to oppose, our activities and our identities as agents of change will be gravely undermined and ineffectual.*

BLACK FEMINISTS BIRTHING AN INTERSECTIONAL TRADITION

One of the primary objectives of the workshop was to help familiarize participants with intermittent interventions by Black feminist women in different historical periods that have helped to advance the practice and the theorizing of intersectionality. In this section, several such interventions are noted and briefly discussed. From their earliest harrowing hours of systematic denigration and abuse in conditions of white settler colonialism, male supremacy, and chattel enslavement; Black women began considering human differences in ways that could enable them to survive and resist their placement in the "New World." Enduring many of the same hardships experienced by their male counterparts, they also witnessed and experienced travails peculiar to their gender and sexualities. Given the gendering and sexualization of their racial abuses, Black women have often been forced to live in situations of harsh solidarity with their families, lovers, and communities, while nonetheless alienated and apart. Amidst such wrenching challenges, many Black women have discerned that to end all their injustices—not only for themselves, but for their people—would require personal and collective struggles against every system denying their humanity. In turn, they and their people would have to learn how to confront and oppose every "dream" of reform that might defend privileges for some while actually denying the full measures of justice and human rights for all.

Throughout the many arduous years of their sojourn(s) in the United States, Afrodescendant peoples forged many expressions of their agency in resisting and directly opposing their subjugation and intergenerational exploitations by Europeans and Euro-Americans. Among the most potent of these expressions, the Black Radical Tradition has proven to have singular significance. This tradition, among others, has served Blacks in our efforts to end the myriad violations of our humanity, as we (have) continually sought more humane and liberated societal relationships. Yet even as major architects and theorists of the Black Radical Tradition have worked to critique U.S. inequalities and envision more expansive and democratic forms of society, this tradition has all too often produced denials, suppressions, and efforts to "police" the humanity of Black women and men who have not lived up to the patriarchal norms and ideals of the broader social order. The experiences, understandings of reality, voices, and resistant and transgressive behaviors of these Black women and men have thus been marginalized. Consequently, painful forms of invisibility[12] have repeatedly emerged amongst Black people(s), and the orientations and actions of patriarchy (in insidious combination with other oppressive systems) have generally contributed to the damaging and underdevelopment of all Black lives. Black feminist scholar Beverly Guy-Sheftall has written regarding this orientation and the historical causes for its continual re-emergence:

> Black women experience a special kind of oppression and suffering in this country which is racist, sexist, and classist because of their . . . racial and gender identity and their limited access to economic resources. . . . This 'triple jeopardy' has meant that the problems, concerns, and needs of Black women are different in many ways from those of both white women and Black men. . . . Black women must struggle for Black liberation and gender equality simultaneously. . . . There is no inherent contradiction in the struggle to eradicate sexism and racism as well as the other 'isms' which plague the human community, such as classism and heterosexism.[13]

INTERSECTIONALITY AND
PEOPLE-CENTERED HUMAN RIGHTS

During the past several years of my teaching and human rights activism, I have frequently discussed *the importance of shifting grassroots (i.e., working-class) organizing and movement-building orientations from the customary leader-centered focus to one that is people-centered.* My own political and organizational experiences during the past several decades (including some study of the work of Ella Baker and SNCC) have convinced me that social justice organizing in the United States must engage and enable the leadership of "those most affected" by oppressions to build sustained struggles for improvements and transformations in society. With such a shift in customary activists' orientations, organizing can more readily and effectively address the effects of interlocking oppressions and discriminations in this country. Moreover, such an orientation, while more intersectional, will also enable human rights activists and advocates to help the members of oppressed groups *to reclaim—and ground themselves within—the past human rights interventions of those groups.* With this approach, organizers can address many of the apprehensions and doubts regarding "human rights" that arise when members of oppressed groups are encouraged to embrace human rights—which are usually regarded as initiatives defined and pursued by more mainstream and elite groups and individuals.

Since most of our workshop participants lived and worked in working-class communities, their own bases of lived experience were precisely what I hoped they would re-examine during our considerations of historical human rights struggles. Ajamu Baraka, the former and founding executive director for the U.S. Human Rights Network, has written incisively and persuasively regarding the people-centered orientation:

> The feature that distinguishes the people-centered framework from all of the prevailing schools of human rights theory and practice is that it is based on an explicit understanding that to realize the full range of the still-developing human rights idea requires: (1) an epistemological break with . . . human rights orthodoxy grounded in Eurocentric liberalism; (2) a reconceptualization of human rights from the standpoint of oppressed groups; (3) a restructuring of prevailing social relationships that perpetuate oppression; and (4) the acquiring of power on the part of the oppressed to bring about that restructuring.[14]

Examining the conditions, consciousness, and agency of Black working-class women (and also women who were firmly committed to working-class empowerment) enabled us in our workshop process to begin (and for some, to continue) a re-centering process providing for radical, "bottom-up" thinking about human rights and movement-building today. As Shelley Wright has noted (and others have frequently confirmed), it was primarily the agency of marginalized people(s) that had actually elevated human rights into "a primary position" within the post-WWII agenda for the United Nations.[15] By focusing on the lives and interventions of Black women in Harlem, then, we could consider lives seldom placed at the center of human rights advocacy and activism. This provided for a reflective process in which participants could begin to consider the arc of the Eurocentric liberalism to which Wright, Baraka, and others have referred. If the interventions of Black working-class women were grounded in oppressive conditions broadly similar to those of workshop participants; perhaps contemporary activists would do well to think beyond the Eurocentric and liberal philosophical groundings that still guide so much of human rights advocacy and activism.

Once participants began to critically consider the historic constraints impeding the respecting, protecting, and fulfilling of human rights for most members of the U.S. body politic; these activists could also think more carefully about the possibility and the urgency of rethinking their previous apprehensions and misgivings about human rights. If impoverished Black women could grasp human rights ideals to frame their own struggles, why can't the dominated groups and individuals in the United States today rethink their own experiences and the potential benefits of framing their political and economic strivings in human rights terms? Moreover, by refocusing attention on the intersectional interventions of Afrodescendant working women, participants could more intentionally shift toward people-centered human rights organizing. Dr. Yolande Tomlinson, former Education Director of the U.S. Human Rights Network notes that, "Intersectionality marries well with a people-centered approach because of: its focus on those who are most affected by oppression; its insistence on the inherent value of their lives; its insistence on the need to address oppressive power in all its forms and to do so collectively; and, its decentering of dominant ideologies and practices."[16]

If, as numerous social movement scholars have noted, the "unmasking and demystifying of the realities of class struggle" is indeed a crucial aspect of learning for social transformation,[17] our FIHRE workshop aided human rights activists in this crucial pursuit. In fact, by engaging participants to think more carefully about the *working-class character of intergenerational Black feminist interventions*; our workshop helped activists to enhance their understanding of how unequal power relations of race, gender, and class have operated in interlocking fashion in a number of instances in which race and gender might have seemed singularly salient. Much more work must be done on this aspect of intersectional explication, however, in light of the profound impact of typical additive explorations of class, race, and gender.[18] In future educational and organizational efforts, we will be more intentional about planning and conducting our workshops as intersectional bridges to people-centered human rights activism.

BLACK FEMINISTS AND GENDERED BLACK POWER

As Black feminist activists grappled with the lack of financial and elite political supports during the late 1960s and early 1970s, they painstakingly sought for the means and the methods to sustain their commitments to Black empowerment; built organizational structures; strengthened and expanded organizational alliances; broke away from larger, more hierarchically-structured, and less grassroots units; developed their political and ideological connections with like-minded feminists; strengthened education and organizing at the grassroots; and strove to evade cooptation.[19]

Human rights activists can learn much from careful study of Black radical women. In considering the organizational challenges with which these feminists wrestled during the years of Civil Rights and Black Power successes, ebbs and declines, what seems most noteworthy is (1) the intergenerational efforts of radical Black women to find their voices; (2) their work to establish necessary organizational processes and forms to address their needs for expanded democracy and power; and (3) their continual organizing to end the systemic violations of the rights and fulfill their human rights. Given their intermittent struggles extending from 1917 to the 1970s, Black feminists had practiced and theorized the intersectional oppositions to injustice that they had begun to forge in the earliest days of their enslavement. Their efforts continue still.

BIBLIOGRAPHY

Andersen, Margaret L., and Patricia Hill Collins. "Shifting the Center." In *Race, Class, and Gender: An Anthology*, edited by Margaret L. Andersen and Patricia Hill Collins, 13–21. Belmont, CA: Wadsworth/Thomson Higher Education, 2004.

Baraka, Ajamu. "'People-Centered' Human Rights as a Framework for Social Transformation," December 10, 2013. http://www.ajamubaraka.com/.

Collins, Patricia Hill. "Moving Beyond Gender: Intersectionality and Scientific Knowledge," In *Revisioning Gender*, edited by Myra Marx Ferree and Judith Lorber, 261–84. Lanham: AltaMira Press, 2000.

Davis, Kathy. "Intersectionality as Buzzword: A Sociology of Science Perspective on What Makes a Feminist Theory Successful." *Feminist Theory* 9, no. 1 (2008): 67–85.

Guy-Sheftall, Beverly. "Introduction." In *Words of Fire: An Anthology of African-American Feminist Thought,* edited by Beverly Guy-Sheftall, 1–22. New York: The New Press, 1995.

hooks, bell. *Feminism Is for Everybody.* Cambridge, MA: South End Press, 2000.

Holvino, Evangelina. "Complicating Gender: The Simultaneity of Race, Gender, and Class in Organization Change(ing)," in *For Gender in Organizations, Simmons School of Management,* Working Paper, No. 14, June 2001.

Kurtz, Sharon. *Workplace Justice: Organizing Multi-Identity Movements.* Minneapolis: University of Minnesota Press, 2002.

McLaren, Peter L., and Colin Lankshear. Eds., *Politics of Liberation: Paths from Freire.* New York: Routledge, 1994.

Wright, Shelley. *International Human Rights, Decolonization and Globalization: Becoming Human.* New York: Routledge, 2001.

NOTES

1. Margaret L. Andersen and Patricia Hill Collins, "Shifting the Center," In *Race, Class, and Gender: An Anthology*, eds. Margaret L. Andersen and Patricia Hill Collins (Belmont, CA:Wadsworth/Thomson, 2004), 13–21.

2. bell hooks, *Feminism Is for Everybody*, Cambridge, MA: South End Press, 2000).

3. The relevance of class and class privilege to an activist's thinking and political practice is often underestimated and/or ignored—even by some espousing feminist commitments. While this can certainly be understood as a consequence of activists working within academic institutions and liberally funded NGOs; the vacillations which attend middle-class orientations and methods can do irreparable harm to social movement-building for radical transformations. Radical educator Donaldo Macedo has written: "By refusing to deal with the issue of class privilege, the pseudo-critical educator dogmatically pronounces to empower students, to give them voices. These educators are even betrayed by their own language. Instead of creating pedagogical structures which would enable oppressed students to empower themselves, they paternalistically proclaim: 'We need to empower students.' This position often leads to the creation of what I call literacy and poverty pimps to the extent that, while proclaiming to empower students, they are in fact strengthening their own privileged position." See Prof. Macedo's "Preface" in *Politics of Liberation: Paths from Freire*, (Eds.), Peter L. McLaren and Colin Lankshear, Routledge, 1994.

4. Poem by M. Thandabantu Iverson, ©2015.

5. See www.ushrnetwork.org.

6. Kathy Davis, "Intersectionality as Buzzword: A Sociology of Science Perspective on What Makes a Feminist Theory Successful," 67. See also "Critical Thinking about Inequality: An Emerging Lens," in *Emerging Intersections: Race, Class, and Gender in Theory, Policy, and Practice*, (Eds.) Bonnie Thornton Dill and Ruth Enid Zambrana (Foreword by Patricia Hill Collins), Rutgers University Press, 2009.

7. Evangelina Holvino, "Complicating Gender: The Simultaneity of Race, Gender, and Class in Organization Change(ing)," Working Paper, No. 14, June 2001, Center for Gender in Organization.

8. Sharon Kurtz's illuminating discussion of "The Single-Identity Problem," in *Workplace Justice: Organizing Multi-Identity Movements*, University of Minnesota Press, 2002. Readers will also benefit considerably from reading "The Concept of Intersectionality in Feminist Theory," Anna Carastathis, Philosophy Compass 9/5 (2014).

9. Patricia Hill Collins, "Moving Beyond Gender: Intersectionality and Scientific Knowledge," in *Revisioning Gender*, ed. Myra Marx Ferree and Judith Lorber (Lanham, Md: Alta Mira Press, 2000). Regarding the complex matter of how to think about the simultaneity and interconnectedness of (forms of) oppressions in our lives, see also a very instructive and earlier discussion in *Inessential Woman: Problems of Exclusion in Feminist Thought*, Elizabeth V. Spelman, Beacon Press, 1988.

10. Sharon Kurtz, *Workplace Justice*.

11. During our collective de-brief organizers of the retreat workshop(s) acknowledged that insufficient time had been allotted for adequate discussion of the complex aspects of the workshop foci of intersectionality and human rights. Clearly, more time should have been allotted—not only because of the complexity of the topics, but also because of the emotionally-charged conversations that are often required when activists address matters of oppression, rights and privilege. Immediately following the workshop, it was clear that more time should have been allotted to discuss *what intersectionality means and requires in the building of organizations and movements*. Yet because of the intensity of conversations that came about when issues and questions of (whiteness) privilege came up; we could not readily shift to discussion about "*how to do intersectionality*" without silencing some participants who needed to be heard.

12. This recurring problem of invisibility has not only diminished the lives of those who have been silenced, ridiculed, and organizationally (and thus, politically) marginalized. As a direct result of recurrent efforts at *policing* the behaviors, morals, and visions of certain Black women and men; Blacks have generally been denied the humanizing contributions 'othered' Black people conscientiously living in opposition to various institutionalized aspects patriarchal and racial capitalism. Such major contributors include (but are certainly not limited to) Anna Julia Cooper, Ida B. Wells-Barnett, Claudia Jones, Lorraine Hansberry, Bayard Rustin, James Baldwin, Ella Baker, Audre Lorde, and Barbara Smith.

13. Beverly Guy-Sheftall, "Introduction" in *Words of Fire: An Anthology of African-American Feminist Thought*, ed. Beverly Guy-Sheftall (NY: The New Press,1995), 2.

14. Ajamu Baraka, "'People-Centered' Human Rights as a Framework for Social Transformation," December 10, 2013. See Baraka's discussion of human rights topics at http://www.ajamubaraka.com/. The reader should note very well that the "restructuring of prevailing social relationships" to which Baraka has referred should properly be understood as an immediate objective, and not merely one to be realized in the future. One of the most telling consequences of attempting to build organizations and struggles that are not intersectional and people-centered (but additive and

leader-centered) is the reproduction of hegemonic relationships and policies—i.e., elitist, undemocratic, exclusionary, patriarchal, ableist, self-serving, and discriminatory relationships and policies that actually undermine human rights.

15. Shelley Wright, *International Human Rights, Decolonization, and Globalisation: Becoming Human*, (New York: Routledge, 2001) 20. See also *Crimes Against Humanity: The Struggle for Global Justice*, G. Robertson, Penguin Press, 1999. On this matter, Ajamu Baraka has also written trenchantly: "The human rights idea and project is not innocent. It emerged in its modern expression as a contested idea at a historical moment when the assumptions, world-views and social practices of Western, liberal, white supremacist, patriarchal, colonial-capitalist states were dominant. The result was that the human rights framework and methods of practice that emerged . . . as universal truths were informed by the . . . experiences, needs and world-views of those states and their intellectual elites." Baraka, "People-Centered Human Rights as a Framework for Social Transformation," at http://www.ajamubaraka.com/.

16. Interview and online conversation with Dr. Yolande Tomlinson, ("Intersectional Human Rights Organizing: A Strategy for Building Inclusive and Transformational Movements"), Tuesday, August 24, 2015.

17. Peter L. McLaren and Colin Lankshear, ed. *Politics of Liberation: Paths from Freire*, (New York: Routledge, 1994). In this volume, the chapter by Peter Findlay is especially helpful.

18. Unfortunately, our customary discussions of principles and systems of oppression and discrimination in the United States undermine clear-sighted analyses of societal conditions. All too often, such discussions obscure the very interlocking features and interactive synergies that render these systems and principles so powerful within our collective and individual lives.

19. See *Living for the Revolution*. In this volume, Kimberly Springer provides a most instructive examination of the organizational development of several Black feminist organizations in her well-researched Chapter 3, "Barbecue and Bake Sales Won't Fund a Movement."

.

Chapter Ten

Working Overtime

My Mother and Black Feminists' Embodied Narrative Inheritance

Marquese McFerguson

"Introduction to Hip Hop Studies"

As a Black masculinity studies scholar and student/teacher, I credit Black feminists and their scholarship for inviting me to rethink how I conceive and perform Black masculinity—in and outside the classroom. Whether it was bell hooks[1] breaking down the role slavery and white supremacy has played in the development of modern-day patriarchal Black masculinity or Robin Boylorn using her scholarship to reimagine the performative possibilities of Black masculinity, Black feminist scholars have often made me question and (re)evaluate how I perform Black manhood in and outside the classroom.

Moreover, as a hip hop studies scholar, many Black feminists/hip hop feminists have (re)formed me and my scholarship. For instance, it is the work of hip hop feminist like Aisha Durham that has equipped me a critical language and lens to analyze representation of racialized gender within hip hop culture. It has been the scholarship of Bettina Love[2] that has given me a template and enabled me to do the seemingly contradictory work of celebrating and in the same breath, sternly and necessarily critiquing hip hop culture. Furthermore, it has been the work of hip hop feminist Joan Morgan[3] who has allowed me

149

to embrace the messy and complicated gray areas in theories and cultures, and (re)imagine concepts and ideas beyond strict Black and white binaries.

Hip hop is an art form born from the margins and Black feminist thought has taught me to listen to the voices that are often situated within the margins of Eurocentric social norms. Acknowledging this, the "Introduction to Hip Hop Studies" course I teach seeks to honor the voices of women of color who experience marginality the most within academic spaces. With a syllabus composed of largely theory and criticism by women of color, the course seeks to push back on and remix canonical and Eurocentric ways of producing knowledge within the "ivory tower" and amplify the voices of scholars positioned in the margins.

The course introduces students to the interdisciplinary field of hip hop studies and invites them to see hip hop as more than "just music." The course critically explores hip hop history, aesthetics, pedagogy, dance, fashion, poetry, visual art, and language in an attempt to illuminate the art form's sonic, social, cultural, and political impact. From the deejay, to the graffiti artist, to the emcee, within this course, each foundational element within hip hop culture will be used as a creative-intellectual lens to investigate how the art form has influenced the ways in which we see, perform, and interpret race, gender, class, religion, sexuality, and lived experiences on a regional, national, and international level. From hip hop feminism, to the Caribbean influences on the early development of hip hop, to hip hop's current international status, this course explores a wide range of voices and identities that exist underneath the umbrella of hip hop culture.

Since its inception in 1973, hip hop has become a global phenomenon that is continually changing the world. In the process of changing the world, hip hop's influence on the mass media, and vice versa, has also impacted how Black identities are portrayed, perceived, and performed. This course explores those portrayals and performances within the scope of popular culture. Ultimately, this course examines how Black bodies within hip hop culture are represented and produced by media makers and interpreted by media audiences to make sense of Blackness.

Throughout the course, students sharpen skills such as their ability to analyze how social, cultural, and political concepts, issues, and beliefs are constituted in various mediated forms by developing the capacities to critically engage with scholarly works and intellectual inquiry related to hip hop culture. Furthermore, students describe multiple dimensions of cultures (e.g., environmental, ideological, linguistic, communicative, historical, geographic, technological, and/or artistic) by acquiring discipline-specific vocabulary, practicing interpretive techniques used in the humanities, and developing a basic understanding of key theories/theorists in the field of hip hop studies.

Conversely, another goal I conceptualized in the course is to exhibit to students the interdisciplinary nature of hip hop studies. Across the fields of education,[4] English,[5] economics,[6] rhetoric,[7] gender studies,[8] music,[9] media studies,[10] and communication,[11] a significant body of scholars have analyzed hip hop in their groundbreaking research. In my interpretive vision of the course, students explore the work of many of these scholars to demonstrate hip hop's significance as a site of self-transformative academic inquiry across disciplines boundaries.

Although I continue to center my focus on academic spaces and my critique of Eurocentric marginality of Black identities—it is the self-transformative power Black feminist thought that not only grounds ways I teach my hip hop studies course, but also it resonates in ways my mother's work ethics molded me as a Black man, student, and teacher. In the writing that follows, I employ autoethnography to contextualize my personal *his-story*. It would be my mother's voice that would perform as the root cause of my becoming a hip hop, Black feminist scholar and teacher committed to engaging voices from the margins.

MY HIS-STORY: BETWEEN A MOTHER, A SON, AND THE MARGINS

In this autoethnographic essay, I explore what Art Bochner[12] defines as narrative inheritance and analyze how the storied experiences of parents are often resurrected in the bodies and behavior of their children. Using the lived experiences of my mother, a working-class black woman, I analyze how her personal narrative accounts of growing up in the Jim Crow South prepared me, her son, for moments of being "othered" within higher education. Like hip hop culture in inner-city New York, as a Black woman in the Jim Crow South, my mother was born on the margins. Yet, like hip hop's early pioneers, my mother believed the margins can be an oppressive space, but beauty could be birthed from those positioned on its borders. I argue, even though my mother never had the opportunity to attend college, it was her narrative inheritance, sharing of stories about growing up in the south and keen sense of understanding the ways in which Black bodies are understood within racialized spaces that became my pedagogical and performative template for navigating predominantly white academic institutions (PWIs) as a Black man. From exploring the framing and violence experienced by Black bodies, to examining the marginalization that can come from and the beauty and persistence that can develop in spite of oppressive environments, my lived experiences within academia and the themes I explore in the "Introduction to Hip Hop Studies" course I teach. They mirror each other and illustrate the beauty and blight that can be birthed amid the marginalized spaces Black female bodies occupied—and the economic workload they had to take on.

REJECTING A FATHER'S INHERITANCE

In *Coming to Narrative*, Art Bochner discusses the narrative inheritance his father passes down to him. As a Jewish youth immigrating to the United States in 1920, Bochner's father and his family fled the oppression they were experiencing in the aftermath of the holocaust in Eastern Europe only to be greeted by alienation upon arriving to America. Bochner elaborates:

> Already poor in 'the old country,' my father's family confronted new forms of cultural and social impoverishment. Stigmatized by the Yiddish jargon he spoke, the odd clothing he wore, and the dirty home environment in which he lived, my father internalized deep-seated feelings of inferiority and social awkwardness that he never overcame. A childhood of deprivations, humiliation, and discrimination took its toll.[13]

Bochner states that the lessons and family stories his father often shared with him were marked with the "despair of growing up poor, insecure, and out of place." These lessons were meant to help Bochner prepare for and endure "discrimination, injustice and suffering" as he moved throughout his community and the world.[14]

The social, cultural, and psychological oppression that Bochner's father lived through affected how he came to view labor. For Bochner's father, work was not supposed to be enjoyable or fun, work represented struggle and commitment. For Bochner's father, "who often referred to himself as someone who worked like a slave . . . he equated work with coercion and sacrifice and made a clear distinction between work and play."[15] This was the narrative inheritance that Bochner's father passed down to him. This was the way Bochner's father understood and experienced the world, and this was how Bochner was to experience it as well. However, Bochner decided to contest his inheritance and reimagine the narrative that was being passed down to him. He asserts:

> I didn't want to be a slave to work. As a kid, I loved to play and hated to work. Was there any work that could also be play, fun or enjoyable? Would work always feel like a form of slavery or coercion, or could one love work as much as play? Could work be play? Must work always be riddled with contradictions.[16]

ACCEPTING MY MOTHER'S VISION OF
WORK AS CULTURAL INHERITANCE

My mother grew up in the Jim Crow South. She grew up in a systematically oppressive culture. A culture that grew out of segregation. My mother and her siblings would often share stories with me about their upbringing. Stories about sharecropping. Stories that echoed slavery. Stories about being forced to pick cotton and vegetables instead of being allowed to attend school. Stories about learning how to smile and persevere in the face of crippling poverty. Stories about understanding what bodies could occupy certain spaces in the segregated South. Growing up in the South in the Jim Crow era, my mother developed a heightened awareness and understanding of spatial and body politics. For her, growing up there was a "white" side of town and a "black" side of town. If you were Black and you ventured to the white side of town, you understood violence could ensue.

My mother, my aunts, and my uncles often told me stories about how hard they had to work as children. They would say, "We used to work from can to can't." Basically, they would enter the fields before the sun rose and work until the sun set. They hated the work. They hated the callouses that developed on their hands. They hated the way the sun beat down their bodies. They hated the fact that they were forced to pick cotton instead of being allowed to attend school. The social, cultural, and psychological oppression that my mother lived through, like Bochner's father, affected how she came to view labor. Hard work and working excessively was a performance her flesh had rehearsed and memorized. At a young age, her body was forced to become accustomed to working overtime. She hated the work she was forced to do as an adolescent; however, as she got older, she used work as a tool to escape the impoverished community of her youth and provide for her own child a chance to have a different existence and opportunities than she had. I can still hear my mother saying, "Always remember, I do this kind of work (janitorial/day labor) so that you won't have to. I don't want you to lift anything heavier than a pen or pencil." My mother did not want me to have a manual labor job. She did not want my hands to become calloused like hers. However, she did let me know that she expected me to *work overtime*.

I know my mother loved me. However, she did not show her love through taking me on extravagant vacations or trips to Disneyland. For my mother, love came in the form of six-day workweeks and fourteen-hour workdays.

I know my mother loved me. However, she did not show her love through purchasing me name-brand clothing. For my mother, love was shown by waking up and traveling to work long before the sun rose and returning home long after the sun had set.

BLACK BODIES WORKING OVERTIME IN ACADEMIA

Scholars have chronicled the challenges Black men have experienced while navigating academia. These challenges include the fear of triggering white fragility and the constant double conscious state of wondering how the emotions they display may be racialized and gendered,[17] continual need to legitimize their existence within academia and among white colleagues/peers,[18] perpetual awareness of how the intersections of their Black masculine identity mark them as "others" on college campuses,[19] struggle to find academic publications that speak to and represent the intersections of their identity,[20] and the pushback they experience when attempting to decenter whiteness and destabilize white supremacy.[21] Each one of these instances speaks to the struggles and insider/outsider status Black men often experience within the culture of academia. This essay extends the work of the aforementioned scholars by exploring the ways in which my Black masculine self has experienced and attempted to reimagine my existence within academic spaces and continuing to mark the lives Black men lead within academia as an important and necessary site of inquiry within communication studies.

When I went off to college, my mother repeated to me the same words I'd heard her say a million times before. It is the same words many black parents have uttered to their children throughout their lives: "Remember, you will always have to work twice as hard as your (white) classmates. You will have to work twice as hard to be seen as half as good."[22] Essentially, my mother was trying to prepare me for working overtime. Although my mother never attended college, she understood the politics of bodies and spaces. From her lived experiences, she understood when Black bodies entered white spaces violence (physical/intellectual/symbolic) could ensue. Like Bochner's father, my mother wanted to prepare me for "discrimination, injustice, and suffering."[23] She wanted to prepare me for working twice as hard as my *white* classmates. She wanted to prepare me for working overtime to be seen as competent. She wanted to prepare me for working overtime to find the work of scholars of color that was often left out of courses I took. She understood my experience in academia would be different from my white classmates. Even while sitting next to each other in the same classrooms, my white classmates and I would experience and process the space differently. She wanted to prepare me for the possibilities of experiencing violence. The narrative inheritance that my mother passed down to me was one of understanding space and working overtime.

According to Horn, Berger, & Carroll,[24] Black men represent less than 5 percent of the student population at four-year institutions of higher education in the United States. Writing in relation to this statistic, Lemons asserts, "While I've been educated in majority-white schools for the greater part of my life, I have never gotten over the feeling of otherness associated with being a 'minority' in them."[25] When I first enrolled as a college student in Ouachita Baptist University (in Arkansas), the average annual cost of tuition was over $20,000. The lawns of the University were manicured and pristine. The academic hallways of the institution were filled with framed pictures of the politicians and businessmen that attended the private university in the past and their children filled the classrooms. None of the people in the pictures looked "black" like me and neither did their children. My mother was not a politician or a businessman. She was a janitor. Unlike one of my freshman classmates, my mother could not afford to buy me a new Jaguar as a high school graduation gift. My mother and I couldn't even afford suitcases or luggage. I used plastic grocery sacks to carry my clothes up to my room when I moved into my dormitory. That first day at Ouachita taught me how poor and I was and how black I was. I felt alone. My skin, my class, both marked me as an outsider. Working overtime.

Watching my mother work sixty-hour workweeks taught me how work could be used as a tool. My road to college was paved with her overtime hours and sacrifices. Upon enrolling in my first semester at Ouachita, I realized that I was enrolled in a class with the governor of Arkansas' daughter. I knew many of my classmates came from private schools, took advanced placement classes, and had higher ACT scores than I did. I did not come from the same communities many of my classmates came from. I did not have many of the privileges my classmates had. However, I did have the privilege of having a mother who prepared me to work overtime and taught me the importance of using work as a tool. I entered that first semester vowing to not let one of my peers study harder than me. If I didn't know anything else, I knew what determination looked like. I saw it every day as my mother left our home before the sun rose. She worked from 8 a.m. to 5 p.m., got off work, and went to her second job from 6 p.m. to 10 p.m., only to return home long after the sun had set. It was a routine that her body had rehearsed since her adolescence. *Working overtime.*

I was studying hard to honor the sacrifices my mother made to get me to college. I was studying hard to prove that I intellectually could compete with my white classmates. I was studying hard to prove that my melanin or how much money my family made did not preclude me from belonging at Ouachita. I was studying hard to prove that people who looked like me belonged at Ouachita even though their pictures couldn't be found in the hallways. I was working to prove all these things. Physically, psychologically and emotionally I was *working overtime*. I finished my first semester at Ouachita with a 3.8 GPA. *Working overtime.*

I was not a member of any of the school's official athletic programs at Ouachita. However, daily, I was asked what sport I played. For my white classmates, me receiving an athletic scholarship was the only way they could make sense of my black body being on the campus. *Working overtime.*

Many of my Black friends (the few of us that were on campus) and I developed comradery through playing intramural sports together. In particular, intramural football. However, when we were on the intramural fields, we would still be reminded of our difference. We would still be reminded that our bodies did not fit the standards for the space we existed within. While I wore frayed t-shirts and second-hand cleats to my intramural games, many of my white classmates wore name brand cleats and customized jerseys with their team logos and names printed on them. While my opponents were often better dressed, my friends and I were often able to athletically outperform them. I remember one game when our opponents took offense to the idea of being beaten by the Black kids. At the end of the game, one the members of the opposing team turned to me and said, "Congratulations on your win. How are y'all gonna celebrate? Are you gonna go to your momma's house to eat fried chicken and watermelon?" In that moment, multiple thoughts ran through my mind. *How should I respond? If I put my hands on this student will I lose my scholarship? What made him feel it was okay to say these words?* Instead, I decided to walk away. I didn't want to jeopardize the academic opportunity my mother worked so hard to afford me. Violence like this was what she was trying to prepare me for. I walked away from the situation on the intramural football field, but the situation did not depart from me. The effects of it lingered. Emotionally and psychologically *working overtime.*

As I sit in the classroom, I sense what is about to happen. The conversation begins to move towards "Black" issues, topics and/or culture. The teacher looks directly at me, making elongated eye contact as if to signal me to speak, as if s/he is waiting on my input. I look away. I bury my eyes in the textbook. I do not feel like answering on behalf of my entire race today. Today, I do not feel like being the classroom's Black cultural informant. Then, the teacher asks the question, "So, how do you feel about this topic, Marquese?" In these moments, I am usually the only Black person in the classroom. In these moments, I am usually one of the only people of color in the classroom. In these moments, I am student and educator. I become the classrooms African American culture aficionado. I become the Black Lives Matter representative. I am expected to know everything about the Civil Rights Movement, Black popular culture, issues facing economically vulnerable communities in the inner city and everything in between. I am expected to have the answer to the "Why do Black people do this?" question. *Working overtime.*

Since entering college (from undergraduate school through finishing a doctoral program), I have developed an interesting habit. I like to google and YouTube the scholars found in course syllabi that I have been given over time. I enjoy learning about them. What is their backstory? Where did they come from? Where have they been? What made them want to do the scholarship they conduct? Do they have multiple areas of expertise? Since beginning this practice, I have noticed a few thematic connections between the courses I have taken over time. In particular—I have noticed that there is a severe lack of people of color scholars in required readings in the courses I have taken throughout my college career.

Pelias states, "Every time a paper is graded, an article for a journal is reviewed, or a scholarly essay is written, scholars are reflecting and affirming what they value."[26] I believe Pelias' claim can be extended to the constructing of syllabi. Knowledge is political. Through the constructing of a syllabus, professors and students affirm what knowledge and which knowledge makers are valuable. When reading articles for classes my mind often drifts. I want to engage with the content, but I often find myself contemplating and reflecting on questions such as: whose knowledge matters[27] and what happens when you are told diversity is valued at an academic institution? However, black/people of color rarely are represented in the syllabi. I know I'm supposed to stay focused on the content. I know I am supposed to stay focused on the theory being discussed. However, my mind drifts. I think about which authors aren't present in the literature and classroom discussions. I think about what professors are communicating to their students when they distribute syllabi that are absent of Black/people of color. I think about who gets to be marked as a producer of knowledge. I think about which voices get to be heard and which are silenced. I think about the question Nobel Peace Prize–winning scholar Saul Bellow asked, "Who is the Tolstoy of the Zulus?"[28] I end up searching for these voices, looking for scholars of color that have discussed the theories and analyzing how and if they access and assess the theoretical concepts differently. Although, I know it adds extra work to my schedule, I feel like it is important to see my "Black" self in the literature. I conduct the regularly assigned readings and search for the voices that go unheard. *Working overtime.*

A (white) classmate or professor makes a racially insensitive remark in class. I wait. I wonder if anyone will say anything. I wonder if anyone else felt the blow of the words. I wait. No one else says anything about the remark. I wonder should I speak up. I wonder how me bringing up the professor's word choice will be received. I wonder if the classroom was filled with Black/ people of color would the professor have made the same statement. I wonder why none of my *white* classmates have said anything. Did they hear the statement? I wonder if I speak up will I be marked as a troublemaker or belligerent in the professor's eyes. I wonder will my comment affect my grade or my relationship with the professor. I wonder will my white classmates get tired of me bringing up issues of race in class. I am *working overtime* . . . I swallow my fear and decide to say something. After class, more than one of my (white) classmates tells me they were offended by the remark the professor made. More than one classmate tells me they thought about saying something but didn't. I wonder why they were not offended enough to say something during class. I smile and tell them it's okay. My words exonerate them of their guilt. *Working overtime.*

THE PERFORMANCE AND INHERITANCE OF FLESH

Our lived experiences write this knowing onto our flesh. Our flesh remembers. My Black mother's lived experiences inscribed themselves onto her body. Experiences of *working overtime*, experiences of growing up in the segregated South, all of these events were written onto and became one with my mother's flesh. These experiences provided my mother's body with a unique set of embodied intelligence and intuition.[29]

The "storied" narratives I have shared thus far illustrate how I have experienced, moved through, and dealt with moments of my experiences of racial oppression within PWI academic spaces. Reflecting on how I responded in these situations, I realize that I not only received a narrative inheritance from my mother, but I also received an embodied inheritance. This embodied intelligence is exemplified in the way that I communicate in and continue to move through the academy. The constantly thinking about how hard I need to work, how my body is seen within PWI academic spaces and what my body can do within these spaces is connected to an embodied legacy that I received from my mother. Pertaining to this belief, Young states the following:

> Within families, memory is passed down, not only as oral lore or material artifacts but also as something that is neither mentifact nor artifact: corporeal disposition. Children apprehend parents' bodies as solutions to the ontological problem of how to be in the world.[30]

For me, replicating the performance of my *Black* mother's body and inheriting the embodied intelligence she passed down to me were the solutions to the question of how to exist within and move through PWI academic spaces.

WORKING OVERTIME AND DOUBLE-CONSCIOUSNESS

W. E. B. Du Bois, in his seminal autoethnographic book about Black identity, *The Souls of Black Folk*, states:

> It is a peculiar sensation, this double-consciousness, this sense of always looking at one's self through the eyes of others, of measuring one's soul by the tape of a world that looks on in amused contempt and pity. One ever feels his two-ness, -an American, a Negro; two souls, two thoughts, two unreconciled strivings; two warring ideals in one dark body.[31]

This theorizing of two-ness by Du Bois, the awareness of seeing yourself through your own eyes and the eyes of others is exemplified multiple times throughout the narratives I have shared. This two-ness is the seeing myself as I see myself and learning to detect when my speaking out in class may mark me as angry and belligerent in the eyes of (white) classmates and professors.[32] It is seeing myself through my eyes and the peculiar sensation of looking at myself through the eyes of *white* classmates who see me as a "chicken and watermelon eating nigger." It is the repetitive action of thinking through and seeing everything twice that my *black* body has rehearsed and intuitively performs. *Working overtime.*

As I have narratively shown, growing up in the South, my mother learned about this two-ness and the link between locations and normative behavior. Edensor[33] states that each space carries within it pre-existing norms that establish how we should perform within them. In the South, understanding which bodies belong in which spaces and what actions they could perform within those spaces was a survival tactic for my mother. She understood the performance that took place between bodies and spaces. My mother understood that my skin color, socioeconomic status, and vernacular would not match the norms found within the PWI college classrooms she was sending me off to. As performers, we often alter our performance to make sure it aligns with the preferred standards set within the spaces we find ourselves within.[34] However, what happens when you are black and the performative norm is whiteness? What happens when the space you find yourself within *Others* you? It is in these moments that you begin to understand how spaces are active and sometimes alienating actors. This is what my mother wanted to prepare me for.

STILL *WORKING OVERTIME*

In the autoethnographic accounts I have shared in this essay, I illustrate how I have learned to activate the inheritance my mother passed down to me. It is a narrative and embodied inheritance that I still carry with me even though my mother has transitioned. It is an inheritance of using work as a tool to overcome oppression and understanding spatial/body politics. My inheritance of *working overtime* is both a burden and survival tactic. It is simultaneously draining and sustaining. It is a performance that my body has rehearsed. It is a consciousness that my black skin has come to know.

As I say these words, I realize this has been a reflective journey that has caused me to revisit events in my past that I had intentionally buried. It is a journey that caused me to relive the oppression that my body has absorbed; relive events that silenced me; relive events that made me feel powerless. However, it was my mother's voice and other *pro*-Black feminist voices from the margins and their experiences that equipped me to not only survive my academic journey in PWI spaces, but also guiding me to teach my "Introduction to Hip Hop Studies" course.

To my mother and these Black/women of color feminists, I am forever grateful.

BIBLIOGRAPHY

Alexander, B. K. "The Cost of a Presumed Public Good," *Cultural Studies Critical Methodologies*, 17, no. 4 (2017): 357–60.

Banks, A. J. *Digital griots: African American rhetoric in a multimedia age.* Carbondale, IL: SIU Press, 2010.

Bochner, A. P. *Coming to narrative: A personal history of paradigm change in the human sciences.* New York: Routledge, 2016.

Bottoms, S., and M. Goulish, *Small acts of repair: Performance, ecology and Goat Island.* New York: Routledge, 2013.

Bowman, M. "Looking for Stonewall's arm: Tourist performance as research method." In *Opening acts: Performance in/as communication and cultural studies*, edited by Judith Hamera, 102–133. Thousand Oaks, CA: Sage Publications, 2006.

Boylorn, R. M. "From Boys to Men: Hip-Hop, Hood Films, and the Performance of Contemporary Black Masculinity." *Black Camera* 8, no. 2 (2017): 146–64.

Bradley, R. N. "Kanye West's sonic [hip-hop] cosmopolitanism." In *The Cultural Impact of Kanye West*, edited by Julius Bailey, 97–107. NY: Palgrave Macmillan, 2014.

Bradley, R. N. "Introduction: Hip-Hop Cinema as a Lens of Contemporary Black Realities." *Black Camera*, 8 no.2 (2017): 141–45.

Carson, A. D. "Trimalchio from Chicago: Flashing lights and the great Kanye in West Egg." In *The Cultural Impact of Kanye West* edited by Julius Bailey, 181–93. NY: Palgrave Macmillan, 2014.

Coates, T. N. *Between the world and me*. New York: Spiegel and Grau, 2015.

Collins, P. H. "Learning from the outsider within: The sociological significance of Black feminist thought." *Social problems*, 33 no.6 (1986): 14–32.

Conquergood, D. and E. P. Johnson. *Cultural struggles: Performance, ethnography, praxis*. Ann Arbor: University of Michigan Press, 2013.

Dimitriadis, G. *Performing identity/performing culture: Hip hop as text, pedagogy, and lived practice*. NY: Peter Lang, 2009.

Du Bois, W. E. B. *The souls of black folk*. edited by Jasmine Griffin. New York: Barnes & Noble Classic, 2003.

Durham, A. *Home with hip hop feminism: Performances in communication and culture*. NY: Peter Lang Publishing Group, 2014.

Edensor, T. "Performing tourism, staging tourism (Re) producing tourist space and practice." *Tourist studies*, 1, no.1 (2001): 59–81.

Fries-Britt, S. and B. Turner. "Uneven stories: Successful Black collegians at a Black and a White campus." *The Review of Higher Education*, 25, no. 3 (2002): 315–30.

Griffin, R. A. "I AM an angry Black woman: Black feminist autoethnography, voice, and resistance." *Women's Studies in Communication*, 35, no. 2 (2012):138–57.

Guiffrida, D. A. "Othermothering as a framework for understanding African American students' definitions of student-centered faculty." *Journal of Higher Education*, 76, (2005):701–23.

Hamera, J. 2006. *Opening acts: Performance in/as communication and cultural studies*. Thousand Oaks: Sage Publications.

Henson, B. "Real recognize real: Local hip-hop cultures and global imbalances in the African diaspora." *Encyclopedia of educational philosophy and theory*, (2016): 1–5.

Hill, M. L. *Beats, rhymes, and classroom life: Hip-hop pedagogy and the politics of identity*. NY: Teachers College Press, 2009.

hooks, b. *We real cool: Black men and masculinity*. London: Psychology Press, 2004.

Johnson, E. P. "'Queer' studies, or (almost) everything I know about queer studies I learned from my grandmother." *Text and Performance Quarterly*, 2, no. 1 (2001): 1–25.

Johnson, A. "Confessions of a video vixen: My autocritography of sexuality, desire, and memory." *Text and Performance Quarterly*, 34, no. 2 (2014): 182–200.

Johnson, J. "Blasphemously Black: Reflections on Performance and Pedagogy." *Liminalities*, 2, no. 4 (2015): 1–13.

Lemons, G. *Black Male Outsider, A Memoir: Teaching as a Pro-Feminist Man*. Albany, NY: SUNY Press, 2008.

Love, B. L. *Hip hop's li'l sistas speak: Negotiating hip hop identities and politics in the new South.* NY: Peter Lang, 2012.

Morgan, J. *When chickenheads come home to roost.* NY: Simon & Schuster, 1999.

Neal, M. A. *Looking for Leroy: illegible black masculinities.* NY: NYU Press, 2013.

Pelias, R. J. *Performance: An alphabet of performative writing.* Walnut Creek, CA: Left Coast Press, 2014.

Richardson, E. 2003. *African American literacies.* London: Routledge Press, 2003.

Smith-Shomade, B. E. "'Rock-a-bye, baby!': black women disrupting gangs and constructing hip-hop gangsta films." *Cinema Journal* (2003): 25–40.

Stoute, S. *The Tanning of America: How hip-hop Created a culture that rewrote the rules of the new economy.* New York: Gotham Books, 2011.

Watkins, S. C. *Hip hop matters: Politics, pop culture, and the struggle for the soul of a movement.* Boston, MA: Beacon Press, 2005.

Watts, E. K. "An exploration of spectacular consumption: Gangsta rap as cultural commodity." *Communication Studies* 48, no. 1 (1997): 42–58.

Weiler, H. N. "Knowledge and Power." *Journal of Educational Planning and Administration,* 25 no. 3 (2011): 205–21.

White, M. *From Jim Crow to Jay-Z: race, rap, and the performance of masculinity.* Urbana, IL: University of Illinois Press, 2011.

Young, K. "The memory of the flesh: the family body in somatic psychology." *Body & Society,* 8, no. 3 (2002): 25–47.

Young, V. A. *Your average nigga: Performing race, literacy and masculinity.* Detroit, MI: Wayne State University Press, 2007.

NOTES

1. hooks, b. *We real cool: Black men and masculinity* (London: Psychology Press, 2004).

2. Love, B. L. *Hip hop's li'l sistas speak: Negotiating hip hop identities and politics in the new South* (NY: Peter Lang, 2012).

3. Morgan, J. *When chickenheads come home to roost* (NY: Simon & Schuster, 1999).

4. See, Dimitriadis, G. *Performing identity/performing culture: Hip hop as text, pedagogy, and lived practice* (NY: Peter Lang, 2009); Henson, B. "Real recognize real: Local hip-hop cultures and global imbalances in the African diaspora." *Encyclopedia of educational philosophy and theory* (2016), 1–5; Hill, M. L. *Beats, rhymes, and classroom life: Hip-hop pedagogy and the politics of identity* (NY: Teachers College Press, 2009); Love, B. L. *Hip hop's li'l sistas speak: Negotiating hip hop identities and politics in the new South* (NY: Peter Lang, 2012); Richardson, E. *African American literacies* (London: Routledge Press, 2003); Watts, E. K. "An exploration of spectacular consumption: Gangsta rap as cultural commodity" *Communication Studies* 48, no. 1 (1997): 42–58.

5. See, for example, Bradley, R. N. "Kanye West's sonic [hip-hop] cosmopolitanism." In *The Cultural Impact of Kanye West,* ed. Julius Bailey, 97–107. NY: (Palgrave

Macmillan, 2014); Bradley, R. N. "Introduction: Hip-Hop Cinema as a Lens of Contemporary Black Realities." *Black Camera*, 8 no.2 (2017): 141–45; White, M. *From Jim Crow to Jay-Z: race, rap, and the performance of masculinity* (Urbana, IL: University of Illinois Press, 2011).

6. Stoute, S. *The Tanning of America: How hip-hop Created a culture that rewrote the rules of the new economy* (New York: Gotham Books, 2011).

7. Banks, A. J. 2010. *Digital griots: African American rhetoric in a multimedia age* (Carbondale, IL: SIU Press, 2010).

8. Neal, M. A. *Looking for Leroy: illegible black masculinities* (NY: NYU Press, 2013).

9. Carson, A. D. "Trimalchio from Chicago: Flashing lights and the great Kanye in West Egg," in *The Cultural Impact of Kanye West*, ed. Julius Bailey (NY: Palgrave Macmillan, 2014), 181–93.

10. Smith-Shomade, B. E. "'Rock-a-bye, baby!': black women disrupting gangs and constructing hip-hop gangsta films," *Cinema Journal* (2003): 25–40.

11. See, for example, Boylorn, R. M. "From Boys to Men: Hip-Hop, Hood Films, and the Performance of Contemporary Black Masculinity." *Black Camera* 8, no. 2 (2017): 146–64; Durham, A. *Home with hip hop feminism: Performances in communication and culture* (NY: Peter Lang Publishing Group, 2014); Johnson, J. "Blasphemously Black: Reflections on Performance and Pedagogy." *Liminalities*, 2, no. 4 (2015), 1–13; Watts, E. K. "An exploration of spectacular consumption: Gangsta rap as cultural commodity." *Communication Studies* 48, no. 1 (1997), 42–58.

12. Bochner, A. P. *Coming to narrative: A personal history of paradigm change in the human sciences* (New York: Routledge, 2016).

13. Bochner, A. P. *Coming to narrative: A personal history of paradigm change in the human sciences*, 27.

14. Bochner, A. P. *Coming to narrative: A personal history of paradigm change in the human sciences*, 29.

15. Bochner, A. P. *Coming to narrative: A personal history of paradigm change in the human sciences*, 29.

16. Ibid., 29.

17. Johnson, J. "Blasphemously Black: Reflections on Performance and Pedagogy," *Liminalities*, 2, no. 4 (2015): 1–13.

18. Young, V. A. *Your average nigga: Performing race, literacy and masculinity* (Detroit, MI: Wayne State University Press, 2007).

19. Alexander, B. K. "The Cost of a Presumed Public Good," *Cultural Studies Critical Methodologies*, 17, no. 4 (2017): 357–60.

20. Johnson, E. P. "'Queer' studies, or (almost) everything I know about queer studies I learned from my grandmother," *Text and Performance Quarterly* 2, no. 1 (2001): 1–25.

21. Lemons, G. *Black Male Outsider, A Memoir: Teaching as a Pro-Feminist Man* (Albany, NY: SUNY Press, 2008).

22. Coates, T. N. *Between the world and me* (New York: Spiegel and Grau, 2015).

23. Bochner, A. P. *Coming to narrative: A personal history of paradigm change in the human sciences*, 29.

24. Horn, Berger, and Carroll. "College Persistence on the Rise? Changes in 5-Year Degree Completion and Postsecondary Persistence Rates Between 1994 and 2000: Postsecondary Education Descriptive Analysis Reports. NCES 2005–156." *National Center for Education Statistics* (2004).

25. Lemons, G. Black Male Outsider, 2008.

26. Pelias, R. J. *Performance: An alphabet of performative writing* (Walnut Creek, CA: Left Coast Press, 2014), 11.

27. Weiler, H. N. "Knowledge and Power," *Journal of Educational Planning and Administration*, 25 no. 3 (2011): 205–21.

28. Coates, T. N. *Between the world and me* (New York: Spiegel and Grau, 2015), 25.

29. Bottoms, S., and M. Goulish, *Small acts of repair: Performance, ecology and Goat Island.* (New York: Routledge, 2013).

30. Young, K. "The memory of the flesh: the family body in somatic psychology," *Body & Society* 8, no. 3 (2002): 25.

31. Du Bois, W. E. B. *The souls of black folk.* edited by Jasmine Griffin (New York: Barnes & Noble Classic, 2003), 9.

32. Griffin, R. A. "I AM an angry Black woman: Black feminist autoethnography, voice, and resistance," *Women's Studies in Communication* 35, no. 2 (2012):138–57.

33. Edensor, T. "Performing tourism, staging tourism (Re) producing tourist space and practice." *Tourist studies*, 1, no.1 (2001): 59–81.

34. Bowman, M. "Looking for Stonewall's arm: Tourist performance as research method." in *Opening acts: Performance in/as communication and cultural studies*, ed. Judith Hamera (Thousand Oaks, CA: Sage Publications, 2006), 102–33.

Chapter Eleven

A Pedagogical Awakening

My Pro-Womanist His-Story

Vincent Adejumo

"WOKE" AND PRO-"WOMANIST"

The term "Woke" is traditionally defined as being "aware of and actively attentive to important facts and issues (especially issues of racial and social justice)."[1] The term within the context of calling attention to awareness particularly became a part of the larger discussion of police brutality in the Black community in 2014, immediately following the shooting of Michael Brown in Ferguson, Missouri. "Woke" then became entwined with the Black Lives Matter movement[2] and subsequently found a permanent place in the social justice lexicon.

From a gender studies perspective, "woke" perfectly encapsulates the very foundation of womanist principals as they pertain to social justice and well-being of Black folk. "Womanist" as originally conceptualized by Alice Walker in *In Search of Our Mother's Garden* is defined as:

A black feminist or feminist of color. From the black folk expression of mothers to female children, "you acting womanish," i.e., like a woman. A woman who loves other women, sexually and/or nonsexually. Appreciates and prefers women's culture, women's emotional flexibility (values tears as natural counterbalance of laughter), and women's strength. Sometimes loves individual men, sexually and/or nonsexually. Committed to survival and wholeness of entire people, male and female.[3]

165

In more of an academic context, Layli Phillips Maparyan defines womanism as "a social change perspective rooted in Black women's and other women of color's everyday experiences and everyday methods of problem-solving in everyday spaces, extended to the problem of ending all forms of oppression for all people, restoring the balance between people and the environment/ nature, and reconciling human life with the spiritual dimension."[4]

Daphne W. Ntiri argues that scholars in recent years have used "womanism as a corrective or alternative to the feminist movement" which historically has "paid scant attention to the social and economic needs of women of African heritage or to discourse on their contributions.[5] From 2014 to 2016, the collective conscious of America was in a constant of awareness surrounding police brutality on a micro level and the overall conditions of Black people at a macro level thanks impart to those unfortunately incidences involving unarmed Black bodies and the agitation provided from groups such as Dream Defenders and Black Lives Matter. My own awareness of "woke" from an academic perspective took shape within this period and influenced much of my scholarship and activity at that time as I completed my graduate studies.

In thinking about what it means to be "woke," I cannot help but think that the purpose of my entire career as an academic and scholar has been not only to awaken the collective conscious of my students on a daily basis, but also to self-reflect continuously about my own biases and conception of societal normativity to ensure that there is room in my soul for growth and understanding. With the explosion of media attention on unarmed Black bodies getting killed by vigilantes and law enforcers primarily of Caucasian descent during the latter years of the Obama presidency, the ideology of "Woke" began to take shape in the streets. This flurry of media attention of an issue that is engrained in American society since its inception, as well as the response from all walks of life, informed many aspects of my personal and professional existence— especially as it pertains to my own pedagogical development as a lecturer.

AFRICAN-CENTERED FAMILY VALUES: MY PATH TO CRITICAL SELF-CONSCIOUSNESS

After receiving my doctorate in 2015, I was appointed as a lecturer of African American studies at the University of Florida. Although the journey to this position was in many ways unorthodox when juxtaposed against traditional means of procuring this type of position at a research one institution, the process that led up to that point played a crucial role in creating what would become the foundation of each course that I currently teach. The process of my being who I profess to be is and of itself a story of social justice and human rights that eventually manifested into my own concept of "woke" pedagogy.

Sharing the evolution of my pedagogical consciousness, I begin by offering my family history. I was born in Tampa Florida. One of parents is from the deep South; the other is directly from Nigeria, I consider the history of my existence a story of tragedy and triumph like all African Americans in this country. As stated, my familial demographic history would ultimately manifest itself in the geographic and conceptual meaning of the "classroom"—as a personal space for learning about oneself. The tragedy I connect to this concept is that on my biological mother's side of the family, it is difficult to trace my family lineage due in part to the ugliness of slavery and how with impunity white slave masters regularly discarded any shred of family life and humanity in the slave quarters, either by means of violence such as whippings and rape or capital by way of selling Black bodies to the highest bidder.

In the "Introduction to African American Studies course" that I teach, students are asked to voluntarily describe themselves as it pertains to identification of race and ethnicity. Most students of Caucasian descent when self-identifying their family heritage can rattle off without much thought their family background, some tracing their lineage as far back as since before America was officially an autonomous state. However, I and students that are of African American descent cannot trace this part of our family and thus it has fueled my ambition to ensure that others in and outside of the classroom are awaken to the intricate process of how this terrible institution was systemically sanctioned and its effects that are still being present today.

The triumph of my existence is that my father is directly from Nigeria, and he is in constant contact with his immediate and extended family, not only those who are still in Nigeria, but others who have migrated throughout the diaspora. When I went to Nigeria a few years ago to lecture at the great University of Ibadan and Bowen University, Iwo, my uncles sat me down and explained exactly my lineage from that side of the family. From the information that they gave me, they can trace the family surname as far back as ancient Egypt. Hearing this information did wonders for my conscious and it was almost as if I was coming out of the womb for the first time, a rebirth.

I had never heard my father speak of this information before making my trip, however when I arrived back to the States, we spent a great amount of time discussing the family heritage and its place in Nigeria. The experience of making my journey to Nigeria, meeting family that I had never met before, learning the history of the family, and then engaging in discussion with my father about the family added another layer in building my personal pedagogy as it pertained to classroom teaching strategies and curriculum development. However, before making my journey to Nigeria, there were certain flashpoint experiences in my life that played a crucial role in my development as an instructor.

In elementary school, I attended a private Black-owned Christian academy from kindergarten to second grade, and while my third- through fifth-grade years were spent at a public school in the neighborhood. It was during my time in private school where I really developed the foundations of my academic skills and began to understand the world around me in more concrete terms. The owners at this school were Black Christian folk and did an excellent job of tailoring the curriculum to the experience of African American children with an all-Black faculty and staff as well as Black and brown characters in the course material while maintaining a standard of excellence in academics for each student.

The owners, faculty, and staff at the school all made an extra effort to get to know each student and their parents on a personal level and were efficient in communicating the needs of each student so that parents could to take the necessary steps to work with the child in these areas when they were away from the school. After my biological parents divorced, I was transferred from this institution to public school. I don't remember whether I was sad or happy to be in public school, however, I did remember having a bit of anxiety before the first day of classes. To this end, the first couple of weeks of third grade was quite an adjustment for me.

Missing were the lessons from the Bible that served as an important framework of the curriculum at the private school that I had attended previously, and I also became more acutely aware of my race due to the presences of Caucasian students which was not the case at the private school. I had also never had teachers of Caucasian descent at the private school nor was there a rigid structure as it pertained to classroom activities. I believe the free-flowing environment of the private school as well as the curriculum that centered the African American and Christian experience developed me into a much more capable academic when I arrived at public school compared to my peers, even though I was the youngest in the classroom due to my parents enrolling me in the private school almost a year before I was supposed to start according to public school age standards.

From the third through fifth grade, in spite of undergoing monumental adjustments in life such as the divorce of my mother and father as well as a not only a new school but new structure for learning, I excelled at the public school, never earning below a B in any of my classes. Despite cruising through the curriculum, I never was "tapped" to receive an invitation for the accelerated or "gifted" courses as my peers who were mostly white. This observance brought upon my initial feelings that my race was a detriment to me being on equal academic footing with my white peers.

I was more made certain of this observation and feeling when the white teachers that I had did not take kindly to the intellectual abilities that I displayed for my age and in some ways felt that they resented me. This was clearer to me in one instance where I was punished for being disruptive in class and the teacher remarked that I would never amount to anything in life. It was from that point forth that I was stricken, or perhaps awaken, with an academic drive to prove to this teacher and my peers who were naysayers of my abilities that I would in fact amount to more than what she and they assumed.

During this time, I also attended the Boys and Girls Club during after school hours. It was at the club where I began to develop my social skills and test my intellectual and physical abilities with debates about current events and sports. I became captain of the football team in the pee wee football league division and captain of the basketball team, all of which was through the Ybor City branch of the Boys and Girls Club. I remember during the basketball games my favorite part would be before the games where the team had to take a test on civics and history for points that would be added on at the beginning of games. Interestingly, someone from my team would find a way to sit close enough to me to copy the answers that were on my sheet and then disseminate the information to the rest of the team. Suffice to say, our team consistently won this part of the competition, and I felt a sense of pride that I was the main culprit responsible.

The Boys and Girls Club also attracted many outside organizations and individuals that wanted to do outreach to "lower income" youth in "urban" areas of town. One such individual was a white man named Chuck that conducted a program called "second step." In my first introduction to Chuck, I was very distrustful as my experiences with white people up to that point were not pleasant. However, in getting to know Chuck and participating in his second step program, I had come to the realization that he was different and subsequently began to open up about my life and how I felt as a Black boy growing up in the environment that I had come from. It was the first time I had felt that comfortable around anybody that was in authority and especially white to that degree of expression.

As I reflect on how I think about the curriculum of courses that I teach currently, those experiences in elementary school and at the Boys and Girls club were invaluable as I learned how a simple game such as competition basketball can be used as an innovative academic tool in artificially encouraging learning. In the courses that I teach currently, I have built in innovative activities that are not normally associated with academia, just as quizzes and test are not normally associated with organized basketball leagues.

ON A COURSE ABOUT "BLACK MASCULINITY":
RESISTANCE FOR INNOVATION

In the "Black Masculinity" course that I teach, I allow students to select a final project that entails creating a musical/spoken word album. When I applied for the course to receive state credit for writing, diversity, and humanities requirement, some on the University of Florida's General Education requirements committee who were white thought this option was strange and not very scholarly. In fact, some mistook this option for the project as the students being forced to make a "rap" album. Obviously, these people associated "Black Masculinity" with rap not taking care to observe that the syllabus only mentioned a spoken word/musical album and did not mention anything about rap. There was another colleague on the committee who was also white, whom I later found out was a feminist scholar, whelped that the content of the course could inspire too many "Malcolm Xs." I politely invited her to sit in on a lecture for the course to see who was enrolled in the class (majority African American women). Unsurprisingly, she did not partake in that offer, however, the course received all necessary General Education requirements that in which I applied for it. I would later go on to be invited by the University Provost himself to serve on the General Education committee to oversee the designation of all General Education requirements of courses at the University of Florida.

In creating the pedagogy for that course, I used not only my first experiences with realizing who I am as Black and masculine in this society, but also centering the African American experience within the curriculum so that all students from all backgrounds get a concrete rather than abstract understanding of masculine expression on Black bodies from a historical, political, sociological, and pop cultural perspective. This has especially proven valuable when teaching students who are not Black, particularly white students.

I draw upon my experiences with Chuck when dealing with white students one on one, especially those who come into my courses not only ignorant of race but refuse to believe that there ever was or continues to be a problem of race in America. As with Chuck dealings with me as a child, I acknowledge our differences to get them warmed up and then allow them the space to express themselves candidly and in return I provide studies and statistics to not try to convince them of anything, but to bring awareness that there is quantifiable validity to the situation proving the contrary in which they are skeptical.

While in middle school, my academic talents steadily developed as well as becoming more acutely aware of what was going on in popular culture as it related to my Blackness. Tupac Shakur was killed and subsequently his rival, the Notorious BIG, was killed the following year. This was the first time in my short time of living that I was cognizant of celebrities that I had idolized due to them looking like me, there bravado, and the admiration and respect that they had from my peers would no longer be on earth. Also, in middle school I became more aware of being attracted to the opposite sex as well as being introduced to LGBTQ concepts with celebrities such as RuPaul and Dennis Rodman as queered Black men becoming a staple of mainstream culture at that time.

Discussing these topics with my peers who were majority Black was very crude because we did not have these conversations with our teachers or with our parents. My middle school years were also the time in which my personality as a goofball developed as well as my penchant for trying to enact certain stereotypical behaviors and gender expressions associated with African American males, such as lowering my pants below my buttocks and perfecting the use of curse words and slang. While creating the Black Masculinity and Mentoring At-risks youth courses, I reflected on these experiences in middle school and took care to carefully implement in the curriculum of those courses noted studies that focus on stereotypes of African American males as well as studies of African American youth.

These experiences were invaluable as far as my teaching style whether it is to a group of college aged students or inquisitive third graders. Understanding how to meet them where they are intellectually and demeanor wise and then present the requisite information in such a way that they may understand has been the foundation of my teaching method, of which I owe a large part to my experiences in middle school.

MY INTRODUCTION TO WOMANISM

Middle school was also the time period when I came to know more about the mother of the woman that my father married after my biological parents divorced. In those days and until her last days, my grandmother was very inquisitive about the everyday happenings in my life. Her character was that of encouragement and transformation which is exemplary of what Ntiri argues as the basis of womanism: "womanism promotes social transformation through common sense and humanistic attributes that oppose oppression and racism and embrace peace and harmony, dialogue, and hospitality, and spirituality and self-help."[6] When my sister and I would stay with her during short periods on the weekends, she was very intent on engaging us in long conversations that not only included the Christian faith, but also what was happening in our everyday lives at school and at home.

She was a great conversationalist, allowing me to express myself in a way that made me feel comfortable about telling her everything that was going on in my life. She would interrupt from time to time to give her opinion and guidance, but for the most part, she was a great listener and remained at attention while I expressed myself. The way should made me feel whenever we had our discussions took on a humanist approach. Humanism is defined by Kwame Gyekeye as "Human needs, interests and dignity are fundamental."[7] Badi Foster views humanism as "concern for human life in relationships between self and others" for the purposes of "service to family, clan, community, or nation" as defining tenets of those interactions.[8]

The key ingredient that my grandmother had when engaging in conversations was the ability to put the interests of the person at the forefront without making any mention of whatever trial and tribulation that she may have been going through. Another important part of my grandmother's approach to conversation was her faith by way of her Christian faith. Indeed, my grandmother wasn't someone who just talked about faith, it was encoded in her very DNA. According to Nkrumah, Africans had a natural conception of spirituality "with certain inward dignity, integrity and value"; the recognition of the "equality of all and the responsibility of the many for one"; and the conviction that "the welfare of people is supreme" over any individualistic or "sectional interest."[9]

Not only did my grandmother express her faith in discussions, she also implemented it through exemplary works. For example, she was a founding member of the Benevolence ministry at the Bible-Based Church of Temple Terrace. On the subject of Benevolence, Fannie Williams in 1896 remarked: "Benevolence [was] the essence of most of the colored women's organizations. The humane side of their natures has been cultivated to recognize the duties they owe to the sick, the indigent and ill-fortuned. No church, school, or charitable institution for the special use of colored people has been allowed to languish or fail when the associated efforts of the women could save it."[10]

This ministry was focused on providing resources for those who demonstrated need regardless of sex, gender, race, etc. This ministry, which was primarily led by Black women, falls in line with what Rosetta Ross in 1997 argues, which is that on what they [Black women] understood as God's provisions in their lives, the women demonstrated fidelity to God by routinely working hard and taking risks as they sought to change repressive traditions, institutions and social conventions that generally hampered the well-being of African Americans.[11]

From my grandmother's perspective, even though the ministry was led by women, her main concern was for the ministry, as Josepine St. Pierre Ruffin argues, "was for the good of women and men, for the benefit of all humanity."[12] Through conversation, my grandmother displayed a sense of responsibility to ensure the welfare of myself, the family and whoever else that she conversed with remained supreme, again giving the impression that she was genuinely interested and concern with the wellbeing of who the she focused her attention on.

I have come to appreciate this style of conversation, and it proves especially useful in the classroom. Allowing students the space and comfort to express themselves on how they truly feel on issues such as race, politics, and sexuality, especially African American students, in all of the classes that I teach have been proven to be therapeutic for them as well as for myself. It has also earned me a reputation as being the "cool" teacher as many of my students express that they are not allowed to candidly express how they feel on these issues in other classes. This is mainly due to their instructors and professors being white, and most of their classmate are white as well. On several occasions, students would visit me in my office hours and vent because a discussion became very spirited about race between students of different races.

However, the instructor did not allow the discussion to progress because they did not feel comfortable, even though the class may deal specifically on the topic of race. In every course I teach, I ensure that students remain respectful during discourse, and in this context encourage rigorous academic discussion and disagreement. From this method, the learning is taking place not only from teacher to student but also from student to student and student to teacher.[13] This form of pedagogy is called "Cross Curricular" according to David Roy, and it is essential in creating a "Woke" paradigm, especially in the context of African-American Studies which by its very nature is the essence of a woke curriculum.

LEARNING TO BE A CONSCIOUS BLACK MAN

Harkening back to my youth, high school was the time in which I felt that I really started to come into my own consciously as being a Black man. My first two years in high school I was transported by bus about ten miles from where I lived to school. I remember finding out in eighth grade that I would be attending this school and was very devastated because most of my classmates were also my neighbors and they received letters that allowed them to attend a school that was only three 3 miles away from where I lived, and I had always wanted to attend that school. The first few weeks of high school was an adjustment due to not only having to wake up before 5 a.m. to ride the school bus, but also because a great majority of the school were of Hispanic/Latino descent and white. It was at this school where I had first taken a serious interest in technology beyond video games and chose a curriculum tract of technology and industry. Learning about the way in which computers functioned and how to repair them gave me great joy and confidence that I was learning a skill that could be applied to something tangible and prove useful in making myself a few dollars. While at this school for two years, I also learned a bit of Spanish as mandated by the state curriculum at that time for all students and had come to appreciate the students who were from my same neighborhood who were also transported by bus to the school.

Every day on the bus was a learning exercise for me, observing how the older students interacted with the younger, the arguments, the fists fights, the love stories, and most importantly, the mentorship. One night, after missing the bus after a late basketball practice, myself and a dear friend of mind named Jah embarked on the treacherous 10-mile journey from the school to our home. We had missed the bus in previous times but was always able to call our parents to come pick us up. For some reason, neither of our parents were able to pick us up, none of our coaches lived near us, and the bus that was operated by the city had finished its route. We were no older than fourteen and fifteen at the time when we decided to make the tract home but thankfully after a six-hour run/walk/jog and enduring the elements, we made our way home. To this day we still laugh about that experience, having now forged a friendship of a lifetime.

What my experience at this school taught me in the larger context of my career is that the most effective of communicators and teachers have gone through the most solemn valley to get to the top of their profession. There were many low points for me while attending the school, mainly due to going through the natural process of maturing and learning about myself at a place that I never really felt comfortable. However, these lows were augmented by the bond that I had built with the children who were also from my neighborhood and had to go through the same plight of being transported to a school that was outside of their familiarity and comfort.

When teaching African Americans at a predominately white institution, I make sure that I consistently integrate the experiences of African American students at PWIs into my pedagogy and instruction by making references to the historical injustices that have happened at these institutions and how those injustices play an important role in attempting to appeal to the needs of African Americans on campus today. Around the same time that I was attending the high school that was miles away, a new high school that was to be named "Middleton High School" was being built and set to open in the neighborhood that I was from. I was excited for this new school to open because I felt that it would give me an opportunity for a fresh start surrounded by peers that I had previously known from my time in elementary, middle school, and the Boys and Girls Club. The school opened during my junior year of high school without any students who were to be incoming seniors.

The first day of school was remarkably different than my old school mainly due to the student population of the school being at least 90 percent African American, and there were also more African American teachers and staff than the previous school that I attended. The teachers and staff were not only African American as it pertains to their skin color, but they also were African American in their thought process and the way in which they taught their courses and advised students. Many of them also had attended and graduated from Historically Black Colleges and Universities. It was at this school where I first noticed the difference in teaching and styles of African American men and women. The men displayed different ranges of gender expressions in their pedagogical style, some with a more sentimental approach while others were hypermasculine, and yet some with a mixture of both.

The women also displayed different ranges of gender performances, taking a stern and professional approach in the student-teacher dynamic while others preferred a motherly kinfolk approach. I gravitated more so to the women that took a motherly approach and to the men that were sentimental. This was especially the case since most of my peers perceived me as not being hypermasculine or "soft" due to my soft-spoken voice and relaxed demeanor. Even though I had understood this aspect of myself to a degree as a young boy, this was more evident as I came into my own in my late teenage years at this particular school.

The African American men and women who I had gravitated towards that displayed the more sentimental expressions helped me understand in greater context my own version of masculinity and how to use it as a driving force as a scholar and mentor. The exception to these types of mentors and teachers was the head coach of the basketball team at that time named Coach Smith. Coach Smith was an affable character who always preached the importance of brotherhood and the values of hard work. His father was the assistant principal of the school and a former basketball coach himself in the first iteration of the school.

CROSSING COLOR LINES: FROM JIM CROW TO DESEGREGATED SCHOOLING

George S. Middleton High School first opened during the Jim Crow era in 1934 in East Tampa and was designated specifically for African Americans. The man for whom it is named after, George S. Middleton, was an African American businessman and noted leader in the Black community originally from South Carolina. During his time in Tampa, Mr. Middleton was "secretary and treasurer of the Central Life Insurance Company, president of the Negro State Fair Association, and founder of the Tampa Service Club of the

Negro YMCA."[14] In his honor, the school board at that time voted to name the school by his namesake.

For about forty years, the school served the predominately Black neighborhoods in East Tampa as the premier neighborhood High School. After President Richard M. Nixon's administration successfully instituted policies to enforce the *Brown vs. Board of Education* 1954 decision,[15] Middleton High School transitioned into becoming a middle school and opened as such in 1971. There were many downsides to reopening Middleton High School as a middle school. As Sherman Dorn expressed in "Schools as Imagined Communities: The Creation of Identity, Meaning, and Conflict in U.S. History," the court order of desegregation placed a disproportionate burden on African American families from lower socioeconomic neighborhoods due to a "mandate of a ratio of black/white of 20/80 of all schools and white parents publicly dissenting against sending their children to predominately black high schools."[16]

This led to Black families already segregated in the south by redlining laws having to capitulate to busing their children to predominately white schools while predominately Black high schools, especially in Tampa such as Middleton High School and Blake High School, transformed into middle schools in which white students in the suburbs were transported to via bus after 1971. Cobb-Roberts and Dorn argue that because of forced integration by busing and the closing of predominately Black high schools reopening as middle schools, the fabric of those communities in which the Black high schools existed changed from "imagined" to "fortresses."[17]

As a child of this neighborhood fortress, attending Middleton (which was reopened as a high school in 2002) allowed me to not only to come into my own from a pre-pubescent teen to a young man, but also to understand how the history and structure of my own neighborhood affected the behaviors of young adults at the school. My stepmother had attended the "old" Middleton High school and told me many stories about the fabric of the school and neighborhood. There were no gangs or sets in the neighborhood and except for the occasional troublemaker, everyone was treated with respect and dignity. After the closing of Middleton as a high school in 1971, many neighborhoods, especially Black neighborhoods in highly populated urban areas, were severely impacted by narcotics such as crack cocaine and diseases such as HIV/AIDs.

According to Freyer and Heaton in "Measuring Crack Cocaine and Its Impact," there was a strong link between crack cocaine and an increase in homicide rates by the young, especially among blacks, in the late 1980s.[18] Many of my relatives, close friends, and associates were in some way affected by the crack cocaine era of the 1980s and early 1990s. Some served harsh sentences in prison for the possession of crack cocaine while others were sentenced to die due to deadly disputes with other individuals pertaining to the substance. Coming of age in the aftermath of this era had a direct impact on my world view with the framework of being a Black male often expressing masculine behaviors as American society deemed it so.

THE BATTLE WITHIN [ME]:
PERCEPTION BY EXPRESSION

Back in high school, I had a propensity to constantly think about the perception that others had of me of being "soft" thanks to my high-pitched voice and relaxed demeanor. I would overcompensate for this perception by growing an "afro" and braiding it down, purposefully walking with a slight limp, and wearing my pants below my buttocks. It was a constant internal battle that I had with myself, trying to appeal to the "cool" sensibilities of my peers while at the same time remaining in character as it pertained to the academic expectations of my parents and faculty at Middleton who, for all intents and purposes, functioned as a secondary set of parents within the fictive kin-folk context.

Basketball also served as a coping mechanism in managing my self-image as I was named captain of the basketball team and garnered a reputation for not necessarily as being the most skilled but having the most heart as it pertained to doing the grunt work on the court such as hustling for loose balls and rebounds. Another interesting dynamic at Middleton High School that played a significant role in developing my understanding of the intersection of race and gender and what would also become the foundation for my work in later years is the separation of Black and white students based on being enrolled in the magnet program. This also had implications as it pertained to economic and social status of student groups on campus as well as division among faculty.

A magnet school in Tampa, Florida, entails "a public elementary, middle, or high school whose curricula are theme-based and technology-rich. Magnet school teachers are specially trained not only in theme integration but also in innovative and rigorous academic instructional methods."[19] During my time at Middleton, most of the white students were there for the magnet program, specifically the curriculum that focused on Science, Technology, Engineering, and Math and were from various suburban areas of town. Most of the Black students were within walking distance of the school and were relegated to a more traditional liberal arts curriculum. There were also a few Black students who were classified as magnet however, those students also typically came from suburban areas of town and did not associate themselves much with Black students in the traditional programs.

Although administration did its best to downplay the division between the magnet and traditional sectors of the school, tension was present each day. There would be days in which I would walk into the administrative offices and disagreements between the magnet and traditional faculty as it pertained to the allocation of resources was spirited. Also, the magnet students and traditional students formed groups or "clicks" that fell along racial and socio-economic lines. It seemed as if the only time in which students from different clicks associated with each other regardless of magnet or traditional label was through sports. Ironically, when I later went on to attend Florida State University for my undergraduate career, I would find this same dynamic as it pertained to the socializing of students along racial and socioeconomic lines, which would also play a key role later in my professional career relating to pedagogical development of the courses I teach.

Reflecting on my time at Middleton High school, I was sort of an enigma in that I was perceived by most of my peers as being in the magnet program because of my "soft" demeanor and pension for high academic achievement in general elective courses in which magnet and traditional students typically were in classes together. However, I was not officially a part of the magnet program, although I did have a few friends who were, and I took a few courses in the computer networking program. In considering these different facets of my existence at Middleton High School, the Black women who worked there such as Ms. Warren, Ms. Booth, Ms. Grooms, and even a white woman named Ms. Frerricks were instrumental through conversations and mentorship in helping me navigate the different spaces of my life as a Black man physically, educationally, mentally, and emotionally. To that end, I was able to complete high school and went on to have a fruitful undergraduate, graduate, and professional career.

MATERNAL ESSENCE: EXPERIENCING THE "GRAND"NESS OF WOMANIST LOVE

While the values that I learned in high school continued to serve as an ideological baseline as I moved forward, the one person that continued to serve as a foundation for an understanding of myself and later be an inspiration for the pedagogical development of courses I teach at UF was my grandmother Evelyn Daniels. Grandmother Evelyn, or as I affectionately called her "Grandma," was raised in Tampa, Florida, in the Jim Crow era. She received her education formally in the 1930s and 1940s at home as was the tradition for most blacks, especially girls during this time in Tampa.

The characteristics that Grandma displayed throughout the time that I have known her reminded me of W. E. B. Du Bois remarked in "The Damnation of

Women" in which he posits that Black women are perceived as the "daughter of sorrows" due to their disadvantage in this society based on sex, gender, and race.[20] This notion would become more apparent as I matured and came to understand how my grandmother became the woman that I would get to know and love. Although she didn't talk much about this time period, when she did, there was always a major lesson at the core with an emphasis on her struggle as being a Black and a woman.

Her strength not only as a Black woman but as a mother was a constant fixture in her interactions and exemplified what Dove states, "The love of the mother for her child, of necessity, challenges the European construction of her child's debased humanity. This love is in itself the seed of revolution because it is antithetical to the dominant belief in white superiority."[21] Indeed, my grandmother made it known that notions of white supremacy on the Black intellect should not be a deterrent for the amount of effort needed to succeed. Despite the reality of de jure racism and sexism that was a major barrier for social and economic uplift of blacks and especially Black women in Tampa at this time, Grandma started her own restaurant in the late 1950s in what is now called the old West Tampa off West Green Street. Although she eventually closed the restaurant and began her career at the University of South Florida, retiring from there in the mid 1990s, she still took pride in the restaurant that she started because she was the sole owner and operator.

Whenever she discussed the restaurant with me her faced lit with joy and pride. She frequently joked that my stepmother hated getting up on Saturday mornings as a child to help setup the kitchen and prep the food for the day as part of her chores. She would often recall that it was hard work, but it was satisfying work because of the sense of community that the restaurant brought to the area. Hearing the stories about her restaurant and her overall philosophy on group economics and the importance of supporting of Black-owned businesses inspired me to create a course based on the history of business ownership from an African American experience perspective. The idea to call the course "Black Wall Street" came into my consciousness due to the conversations that I had with Grandma regarding the Black business district in Tulsa, Oklahoma, and her constant reminder that Tampa also had Black business districts on Central Avenue and in West Tampa that she was proudly apart of as a business owner. In 2017, I applied for grant funding through the UF Center for Race and Race relation to build the Black Wall Street course at the University of Florida.

I was awarded the grant and immediately began to correspond more often with Grandma as far as her experience as a business owner. The single most thing that struck me most from her experiences were the reasons why she eventually closed the restaurant. According to her, she believed that at a certain point after the veil of Jim Crow was legally lifted in Tampa, many of the new generation blacks in the 1960s did not see the value of patron-izing Black-owned businesses. This was in part due to the situation that most blacks up until that point had never stepped foot in a white owned business unless they were employed in menial positions such as janitors or cooks. In fact, I recall Grandma saying that Black employees who did work in white owned establishments had to enter said business through the back door, never the front. With Blacks gaining the freedom to patronize white-owned businesses after the civil rights and voting rights act, the tradition of supporting Black-owned establishments withered away from the collective conscious of the Black community and with it, Black-owned businesses dis-sipated. Unfortunately, my grandmother's business was a result of this plight. Grandma said that it was tough to try to continue the business in this new climate of freedom since her former customers who were Black now had the freedom to eat at establishments that they could not eat at before. My step-mother also supports this point, remarking that her generation not only found a sense of freedom in patronizing businesses that they could not before, but they also did not see much value in owning a business that entailed what they deemed as "old school" work such as occupations in trades or food service as they desired to have "white collar" jobs like their white counterparts.

TEACHING "BLACK WALL STREET" IN THE IVORY TOWER

In hearing these points made, this further motivated me to shape the curricu-lum of the "Black Wall Street" course not only from a position of the tradi-tion of Black business ownership in America, but also from the perspective of natural cultural resources being developed into tangible entrepreneurial skills to oppose the larger dominant hegemonic society. From an intersec-tional womanist perspective, I partly focused the course specifically on the entrepreneurial and business contributions of Black women from every aspect of society since the founding of this country as slave, free people, and every class of citizen.

Some of the women include Madame C.J. Walker, Oprah Winfrey, and Mary Church Terrell. The course also critically interrogates the role of Black women who were slave entrepreneurs as dressmakers, maids, cooks, etc., as well as the entrepreneurial activities of Black women in the Civil Rights and Black Power Movements. More broadly, as history has revealed, the develop-ment of Black entrepreneurship and Black enterprise since the founding of the United States has played an integral role in the advancement of American society today. Without the enterprise contributions of key African American figures, especially those that are women, many of the social and cultural commodities that all Americans identify with and enjoy would not have been a reality.

Black culture as a commodity provides a conceptual paradigm to examine entrepreneurship via the theory of "self-help" which sets the foundation for "Black Wall Street" and other predominantly Black communities and collectives. "Black Wall Street" was a predominantly Black business district located outside of Tulsa, Oklahoma, and was considered an exemplar of Black entrepreneurial success with over three hundred thriving Black businesses before it was burned down during the Tulsa race riots in 1921. The course focuses primarily on critically examining the state of African American entrepreneurship from a historical perspective with "Black Wall Street" serving as a baseline as well as it's strategies for advancement, tangible practices, and the current state of Black business development.

The course creates a bridge between the experiences of students and real-world strategies for financial uplift via literature, data sources, and discursive techniques for conducting empirical research on the dynamics of enterprise, entrepreneurship, and Black business advancement. A critical component of the course is to examine and interrogate the impact of cultural, economic, and societal factors in the twenty-first century that are essential for Black business development, propelled by new technologies in a market economy within the context of globalism. Special attention is given to how globalism impacts the prospects of Black enterprise and Black entrepreneurship in the United States.[22]

To this end, the overall objective of the course is to examine the historical nature of African Americans establishing enterprise at certain points in American history while at the same time focusing on theories and policies that effect the value of the Black dollar compared to other minority community groups. For example, minorities in 2014 owned more than 949,000 businesses, which amounted to roughly 11 percent being Black owned. In contrast, 32 percent of minority owned businesses were Hispanic and about 53 percent were Asian. Using "Black Wall Street" as a baseline, students critically analyze the underlying factors that created the historical conditions that serves as a hurdle for African Americans from initiating and maintaining viable businesses at the same rate as other racial minority groups in America as well as to examine the overall larger dominant hegemonic societies' perception of Black business owners and entrepreneurs.

In the first part of the course, students become acquainted with the theories and general academic rhetoric of entrepreneurship and enterprising in America. The second part of the course entails a historical overview of specifically the history of entrepreneurship and enterprising as it pertains to African Americans, again with "Black Wall Street" serving as the foundation for discourse. The third part of the course examines the current state of Black business development in America today in the context of entertainment, sports, and corporate America. The last part of the course are workshops that are conducted by Black men and women who are businesses owners and entrepreneurs, sharing their experiences as it pertains to the intersection of being Black, gender expression, and perceptions of what they encounter from all segments of society that patronize their business and/or services.

Major assignments that are required for students to complete to realize the goals and objectives of the course include creating a business plan and "snap-a-business." The business plan requires each student to write a professional business plan of at least ten pages. Part of the business plan also entails interviewing a business owner/enterpriser/ entrepreneur and receiving tangible feedback on how they can improve their plan. The "snap-a-business" assignment requires students to patronize a Black-owned business and submit a detailed review of the establishment which ultimately helps them devise innovative ideas for business ownership and entrepreneurial pursuits in their collegiate and professional careers.

In its first semester offered, the Black Wall Street course has made a tremendous impact in the lives of students at the University of Florida. According to course evaluation data, the class on average scored at or higher than the mean college score on thirteen of fifteen categories. As it pertains to qualitative data, one student remarked of the course "The course, and all of its content, not only is a need at this university, but at any university and college. It truly provides tools and skills when matriculating out of college."[23]

REIMAGINING THE CLASSROOM— STUDENTS WAKE UP!

In addition to the "Black Wall Street" course, other courses that I teach that have been inspired by the "woke" conversational women in my life include "Black Masculinity," "The Wire," "Mentoring At-risk Youth," and the "Fundamentals of Reading and Writing" course. To this end, the DNA of each course that I have taught and will continue to teach is grounded in "wokeness" as it pertains to reimagining the classroom to awaken the collective conscious of students who take the course not only to systematic barriers that were and continue to be implemented by the larger dominant hegemonic society to impede the economic and social mobility of Blacks, but also the cultural resources that were and continue to be available to them within the framework of Western capitalism to counter those barriers with a tradition of protest, planning, and uplift.

These courses are a defense of my own version of the classroom as a strategic location for teaching critical-consciousness and self-actualization grounded in a politics of difference as it pertains to Blacks controlling their own resources using culture and capital as a base. The lessons from my "grandma" and other important women in my life such as both of my mothers, Auntie Bobbi, Ms. Wiggins, Ms. Booth, Ms. Rhone, Ms. Phillips, Ms. Hornsby, Ms. Warren, Ms. Bertha, Ms. Eartha, and countless more have played an integral role in my upbringing and unlocking the radical wokeness within me—so that I may continue to inspire future generations of students via Black feminist and womanist pedagogical practices.

BIBLIOGRAPHY

Adejumo, Vincent. "Black Wall Street" Syllabus, 2018.

Carby, Hazel. V. *Reconstructing womanhood: The Emergence of the Afro-American Woman Novelist.* New York: Oxford University Press, 1987.

Cobb-Roberts, Deirdre, and Sherman Dorn. *Schools as Imagined Communities: The Creation of Identity, Meaning, and Conflict in U.S. History.* Palgrave Macmillan, 2006.

Colin, Scipio., III. *White privilege and racism: Perceptions and actions.* New directions for adult and continuing education, no. 125, San Francisco, CA: Jossey-Bass, 2010.

Collins Hill, Patricia. "What's in a name? Womanism, Black feminism and beyond." *The Black Scholar*, 26: 9–15, 1996.

Dove, Nah. "African Womanism: An Afrocentric Theory." *Journal of Black Studies*, vol. 28, no. 5, 1998: 515–39. *JSTOR*, www.jstor.org/stable/2784792.

Du Bois, W.E.B. "The Damnation of Women" 1920, *Darkwater: Voices from Within the Veil.* New York Dover, 1999.

Foster, Badi. "Toward a definition of Black referents" in *Beyond Black or White*, Vernon Dixon & Badi Foster, eds., Boston: Little, Brown, 1971.

Gyekeye, Kwame. *African philosophical thought.* Philadelphia: Temple University Press, 1995.

Gyekeye, Kwame. *An essay on African philosophical thought: The Akan conceptual scheme.* New York: Cambridge University Press, 1990, original work published 1987.

Harvell, Valeria G. "Afrocentric Humanism and African American Women's Humanizing Activism." *Journal of Black Studies*, vol. 40, no. 6, 2010: 1052–74. *JSTOR*, www.jstor.org/stable/25704075.

Nkrumah, Kwame. *Consciencism: Philosophy and ideology for decolonization* (Rev. ed.). New York: Monthly Review Press, 1964, 1970.

Ntiri, Daphne W. "Adult Literacy Reform Through a Womanist Lens: Unpacking the Radical Pedagogy of Civil Rights Era Educator, Bernice V. Robinson." *Journal of Black Studies*, vol. 45, no. 2, 2014: 125–42, www.jstor.org/stable/24572922.

Phillips, Layli. ed., *The Womanist Reader.* New York, NY: Routledge, 2006.

Ross, Rosetta E. (1997). "Womanist work and public policy": 41–53 in *Embracing the spirit: Womanist perspectives on hope, salvation & transformation*, E. M. Townes, ed., New York: Orbis Books. University of Florida Spring 2018 Evaluations.

Walker, Alice. "'In Search of Our Mothers' Gardens' (1983)." *Available Means: An Anthology Of Women's Rhetoric(s)*, 2001: 315–22, University of Pittsburgh Press doi:10.2307/j.ctt5hjqnj:53.

Warren, Nagueyalti. "His Deep and Abiding Love: W.E.B. Du Bois, Gender Politics, and Black Studies." *Phylon (1960-)*, vol. 51, no. 1, 2014:18–29. *JSTOR*, www.jstor .org/stable/43199118.

Williams, Delores. S. *Sisters in the wilderness: The challenge of womanist god-talk*. Maryknoll, NY: Orbis Books, 1993.

Williams, Frances B. "The intellectual progress of the colored women of the United States since the Emancipation Proclamation" in *Black women in Nineteenth-century American life*, J. Loewenberg and R. Bogin, eds., University Park, PA: Pennsylvania State University Press, 1976, original work published 1893.

———. "The awakening of women" in *Can I get a witness? Prophetic religious voices of African American women: An anthology*, M. Riggs, ed., Maryknoll, NY: Orbis Books, 1997a., original work published 1896–1897.

———. (1997b). "The club movement among colored women of America" in *Can I get a witness? Prophetic religious voices of African American women: An anthology*, M. Riggs, ed., Maryknoll, NY: Orbis Books, original work published 1900.

NOTES

1. https://www.merriam-webster.com/dictionary/woke.

2. https://www.merriam-webster.com/words-at-play/woke-meaning-origin.

3. Alice Walker, "'In Search of Our Mothers' Gardens' (1983)," *Available Means: An Anthology Of Women's Rhetoric(s)*, 2001, 315–22 (University of Pittsburgh Press doi:10.2307/j.ctt5hjqnj), 53.

4. Layli Phillips, ed., *The Womanist Reader* (New York, NY: Routledge, 2006); Daphne W. Ntiri, "Adult Literacy Reform Through a Womanist Lens: Unpacking the Radical Pedagogy of Civil Rights Era Educator, Bernice V. Robinson." *Journal of Black Studies*, vol. 45, no. 2, 2014, www.jstor.org/stable/24572922: 127.

5. See Ntiri 1993, 1998, 2007; Hudson-Weems 1993, 2007; Collins 1996; Colin 2010; Tsuruta 2012; Ntiri 2014.

6. Daphne W. Ntiri, "Adult Literacy Reform Through a Womanist Lens . . . ," 128.

7. Kwame Gyekeye, *African philosophical thought* (Philadelphia: Temple University Press. 1995), 143.

8. Badi Foster, "Toward a definition of Black referents" in *Beyond Black or White* (7–22), Vernon Dixon and Badi Foster, eds. (Boston: Little, Brown, 1971), 10.

9. Kwame Nkrumah, rev. ed., *Consciencism: Philosophy and ideology for decolonization* (New York: Monthly Review Press, 1964, 1970), 68–69.

10. Frances B. Williams, "The intellectual progress of the colored women of the United States since the Emancipation Proclamation," 270–79, in J. Loewenberg and R.

Bogin, eds., *Black women in Nineteenth-century American life* (University Park, PA: Pennsylvania State University Press, 1976; original work published 1893), 273–74; Valeria G. Harvell, "Afrocentric Humanism and African American Women's Humanizing Activism," *Journal of Black Studies*, vol. 40, no. 6, 2010, 1052–1074,*JSTOR*, www.jstor.org/stable/25704075: 1063.

11. Rosetta E. Ross, "Womanist work and public policy" in E. M. Townes, ed., *Embracing the spirit: Womanist perspectives on hope, salvation & transformation* (New York: Orbis Books, 1997), 41.

12. Hazel. V. Carby, *Reconstructing womanhood: The Emergence of the Afro-American Woman Novelist* (New York: Oxford University Press, 1987). 117.

13. This pedagogical concept was envisioned by David Roy as discussed in his article "Implementing a cross-curricular approach," July 2016, www.researchgate.net.

14. http://middleton.mysdhc.org/School_information.

15. https://www.nixonfoundation.org/2017/08/nixons-record-civil-rights-2/.

16. Deirdre Cobb-Roberts and Sherman Dorn, *Schools as Imagined Communities: the Creation of Identity, Meaning, and Conflict in U.S. History* (Palgrave Macmillan, 2006), 134.

17. Deidre Cobb-Roberts and Sherman Dorn, *Schools as Imagined Communities*, 137.

18. https://scholar.harvard.edu/files/fryer/files/fhlm_crack_cocaine_0.pdf.

19. https://www.sdhc.k12.fl.us/departments/70/magnet-schools-education/about/.

20. W.E.B. Du Bois, "The Damnation of Women," *Darkwater: Voices from Within the Veil* (New York: Dover, 1999, originally published in 1920), 96; Nagueyalti Warren, "His Deep and Abiding Love: W.E.B. Du Bois, Gender Politics, and Black Studies." *Phylon* (1960-), vol. 51, no. 1, 2014:18–29. *JSTOR*, www.jstor.org/stable /43199118, 19.

21. Dove, Nah. *"African Womanism: An Afrocentric Theory."* *Journal of Black Studies*, vol. 28, no. 5, 1998: 515–39. *JSTOR*, www.jstor.org/stable/2784792: 534.

22. I taught the "Black Wall Street" course in 2018.

23. University of Florida Spring Evaluations, 2018.

Chapter Twelve

The Past and Future Diversities of HBCUs

Queerness and the Institutional Fulfillment of Black Studies

Roderick A. Ferguson

Unlike the days in which Black LGBTQ students primarily existed within the closets of historically Black colleges and universities (HBCUs), those students are often now visibly apart of HBCU environments. For teachers and leaders within those institutions, the presence of LGBTQ students should not simply be regarded as a demographic fact, however. Indeed, in the spirit of this volume, the presence of queer and trans students on HBCU campuses should provoke us to exercise an aspect of Black feminism and womanism, that element of its vision that sees gender and sexual embodiment as reasons for intellectual and institutional insurrections. Looked at this way, the fact of Black LGBTQ difference as it is lived at HBCUs can be a way of deepening our pedagogical and scholarly engagements with the intersections of race, gender, sexuality, class, and so on.

This essay, thus, argues that basing institutional change on the presence of LGBT students is actually consistent with the critical vision of Black Studies, especially as that vision has been outlined by Black feminist scholars. Indeed, this essay understands Black Studies as not only a field but a critical formation with an intellectual, political, ethical, and institutional imperative. The circumstances of Black queer students become the reason to revive this powerful feature of Black studies. The paper will, therefore, argue that in order to build academic institutions that affirm gender and sexual diversity, we must address the gendered history of Black Studies—that is, its masculinist foundations—and put forth a version of Black Studies first articulated by Black feminist intellectuals. To this end, the chapter concludes by making recommendations for institutional and intellectual change within HBCUs, seeing that change as part of a new administrative and social ethic for Black college campuses.

The essay proceeds by considering the contradictory nature of queer sexuality at HBCUs, contradictory because of both the presence and regulation of LGBT persons. The chapter later examines how the social regulations put on queer members of Black colleges and universities are in some instances powerfully driven by pressures that are external to HBCUs. I conclude my essay by designating the study and institutionalization of gender and sexual diversity as one of the most exciting frontiers in American higher education and one that could be most powerfully elaborated at HBCUs.

THE INSTITUTIONAL AND POLITICAL IMPERATIVES OF BLACK STUDIES

Any project of institutional transformation involving HBCUs—even a project organized around sexual and gender transformation—would begin with the broad changes engendered by the emergence of Black Studies. Indeed, the institutional history of Black Studies reveals that it has always exceeded the characteristics of a conventional discipline; objectively speaking, Black Studies has been a critical formation with multiple and overlapping imperatives, imperatives organized around simultaneously ethical, political, epistemological, and institutional interests and demands. Those imperatives emerged out of the conditions of institutional racism within American institutions. Discussing that institutional context, Johnnetta B. Cole argues in her article, "Black Studies in Liberal Arts Education,"

> A political perspective is essential to an understanding of the most comprehensive meaning of Black Studies: the development of a fundamentally new way for Black people to look at themselves and be looked at by others; and a fundamentally new way for Black people to be actively involved in effecting positive changes in their condition, and thus in their society and in the world.[1]

Unlike traditional disciplines, Black Studies—as a field—emerged with an explicit political investment in rather than a disinterested regard for its object of study. As Cole suggests, the institutional mission of Black Studies began by helping to articulate new meanings of blackness for Black communities, the larger U.S. society, and the world. Black Studies' own institutional imagination was part of larger political and cultural efforts that identified

Black people as historical actors who could intervene into the social world. Institutionalizing Black Studies meant more than inaugurating a field; it meant creating spaces within racially exclusive institutions for the talents and intelligence of Black students and faculty.

One of the institutions within the United States that was characterized by such exclusions is the American Academy. Indeed, as Manning Marable has argued, the institutionalization of Black Studies was part of historic efforts to create educational possibilities for Black people. Writing about how the Civil Rights and Black Power Movements ushered in those possibilities and occasioned the birth and justification for Black Studies, Marable writes,

> In 1960, there were barely two hundred thousand African-Americans enrolled in college, and three-fourths of that number attended historically black universities and colleges. By 1970, 417,000 black Americans between ages 18 to 24 were attending college. Three fourths of them were now at predominantly white institutions. Five years later, 666,000 African Americans age 18 to 24 were enrolled in college, more than one out of every five blacks in their age group.[2]

Discussing the wide-ranging institutional effects that anti-racist movements had for Black people, Marable goes on to write,

> The percentage of all African-Americans completing four years of high school more than doubled in only 15 years, from 20 percent in 1960 to 43 percent in 1975. The total number of African-Americans under age thirty-five who held college degrees more than tripled in these same years from 96,200 in 1960 up to 341,000 by 1975.[3]

As Marable suggests, Black Studies was thus part of a profound institutional adventure within U.S. society, an adventure that attempted to both imagine and install young people from a marginalized group within institutional realms riddled with social exclusions. In his own discussion of that adventure, historian V.P. Franklin argues, "Students, who in the early 1960s played a significant role in the nonviolent direct action protests associated with the Civil Rights Movement, soon turned their attention and energies to the social and educational conditions on college campuses and demanded significant change."[4]

Given this history, we can see how the intellectual interventions of Black Studies were simultaneous with the institutional transformations that it supported and fostered. In fact, the field would emerge as part of an effort to make inequalities around race part of intellectual analysis *and* institutional redress. During the period of its inception, students exhibited a broad and critical understanding of American institutions and their various elements. Efforts to institutionalize a Black presence meant militating for outcomes that exceeded mere demographic increases. Indeed, activists understood that Black presence as the inspiration for broad social changes. Suggesting the breadth of that interest, for example, Franklin argues,

> Many students who had been active in the Congress of Racial Equality (CORE), the Student Nonviolent Coordinating Committee (SNCC), and other civil rights groups joined with the members of Students for a Democratic Society (SDS) to bring about the end to parietal regulations ("in loco parentis" rules), greater choice in courses of study, the end of university participation in military research, as well as the hiring of women and minority faculty members and creation of women's and ethnic studies programs.[5]

In a similar spirit, June Jordan used Black communities as a springboard for institutional and intellectual transformations in an article written in 1969. In "Black Studies: Bringing Back the Person," she discussed the role of Black Studies in the Open Admissions movement at City College, how that then emergent field joined forces with the Open Missions movement to call for an institutional transformation of City College, a transformation based on the dynamic presence of Black and Puerto Rican communities within New York City. She wrote,

> Serving the positive implications of Black Studies (Life Studies), students everywhere must insist on new college admission policies that will guide and accelerate necessary, radical change at all levels of education. Universities must admit the inequities of the civilization they boast. These inequities mean that the children of Other America have been vanquished by the consequences of compulsory, hostile instruction and inescapable, destructive experience. It is appropriate that the university should literally adopt these living consequences as its own humane privilege, for service.[6]

In this passage and throughout her essay, Jordan illuminates the ethical imperative of Black Studies—that is, acknowledging the inequities of modern civilization and providing institutional deliverance for those who suffer those inequities. As Jordan implies, that ethical imperative involves deliberating on the difficult question of how those inequalities affect the lives of real people. In addition, the ethical requirements of that imperative compel us to inspire academic institutions to provide marginalized constituencies with new chances for the most robust lives possible.

Advancing the broadest definition of Black Studies and its communities has been historically impeded by at least two forces—one the crippling masculinism of the field of Black Studies and the administrative marginalization of that field in American colleges and universities. In their discussion of the history of Black Women's Studies and the gender, racial, and sexual exclusions of Black Studies and Women's Studies, Stanlie M. James, Frances Smith Foster, and Beverly Guy-Sheftall write in the introduction to *Still Brave: The Evolution of Black Women's Studies*, "Although Black women had been instrumental in helping establish Black Studies, the field remained male centered, while Women's Studies privileged middle-class white women as the norm for what it meant to be female."[7]

The patriarchal and heterosexist tendencies of Black Studies have had deep institutional and epistemological reverberations. For example, the masculinism of the field has, unfortunately, led to the marginalization of Black gays and lesbians as well as Black straight women and has alienated critiques of gender and sexuality from the field's central concerns.[8] Discussing these overlapping marginalizations, scholars E. Patrick Johnson and Mae G. Hendersen write,

> Given the status of women (and class not lagging too far behind) within black studies, it is not surprising that sexuality, and especially homosexuality, became not only a repressed site of study within the field, but also one with which the discourse was paradoxically preoccupied, if only to deny and disavow its place in the discursive field of black studies.[9]

In addition to its internal debilities, Black Studies has been structurally marginalized both in predominantly white institutions and in HBCUs. While most HBCUs offer courses in Black studies, only two campuses have Black Studies departments, according to a recent article.[10] Moreover, only two HBCU campuses have institutions devoted to black feminism—that is, Spelman's Women's Research and Resource Center and Clark Atlanta's Department of African and African American Studies and Africana Women's Studies. The consequence of neglecting to institutionalize Black Women's Studies, in particular, has led HBCU's to miss out on the vast institutional transformations that Black Women's Studies has ushered into the American academy. As James, Foster, and Guy-Sheftall argue,

> Because Black Studies and Women's Studies failed to adequately address the unique experiences of women of African descent in the United States and around the world, a few brave women created a new field—Black Women's Studies—to provide a conceptual framework for moving women of color from the margins to the center of Women's Studies; for incorporating gender analyses into Black Studies; and to be a catalyst for initiatives such as bringing "Minority Women's Studies" (as it was called) into core curricula in diverse academic settings.[11]

As founding Black Women's Studies texts like *All the Women are White, All the Blacks are Men, But Some of Us are Brave: Black Women's Studies* and *Home Girls: A Black Feminist Anthology* argued for the analytical importance of sexuality in Black social formations, we might also say that Black Women's Studies was the first to incorporate examinations of queer sexuality into black studies as well. As HBCUs have deprived themselves of the benefits of Black Women's Studies, they have also generated the very conditions that prevent a healthy institutional and intellectual engagement with Black queer students, staff, and faculty.

In order to produce the conditions for a version of Black Studies that can motivate HBCUs to embrace their gender and sexual diversity, we must advance a Black feminist and queer vision for Black Studies and provide that vision with material and administrative support. The broad—institutional, epistemological, political, and ethical—imperative of Black Studies is precisely what must be brought to bear on the question of queer sexuality at HBCUs. Indeed, we can take the breadth of that imperative and embark on the "long and difficult process of change" for yet another constituency of Blacks—that is, Black queer people. If the rise of Black Studies was occasioned by the "old wrong" of anti-Black racism, the circumstances of Black queer youth in HBCUs suggest that there are other wrongs that Black Studies—and its institutions—must rectify.

QUEERNESS AT HBCUs

Contrary to popular characterization and despite very real restrictions around homosexual expression, Black queer folk have always studied, taught, worked, and lived at HBCUs. Indeed, despite the recency of the media coverage of Black queer life at HBCUs, gay, lesbian, bisexual, and transgender persons and communities have been historic parts of the campus cultures of historically Black colleges and universities. In fact, the reality of Black queer life at HBCUs is both an historic and contemporary observation. As Black queer scholar E. Patrick Johnson argues in *Sweet Tea: Black Gay Men of the South*, HBCUs are campuses in which "homosex is not only common, but in some cases encouraged."[12] Indeed the informants for Johnson's study—several of whom were HBCU alumni—report of campuses in which Black gay men are "incorporated into the fabric of student life . . . and sometimes they are cordoned off into their own discrete and discreet organizations."[13]

Johnson's book and the circumstances of Black queer students suggest that HBCUs are contradictory environments where queer sexualities are concerned. Black gay, lesbian, bisexual, and transgender cultures at HBCUs have existed both formally and informally, within a diverse range of organizations—fraternities and sororities, gospel choirs, fashion shows—and within casual networks. In addition, the men that Johnson interviewed tell of a "much more tolerant" climate for homosexuality and homosex during the 1950s and 1960s than in the 1980s and afterward.[14] But as the stories of current students and recent alumnae suggest, even within conservative climates queer communities still manage to exist.

For example, social groups and organizations for Black queer students have also arisen on HBCU campuses. There is the Bisexual, Lesbian, and Gay Organization of Students at Howard University, the groups Safe Space and the Plastics at Morehouse, the Gay Straight Alliance at Tennessee State and Fisk universities, and the African American Alliance for Gay and Lesbian Education at Johnson C. Smith. These groups are just a few examples of a newly assertive gay, transgender, bisexual and lesbian constituency at HBCUs, groups that help to illuminate the sexual and gender contradictions at Black colleges and universities.

Many of these groups have risen alongside of the emergence of anti-discrimination policies at various campuses. Indeed, in 2009, the state of North Carolina could boast that "four of the five public historically Black colleges and universities . . . have policies that include sexual orientation," an improvement from zero in 2006.[15] Other campuses have also followed suit, campuses such as Howard, Fisk, Spelman, Winston-Salem State, and Morehouse. As a matter of fact, 20 percent of HBCUs now have such policies or have student organizations for their gay, lesbian, bisexual, and transgender community members. In sum, the development of formal policies and the rise of groups for LGBT students has helped to foster HBCUs as institutions not only characterized by gender and sexual regulation but by LGBT expression as well.

RESPECTABILITY, LEADERSHIP, AND THE REGULATION OF BLACK SEXUALITIES

While HBCU campuses have often had robust—often subcultural—queer communities and while several colleges and universities have adopted policies that protect sexual orientation, those institutions are still very much characterized by social practices that attempt to regulate and eradicate gender and sexual diversity. For instance, many of the non-discrimination policies adopted by various HBCUs were motivated by homophobic violence that marred at least three HBCUs. The most notorious of those incidents was the brutal beating of a student at Morehouse College in 2002. And as we will see, the social conservatism at HBCUs around sexuality and gender produces a range of negative consequences for queer students especially.

In their article, "Consequences of Conservatism: Black Male Undergraduates and the Politics of Historically Black Colleges and Universities," education scholars Shaun R. Harper and Marybeth Gasman detail the risks of socially conservative policies and practices upon matriculation at HBCUs, underlining how research of this type is significant given that the issue of social conservatism's consequences for students has not garnered sufficient concern in the realms of scholarship or administration. As they argue, the "ways in which students experience [authoritarian policies and practices], particularly among those who are most vulnerable to discontinuing matriculation prior to degree attainment, remains understudied."[16]

Pointing to the social conservatism at HBCUs, a 2006 report released by the Thurgood Marshall College Fund illuminated the conservative nature of public Black colleges around issues of gender and sexuality. The report presented student surveys that reported "witnessing faculty members treating students differently due to their actual or perceived sexual orientations, specifically discriminating against gay male students."[17] In addition, Harper and Gasman go on to note that the rise of Black gay and lesbian student organizations has been met with both support and opposition, some of which has culminated in actual death threats to students.

In addition to informal modes of regulating gender and sexual diversity at HBCUs, there are also formal—and perhaps unwitting—means of regulating that diversity. For instance, many students have pointed to the dress codes that operate at Morehouse College, Hampton University, and Paul Quinn College as examples of a formal and indirect method of disciplining transgender students, particularly. In the case of Morehouse, in 2009 the college instituted a broad dress code-policy that banned the wearing of caps, do-rags, hoodies, sunglasses, and saggy pants in classrooms or at formal events. The rule also includes a ban on "clothing usually worn by women (dresses, tops, tunics, purses, pumps, etc.)."[18] This particular stipulation has drawn the ire of some students at Morehouse who believe that the real targets of the dress code are gay and transgender students.

One such group of students goes by the name of the Plastics. Located at Morehouse College, the Plastics is a group of biologically male students who maneuver feminine aesthetics and clothing styles to evolve identities that cross the boundaries of traditional gender distinctions. As a recent *Vibe* magazine article put it, "The Plastics all assume that the recent appropriate attire policy was aimed directly at their personal freedom of expression, which includes foundation, cross-dressing, and even taking female hormones."[19]

For Morehouse administrators, the dress code is part of a larger issue around defining the Morehouse Man. As Morehouse president Dr. William Bynum argues, "'We expect our young men to be Renaissance Men. . . . When people go about campus, we want them to represent the college in an appropriate manner.'"[20] Indeed, as President Bynum argues, the dress code is a way of defining and regulating proper manhood. He states, "'We respect the identity and choices of all young men at Morehouse. . . . However, the Morehouse leadership development model sets a certain standard of how we expect the young men to dress, and this attire [from the Plastics] does not fit within the model. Our proper attire policy expresses that standard."[21] As President Bynum implies, the dress code policy promotes a model of leadership based on an ideal of Black manhood. As that model determines what a proper Black man is, it also defines implicitly what an improper Black man is as well, using clothing as a litmus for that ideal. In doing so, the dress code prescribes not only a standard of masculinity but a vision of proper leadership also. As such, the dress code and the leadership model can only imagine transgender persons as improperly gendered and as categorically incapable of being leaders at Morehouse.

In contrast to a restrictive Renaissance model, we might remind ourselves of the capacious ideal of erudition advocated by Black intellectuals during the Harlem Renaissance, an ideal that embraced gender and sexual diversity rather than eschewed it. Here we might cite such towering figures as Claude McKay, Wallace Thurman, and Richard Bruce Nugent. To this end, we might invoke the Harlem Renaissance as a period in which the erudition associated with the Renaissance Man was redefined in favor of gender and sexual experimentation.[22] For instance, McKay's *Home to Harlem* and the journal *Fire!!* represented—in the language of Black queer literary scholar Marlon Ross—an "experimental literary expression of same-sexuality."[23] Indeed, the Harlem Renaissance produced a model of the Renaissance Man that was able to parlay gender and sexual experimentation into a testing of artistic and intellectual forms.

As suggested earlier, Morehouse does not at all have a monopoly on dress code practices. Indeed, Harper and Gasman identify Hampton University and Paul Quinn College as having similar practices. Discussing a 2007 news story about Paul Quinn College's dress code restrictions, the authors write,

> Michael J. Sorrell, the College's president, developed a policy requiring students to dress in business casual clothing between the hours of 8:00 a.m. and 5:00 p.m. Those who dressed in loungewear, casual outfits, or athletic attire were not permitted to attend classes or eat in the dining hall on campus. . . . The story went on to describe how first offenders were sentenced community service, and those who violated the policy a second time were required to jog with President Sorrell on Saturday mornings.[24]

As the example above shows, HBCU dress codes potentially circumscribe the personal freedoms of a variety of students, not just queer students. But the effect that the dress codes have on gay, bisexual, lesbian, and transgender students—their freedom of cultural and gender expression, particularly—is precisely what has led opponents to label the dress codes as "homophobic."

At issue is the gender and erotic autonomy of students as well as their ability to define and shape the ideals of their various institutions. While the college presents itself as the authority of what constitutes the Morehouse Man, the Plastics and other students present themselves as equally viable authorities on the definition, constitution, and broadening of the Morehouse man ideal. As a matter of fact, the students' presumption that they are just as much the authors of the institutional culture of the colleges is part of the genealogies of student protest at HBCUs and of the field of Black studies. We might, also, frame the efforts of Black queer students to seize authority over their own experiences at HBCUs as part of the history of protests by HBCU students in the 1920s at Fisk University and Hampton Institute, protests over the prohibition of "student dancing, the enforcement of student codes of conduct with regard to sexuality, and the institutions' support of Jim Crow student entertainment for local Whites."[25] Indeed, if the Black studies movement authorized Black students to write the future of institutions of higher learning, we might understand the Plastics and others as working to write the future not only of Morehouse College but of other HBCUs as well.

BLACK QUEER STUDENTS AND THE EVOLVING HISTORY OF BLACK QUEER STUDIES

We might, also, see Black queer students and their straight allies at HBCUs as inheritors of the critical maneuvers of Black queer artists and intellectuals in the twentieth and twenty-first centuries. Work on Black queer history and criticism has done much to demonstrate the primary role that Black gays and lesbians have had in the development of twentieth century Black culture in general.[26] Much of the scholarship on Black queer sexualities in the nineteen nineties took dominant models of Black leadership to task for basing themselves on notions of bourgeois respectability, notions that ended up regulating and excluding Black straight women as well as Black LGBT folks. For instance, in their introduction to the 2000 special issue of the journal *Callaloo*, an issue that dealt with the politics of sexuality in Black communities, Black queer scholars Jennifer Devere Brody and Dwight McBride argued,

> Much of the way in which African-American literary and cultural discourse or black anti-racist discourse developed had a good deal to do with a kind of representational or a representative model of blackness—of ideal blackness in a very DuBoisian "talented tenth" sense. The logic is that blacks have to put their best foot forward and to lead a struggle for liberation by example to both whites

and to other blacks, not to mention to a worldwide global audience. As much of black feminism has demonstrated, putting one's best foot forward required a straight-laced male guise."[27]

Putting one's best foot forward, as Brody and McBride argue, became the norm of Black leadership with gender and sexual consequences. Talking about how those consequences emerge from the dominant discourse of Black leadership, they write,

> Contributions of black gays and lesbians who have been concerned with fighting anti-racist struggles and who have made significant contributions to black literary and cultural studies have been devalued in rhetoric and reality by movements both major and marginal. As a result the kind of exclusion that black gays and lesbians meet in the black community when they attempt to occupy the role of "race man" or "race woman" is neither aberrant nor accidental. It is built into the history of the discourse itself.[28]

Put within the context of critiques like Brody and McBride's, we can get a sense of how the dominant leadership models at work in HBCUs may indeed nestle ideologies of gender and sexuality that proscribe gender and sexual identities and practices that deviate from norms of respectability and uplift.[29] Historically Black colleges and universities emerged out of this leadership model as it was articulated in the nineteenth century. For example, in a speech given on March 21, 1899, Booker T. Washington argued that Tuskeegee would help young Blacks to "see and appreciate the physical and moral conditions" of family and neighborhood, educating them for the relief of those conditions.[30] Given this background, it is not difficult to see how the various dress codes at HBCUs arise out of this institutional history.

While HBCUs negotiate with the aforementioned history of gender and sexual expression and regulation, Black scholars outside of HBCUs, primarily, have been shaping an entirely different history of gender and sexual expression and theorization. This new history has been articulated under a variety of rubrics—queer of color critique, queer diaspora, and Black Queer Studies. Each one has attempted to rewrite the histories of race and empire through frameworks around sexuality. In particular, the formation known as Black Queer Studies has attempted to interlace the critical universes of Black Studies with those of queer theory and gay and lesbian studies. As E. Patrick Johnson and Mae Gwendolyn Henderson argue in their pioneering text *Black Queer Studies: A Critical Anthology*, an interest in creating the intellectual conditions for an institutional interest in Black queer sexualities was inaugurated at the Black Queer Studies in the Millennium Conference in April of 2000 at the University of North Carolina at Chapel Hill. The conference brought together the then leading black queer scholars working within predominantly white universities. In that same year, my article "The Parvenu Baldwin and the Other Side of Redemption: Modernity, Race, Sexuality, and the Cold War" won the Modern Language Association's Crompton-Noll Award for Best Essay in Lesbian, Gay, and Queer Studies in the Modern Languages, becoming the first essay written by a Black person to win the title. In 2006, the Ford Foundation also convened a two-year workshop on Black and Latino Sexualities, a workshop that resulted in the 2008 conference "Race, Sex, and Power" in Chicago and the 2009 publication of the anthology *Black Sexualities: Probing Powers, Passions, Practices, and Policies.*

Toward the end of the twentieth century and during the first decade of the twenty first century, there was a veritable explosion of research on the topic of Black queer sexualities by Black queer scholars. In addition to the aforementioned texts, in 1998 literary scholar Phillip Brian Harper published *Are We Not Men: Masculine Anxiety and the Problem of African American Identity.* Dwight McBride's anthology *James Baldwin Now* was published the year after. In that year as well political scientist Cathy Cohen offered *The Boundaries of Blackness: AIDS and the Breakdown of Black Politics.* In the year 2000, cultural and American Studies scholar Sharon Holland published *Raising the Dead: Readings of Death and (Black) Subjectivity*; in 2001 Robert Reid-Pharr would debut *Black Gay Man: Essays.* The year 2003 would see the publication of historian Martin Summers's *Manliness and Its Discontents: The Black Middle Class and the Transformation of Masculinity* as well as performance studies scholar E. Patrick Johnson's *Appropriating Blackness: Performance and the Politics of Authenticity.* The following year would witness the publication of Marlon Ross's *Manning the Race: Reforming Black men in the Jim Crow Era* and my book *Aberrations in Black: Toward a Queer of Color Critique.* In 2007 pioneering Black queer feminist theorist M. Jacqui Alexander would bring out *Pedagogies of Crossing: Meditations on Feminism, Sexual Politics, Memory, and the Sacred.* That same year film theorist Kara Keeling debuted *The Witch's Flight: The Cinematic, the Black Femme, and the Image of Common Sense.* Also, cultural theorist Michelle Wright co-edited the anthology *Blackness and Sexualities* through the Forum for European Contributions to African American Studies, an anthology that includes the renowned Black queer Canadian theorist Rinaldo Walcott. And finally, this year Black queer theorist Darieck Scott released his book *Extravagant Abjection: Blackness, Power, and Sexuality in the African American Literary Imagination.*

For the last thirty years, the American Academy has been reshaped by a burgeoning interest in work by queer scholars of color, in general, and black queer scholars, in particular, work that demonstrates that the issue of sexuality is much more than a matter of style and taste but an intellectual inquiry deeply implicated in a range of cultural, political, and intellectual formations.[31] Such work contests the notion that Black gay, lesbian, bisexual and transgender persons are incapable of leadership roles in and beyond Black communities. Indeed, the history of Black gay and lesbian cultural workers is itself the history of how models of leadership and intellection have developed in Black communities and institutions without recourse to restrictive notions of gender and sexual identity. As such this work finds itself in alignment with students like 2009 Morehouse alumnus and former president of Safe Space Michael S. Brewer, who argues that colleges like Morehouse can be a "beacon of light" for progressive change around sexuality, especially given that Morehouse—like so many HBCUs—"'has stood for radical change in the face of injustice.'"[32] Brewer and students like him represent HBCU members who, in their own ways, are pressing for more expansive and democratic models of leadership and the life of the mind.

HOMOPHOBIA AS AN EXTERNAL PRESSURE

Eradicating gender and sexual regulation can also be seen as part of the institutional transformation of HBCUs and as part of the mandate of anti-racist struggle. Indeed, much of the work by feminist and queer of color scholars has focused on the ways in which norms of heterosexual respectability actually have their roots within conditions of colonial domination and white supremacy.[33] This work has attempted to question the notion that heterosexism and homophobia are the "natural" operations of people of color communities. A critique such as this one has a powerful resonance for HBCUs, institutions often constructed as naturally heterosexist and therefore obviously opposed to gay, lesbian, bisexual, and transgender practices and identities. As previous sections illustrated, the sexual contradictions of HBCU campuses demonstrate that they are environments that actually defy interpretations that posit them as culturally and therefore naturally opposed to homosexuality. As Howard University graduate and former board of trustee member Victoria Kirby argues, "I actually did my senior thesis on being gay or lesbian at an HBCU and what I found was that it wasn't Howard's environment that made people not want to come out but the fact that we have labeled the Black community as homophobic so people are afraid of rejection."[34] Kirby points to how the presumably homophobic nature of HBCUs is a partly contrived and often externally encouraged discourse.

As an example of an external force that masquerades as a seemingly indigenous homophobic climate on HBCU campuses, we might simply turn our attention to recent state politics. For instance, in March 2010 the state of Virginia's attorney general Kenneth Cuccinelli issued a legal opinion that would nullify any protections erected by public colleges that would bar discrimination against gays and lesbians. In effect, the legal opinion would devastate anti-homophobic efforts by public HBCUs in the state of Virginia, efforts like those of Norfolk State University, which has had a policy banning discrimination on the basis of sexual orientation since 2000 and has had a college-approved student group for gay, lesbian, and transgender students since 2005.[35] Administrators, students, and faculty at Norfolk state worry that the attorney general's policy will work to deter gay, lesbian, and transgender talent from HBCUs. As interim associate dean at Norfolk State Charles Ford argued, "'We were really starting to make progress on this and now we're set back.'"[36]

Situations like the one that Norfolk State and other Virginia HBCUs face are telling for a number of reasons. First, they demonstrate that several HBCUs have been formally deliberating on the issue of homophobia at their institutions for a number of years and have made real strides in the way of legal protections for gay, lesbian, bisexual and transgender students, faculty and staff. Secondly, situations like the one in Virginia demonstrate that homophobia is not entirely a "home-grown" phenomenon but also an externally encouraged crisis. Thirdly the Virginia legal opinion shows that homophobia on HBCU campuses is in dialogue with homophobic currents outside of HBCUs themselves. Put plainly the Virginia opinion exposes the lie that HBCUs are simply pre-modern institutions that—because of their homophobia—have not caught up with modern orientations on homosexuality. Indeed, the Virginia opinion demonstrates that homophobia is a modern (and very much alive) mode of discrimination that stretches across a wide swath of communities and is by no means the special problem of Black folks or their institutions. In fact, Cuccinelli's legal opinion shows how aggressively invested various levels of government are in maintaining and encouraging discrimination on the basis of sexuality. We might go even further to say that the Virginia state government is attempting to control administrative and campus life at HBCUs precisely by compelling those institutions to conform to homophobic dictates. The Virginia opinion, in this sense, works to ensure that the institutional legitimacy of Virginia HBCUs is brokered through the enforcement of heterosexual respectability and homophobic regulation.

The Virginia opinion shows, therefore, that homophobia is not a sign of the integrity of Black institutions but a symbol of how much they are yoked to predominantly white governing bodies and authorities. Indeed, as Johnnetta B. Cole and Beverly Guy-Sheftall have argued, homophobia is one way by which Black America has attempted to accommodate itself to "mainstream gender ideologies and resist constructions of ourselves as sexually deviant or pathological."[37] If the point of the Black Studies movement as well as the decolonization and national liberation movements in Africa and the Caribbean was to challenge the vestiges of white supremacy and colonial domination, then challenging the ways in which those vestiges are secreted in our gender and sexual norms must become one of our institutional priorities.

BLACK QUEER SEXUALITIES AND THE
REINVENTION OF THE HBCU

In her classic article "Erotic Autonomy as a Politics of Decolonization: An Anatomy of Feminist and State Practice in the Bahamas Tourist Economy," M. Jacqui Alexander argues this about decolonization:

> Since colonization has produced fragmentation and dismemberment at both the material and psychic levels, the work of decolonization has to make room for the deep yearning for wholeness, often expressed as a yearning to belong, a yearning that is both material and existential, both psychic and physical, and which, when satisfied, can subvert and ultimately displace the pain of dismemberment.[38]

If homophobia is part of the legacy of racial domination, then Alexander's words beg us to consider how homophobia has dismembered and fragmented the diverse communities that live and breathe on HBCU campuses. Moreover, the passage asks us to dwell on the question of how to speak to the yearnings of Black gay, lesbian, bisexual, and transgender students, staff, and faculty at HBCUs, speaking to those dreams and yearnings in an effort to subvert and displace the formal and informal means of dismemberment. Put simply, if we were to make Alexander's broad conception of decolonization into an imperative for transforming HBCU campuses, what would those institutions look like?

A politics of decolonization interested in erotic autonomy would neces-sarily mean broadening and revising the ethical, institutional, and political imperatives of Black studies discussed earlier. For instance, in the same way that Black studies was both used to assess and promote institutional transfor-mations concerning Black Studies, we need a similar critical and scholarly framework to assess and promote the existence of Black queer life at HBCUs.

A comprehensive politics of decolonization would involve representing the critical universes established by past and recent work on Black gender and sexual formations. One way of representing those critical universes for the benefit of the communities at HBCUs would be through curricular changes that exhibited a deep interest in Black genders and sexualities. In this way, the histories of Black gender and sexual formations would cease to be marginal issues at HBCUs and become foundational to the liberal arts education at Black colleges and universities. A curricular change of this type would help to produce a social and intellectual climate that could engage Black LGBT community members in the most intelligent ways possible.

A transformation of this sort would necessarily mean institutionalizing a curricular interest in black feminism as well. Indeed, Black feminism has had the longest engagement with the issue of Black sexuality. One need only look at anthologies such as *Home Girls* and *But Some of Us are Brave* as well as the writings of Michelle Cliff, Alexis Deveaux, Jewell Gomez, Gayl Jones, Audre Lorde, Toni Morrison, Alice Walker, and others to see how sexual autonomy was central to Black feminist critical and creative production. The Black gay poet Essex Hemphill echoes the foundational status of Black feminism to analyses of Black racial and sexual formations. In 1990, he wrote in the introduction to the classic Black gay male anthology *Brother to Brother*,

> Perhaps the second Renaissance in African American literature occurred when black women claimed their own voices from the post-sixties, male-dominated realm of the "black experience," a realm that at times resembled a boxing ring restricting black women to the roles of mere spectators. What black women, especially out black lesbians, bravely did was break the silence surrounding their experiences. No longer would black men, the sole interpreters of race and culture, presume to speak for (or ignore) women's experiences. Black women opened up new dialogues and explored uncharted territories surrounding race, sexuality, gender relations, family, history, and eroticism. In the process, they angered some black male writers who felt they were being culturally castrated and usurped, but out of necessity, black women realized they would have to speak for themselves—and do so honestly. As a result of their courage, black women also inspired many of the black gay men writing today to seek our own voices so we can tell our truths. Thus, we are at the beginning of completing a total picture of the African American experience.[39]

Any institutional change on behalf of Black queer formations would necessarily be a recommitment to the insights of Black feminism.

The histories of Black gays and lesbians from the nineteen eighties onward illustrate how Black queer communities were announced and clarified through textual production—that is, through the penning of poems, the writing of novels, the conducting of scholarship, the making of films, and the editing of anthologies. In doing so, those communities confirm that every community presumes a set of texts to read, to interpret, and to write. Likewise, Black queer students at HBCUs presume such an endeavor. *More to the point, a curricular change at the level of race, gender, and sexuality means also institutionalizing a black queer presence at HBCUs. That institutionalization could take place through concerted efforts to recruit and retain students and faculty. It would also mean establishing counseling services for those students and founding postdoctoral opportunities for scholars working out the most complex analyses of Black sexuality.* Such an institutionalization would be a way of seeing a politics of decolonization—one that protects and promotes gender and erotic autonomy—as an extension of the institutional imagination of Black Studies and Black feminism. In truth, the history of the ethnic studies was one in which people gave their imaginations to this question: how to make a despised, marginalized, and patronized constituency into a resource for intellection. The situation of Black LGBT youth is yet another occasion to renew that founding motivation.

As the 2010 two-day symposium on the status of HBCUs made clear, the survival of Black colleges and universities depends upon their ability to make positive change. Ours is a world that is increasingly measuring its modernity in terms of its relationship to homosexuality. Making meaningful and broad transformations in the areas of sexuality and gender would be a powerful way for Black colleges and universities to place themselves at the vanguard of institutions of higher education.

Rather than figures of institutional embarrassment, we might see Black queer and allied students as akin to African spirits, represented in masks and primed for ceremony, demanding their right to embodiment, insisting on difficult and necessary transformations. Those students call for a Black college experience that is capacious, accommodating many different forms of blackness, forms in which gender and sexual differences are celebrated and encouraged rather than pathologized and denied. As we deliberate upon their potential to inspire new ways to imagine our institutional arrangements and our liberal arts, let us remember the ethical injunction of our most esteemed institutional achievements—the consecration and preservation of the person.[40]

BIBLIOGRAPHY

Alexander, M. Jacqui. *Pedagogies of Crossing: Meditations on Feminism, Sexual Politics, Memory, and the Sacred* (Durham and London: Duke University Press, 2005).

Beale, Frances. "Double Jeopardy: To Be Black and Female," in Toni Cade Bambara (ed.) *The Black Woman: Anthology* (New York: Signet, 1970).

Beam, Joseph (ed.) *In the Life: A Black Gay Anthology* (Boston: Alyson Publications, Inc., 1986).

Brody, Jennifer DeVere and Dwight McBride, "Introduction," Callaloo Vol. 23, No. 1, *Gay, Lesbian, Bisexual, Transgender: Literature and Culture* (Winter, 2000): 286–88.

Byrd, Rudoph P., Johnetta Betsch Cole, Beverly Guy-Sheftall (eds.), *I am Your Sister: Collected and Unpublished Writings of Audre Lorde* (Oxford and New York: Oxford University Press, 2009).

Carby, Hazel. *Race Men* (Cambridge: Harvard University Press, 2000).

———. *Reconstructing Womanhood: The Emergence of the Afro-American Woman Novelist* (Oxford: Oxford University Press, 1989).

Cole, Johnetta B. "Black Studies in Liberal Arts Education," in *The Black Studies Reader*, ed. Jacqueline Bobo, Cynthia Hudley, and Claudine Michel (New York and London: Routledge, 2004).

Cole, Johnnetta B. and Beverly Guy-Sheftall, *Gender Talk: The Struggle for Women's Equality in African American Communities* (New Yor: One World//Ballantine, 2003).

D'Emilio, John. *Lost Prophet: The Life and Times of Bayard Rustin* (Chicago: University of Chicago Press, 2004).

Davis, Angela. *Blues Legacies and Black Feminism: Gertrude 'Ma Rainey, Bessie Smith, and Billie Holiday* (New York: Vintage Books, 1998).

———. *Women, Race, and Class* (New York: Vintage, 1983).

Ferguson, Roderick A. "Of Our Normative Strivings: African American Studies and the Histories of Sexuality," in *Social Text* 84–85, Vol. 23, Nos. 3–4, Fall–Winter 2005: 85–100.

———. *Aberrations in Black: Toward a Queer of Color Critique* (Minneapolis: University of Minnesota Press, 2004).

Franklin, V.P. "Hidden in Plain View: African American Women, Radical Feminism, and the Origins of Women's Studies Programs, 1967–1974," in *Journal of African American History* Autumn 2002: 433–45.

Gaines, Kevin. *Uplifting the Race: Black Leadership, Politics, and Culture in the Twentieth Century* (Chapel Hill: The University of North Carolina Press, 1996);

Galuszka, Peter. "Virginia HBCU's Struggle with Legal Opinion that Bars Protection for Gays." Accessed 11/11/10. http://diverseeducation.com/cache/print.php?articleId=13612.

Glave, Thomas (ed.), *Our Caribbean: A Gathering of Lesbian and Gay Writing from the Antilles* (Durham and London: Duke University Press, 2008).

Gopinath, Gayatri. *Impossible Desires: Queer Desires and South Asian Public Cultures* (Durham and London: Duke University Press, 2005).

Harper, Shaun R. and Marybeth Gasman, "Consequences of Conservatism: Black Male Undergraduates and the Politics of Historically Black Colleges and Universities," *The Journal of Negro Education*, 77 (4): 336–51.

Hemphill, Essex. "Introduction" in *Brother to Brother*, ed. Essex Hemphill (Boston: Alyson Publications, 1991).

———. (ed.) Brother to Brother: New Writings by Black Gay Men (Boston: Alyson Publications, Inc., 1991).

Hull, Gloria T. Patricia Bell Scott, Barbara Smith (eds), *All the Women are White, All the Blacks are Men, But Some of Us are Brave: Black Women's Studies*, ed. Gloria T. Hull, Patricia Bell Scott, and Barbara Smith (New York: The Feminist Press, 1982).

James, Stanlie M. Frances Smith Foster, and Beverly Guy-Sheftall, *Still Brave: The Evolution of Black Women's Studies* (New York: The Feminist Press, 2009).

Jenkins, Candice M. *Private Lives, Proper Relations: Regulating Black Intimacy* (Minneapolis: University of Minnesota Press, 2007).

Johnson, E. Patrick and Mae G. Hendersen, "Introduction: Queering Black Studies/'Quaring' Queer Studies," in *Black Queer Studies: A Critical Anthology*, ed. E. Patrick Johnson and Mae G. Hendresen, (Durham and London: Duke University Press, 2005).

———. *Sweet Tea: Black Gay Men of the South* (Chapel Hill, University of North Carolina Press, 2008).

Jordan, June. *Moving Toward Home: Political Essays* (London: Virago Press, 1989).

King, Aliya S. "The Mean Girls of Morehouse." Accessed October 3, 2010. http://www.vibe.com/content/mean-girls-morehouse.

Mann, Aleesa. "The Struggle for Black Studies at HBCUs." http://www.theroot.com/views/hbcu-black-studies.

Marable, Manning. "Beyond Brown: The Revolution in Black Studies," *The Black Scholar*, Volume 35, no. 2: 11–12.

McBride, Dwight (ed.). James Baldwin Now (New York: New York University Press, 1999),

Oguntoyinbo,Lekan. "Non-Discrimination Policies and Support Groups Help Ease Campus Life for Gay and Lesbian Students at HBCUs." Accessed from http://diverseeducation.com/article/12697/ on July 7, 2009.

Reddy, Chandan. "Asian Diasporas, Neoliberalism, and Family: Reviewing the Case for Homosexual Asylum in the Context of Family Rights," *Social Text* 2005 23(3–4 8–85):101–19.

Reid-Pharr, Robert. *Black Gay Man* (New York: New York University Press, 2001).

Ross, Marlon. *Manning the Race: Reforming Black Men in the Jim Crow Era* (New York: New York University Press, 2004).

Simon, Mashaun D. "Morehouse Dress Code Seeks to "Get Back to the Legacy." *The Atlanta Journal and Constitution.* Accessed December 19, 2010. https://www.ajc.com/news/local/morehouse-dress-code-seeks-get-back-the-legacy/4BQeGNx4kTckXgxmlUaJnN/#targetText=Young%20men%20of%20Morehouse%2C%20pull,they%20are%20no%20longer%20permissible.

Smith, Barbara. *Home Girls: A Black Feminist Anthology* (New York: Kitchen Table Press, 1983).

Springer, Kimberly. *Living for the Revolution: Black Feminist Organizations, 1968–1980* (Durham and London: Duke University Press, 2005).

Summers, Martin. *Manliness and its Discontents: The Black Middle Class and the Transformation of Masculinity*, 1900–1930 (Chapel Hill: The University of North Carolina Press, 2003).

Vogel, Shane. *The Scene of the Harlem Cabaret: Race, Sexuality, Performance* (Chicago: University of Chicago Press, 2009).

NOTES

1. Johnnetta B. Cole, "Black Studies in Liberal Arts Education" in *The Black Studies Reader*, eds., Jacqueline Bobo, Cynthia Hudley, and Claudine Michel (New York and London: Routledge, 2004), 21.

2. Manning Marable, "Beyond Brown: The Revolution in Black Studies," *The Black Scholar*, Volume 35, no. 2, 11.

3. Ibid.

4. V.P. Franklin, "Hidden in Plain View: African American Women, Radical Feminism, and the Origins of Women's Studies Programs, 1967–1974," *Journal of African American History*, 433.

5. Ibid.

6. June Jordan, Moving Toward Home: Political Essays (London: Virago Press, 1989), 28.

7. Stanlie M. James, Frances Smith Foster, and Beverly Guy-Sheftall, *Still Brave: The Evolution of Black Women's Studies* (New York: The Feminist Press, 2009), xiii.

8. See Hazel Carby's *Race Men* (Cambridge: Harvard University Press, 2000).

9. E. Patrick Johnson and Mae G. Hendersen, "Introduction: Queering Black Studies/'Quaring' Queer Studies," in *Black Queer Studies: A Critical Anthology*, ed. E. Patrick Johnson and Mae G. Hendersen, (Durham and London: Duke University Press, 2005), 4.

10. See "The Struggle for Black Studies at HBCUs at http://www.theroot.com/views/hbcu-black-studies. Accessed January 31, 2001.

11. James, Foster and Guy-Sheftall, xiii.

12. E. Patrick Johnson, *Sweet Tea: Black Gay Men of the South* (Chapel Hill, University of North Carolina Press, 2008), 284.

13. Ibid., 285.

14. Ibid.

15. Michael Hewlett, "Gay Rights Making Gains," Winston-Salem Journal, May 4, 2009. Accessed 11/11/10. http://www2.journalnow.com/news/2009/may/04/gay-rights-making-gains-ar-152077/.

16. Shaun R. Harper and Marybeth Gasman, "Consequences of Conservatism: Black Male Undergraduates and the Politics of Historically Black Colleges and Universities," *The Journal of Negro Education*, 77 (4), 336–51.

17. Harper and Gasman, 338.

18. Mashaun D. Simon, "Morehouse Dress Code Seeks to "Get Back to the Legacy." *The Atlanta Journal and Constitution*. Accessed December 19, 2010. http://www.ajc.com/news/morehouse-dress-code-seeks-164132.html.

19. Aliya S. King, "The Mean Girls of Morehouse." Accessed October 3, 2010. http://www.vibe.com/content/mean-girls-morehouse.

20. Mashaun D. Simon, "Morehouse Dress Code Seeks to "Get Back to the Legacy." http://www.ajc.com/news/morehouse-dress-code-seeks-164132.html.

21. King, http://www.vibe.com/content/mean-girls-morehouse.

22. See Marlon Ross's *Manning the Race: Reforming Black Men in the Jim Crow Era* and Martin Summers's *Manliness and Its Discontents*.

23. Ross, 268.

24. Harper and Gasman, 338.

25.Ibid., 337.

26. See for instance, Gloria T. Hull, Patricia Bell Scott, Barbara Smith (eds), *All the Women Are White, All the Blacks Are Men, But Some of Us Are Brave: Black Women's*

Studies, ed. Gloria T. Hull, Patricia Bell Scott, and Barbara Smith (New York: The Feminist Press, 1982); Barbara Smith, *Home Girls: A Black Feminist Anthology* (New York: Kitchen Table Press, 1983); Joseph Beam (ed.) *In the Life: A Black Gay Anthology* (Boston: Alyson Publications, Inc., 1986); Essex Hemphill (ed.) *Brother to Brother: New Writings by Black Gay Men* (Boston: Alyson Publications, Inc., 1991); *James Baldwin Now* (New York: New York University Press, 1999), ed. Dwight McBride; Robert Reid-Pharr's *Black Gay Man* (New York: New York University Press, 2001); Roderick A. Ferguson, *Aberrations in Black: Toward a Queer of Color Critique* (Minneapolis: University of Minnesota Press, 2004).M. Jacqui Alexander, *Pedagogies of Crossing: Meditations on Feminism, Sexual Politics, Memory, and the Sacred* (Durham and London: Duke University Press, 2005); E. Patrick Johnson and Mae Gwendolyn Henderson (eds.) *Black Queer Studies: A Critical Anthology* (Durham and London: Duke University Press, 2005); Kimberly Springer, *Living for the Revolution: Black Feminist Organizations, 1968–1980* (Durham and London: Duke University Press, 2005); Thomas Glave (ed.), *Our Caribbean: A Gathering of Lesbian and Gay Writing from the Antilles* (Durham and London: Duke University Press, 2008); Rudoph P. Byrd, Johnnetta Betsch Cole, Beverly Guy-Sheftall (eds.), *I am Your Sister: Collected and Unpublished Writings of Audre Lorde* (Oxford and New York: Oxford University Press, 2009).

27. Jennifer DeVere Brody and Dwight McBride, "Introduction, Callaloo Vol. 23, No. 1, Gay, Lesbian, Bisexual, Transgender: Literature and Culture (Winter, 2000), 286–87.

28. Ibid., 287.

29. For further discussion about respectability and black social formations, see M. Jacqui Alexander's *Pedagogies of Crossing* and "Not Just (Any) Body Can be a Citizen: The Politics of Law, Sexuality, and Postcoloniality in Trinidad and Tobago and the Bahamas," *Feminist Review*, No. 48, (Autumn, 1994), 5–23; Kevin Gaines, *Uplifting the Race: Black Leadership, Politics, and Culture in the Twentieth Century* (Chapel Hill: The University of North Carolina Press, 1996); Hazel Carby, *Race Men* (Cambridge: Harvard University Press, 2000); Martin Summers, *Manliness and its Discontents: The Black Middle Class and the Transformation of Masculinity, 1900–1930* (Chapel Hill: The University of North Carolina Press, 2003); Marlon Ross, *Manning the Race: Reforming Black Men in the Jim Crow Era* (New York: New York University Press, 2004); Candice M. Jenkins, *Private Lives, Proper Relations: Regulating Black Intimacy* (Minneapolis: University of Minnesota Press, 2007).

30. See "Booker T. Washington, "The Influence of Object-Lessons in the Solution of the Race Problem," in Booker T. Washington Papers, Library of Congress, Box 541. For a discussion of this speech and its role in discourses of Black leadership and sexuality, see Roderick A. Ferguson's "Of Our Normative Strivings: African American Studies and the Histories of Sexuality," in *Social Text* 84–85, Vol. 23, Nos. 3–4, Fall–Winter 2005.

31. See for instance, Angela Davis, *Blues Legacies and Black Feminism: Gertrude 'Ma Rainey, Bessie Smith, and Billie Holiday*, (New York: Vintage Books, 1998); John D'Emilio, *Lost Prophet: The Life and Times of Bayard Rustin* (Chicago:

University of Chicago Press, 2004); Shane Vogel, *The Scene of the Harlem Cabaret: Race, Sexuality, Performance* (Chicago: University of Chicago Press, 2009).

32. King, http://www.vibe.com/content/mean-girls-morehouse.

33. See M. Jacqui Alexander's *Pedagogies of Crossing* and "Not Just (Any) Body Can Be a Citizen"; Frances Beale, "Double Jeopardy: To be Black and Female," in Toni Cade Bambara (ed.) *The Black Woman: Anthology* (New York: Signet, 1970); Hazel Carby, *Reconstructing Womanhood: The Emergence of the Afro-American Woman Novelist* (Oxford: Oxford University Press, 1989); Angela Davis, *Women, Race, and Class* (New York: Vintage, 1983); Roderick Ferguson *Aberrations in Black*; Gayatri Gopinath, *Impossible Desires: Queer Desires and South Asian Public Cultures* (Durham and London: Duke University Press, 2005); Chandan Reddy, "Asian Diasporas, Neoliberalism, and Family: Reviewing the Case for Homosexual Asylum in the Context of Family Rights," *Social Text* 2005 23(3–4 84–85):101–19.

34. Lekan Oguntoyinbo, "Non-Discrimination Policies and Support Groups Help Ease Campus Life for Gay and Lesbian Students at HBCUs." Accessed from http://diverseeducation.com/article/12697/ on July 7, 2009.

35. Peter Galuszka, "Virginia HBCU's Struggle with Legal Opinion that Bars Protection for Gays." Accessed 11/11/10. http://diverseeducation.com/cache/print.php?articleId=13612.

36. Ibid.

37. Johnnetta B. Cole, and Beverly Guy-Sheftall, Gender Talk: The Struggle for Women's Equality in African American Communities (One World//Ballantine, 2003), 155.

38. M. Jacqui Alexander, *Pedagogies of Crossing: Meditations on Feminism, Sexual Politics, Memory, and the Sacred* (Durham and London: Duke University Press, 2005), 281.

39. Essex Hemphill, "Introduction" in *Brother to Brother*, ed. Essex Hemphill (Boston: Alyson Publications, 1991), xxvii.

40. See June Jordan's "Black Studies: Bringing Back the Person" in *Moving Toward Home* for a theory of Black Studies as the preservation and consecration of minoritized persons.

Chapter Thirteen

Postscript

*Professing Our Love for Social
Justice "Committed to Survival
and Wholeness of Entire People"*

Gary L. Lemons and Cheryl R. Rodriguez

IN DIALOGUE ON A COURSE TO FREEDOM
WITH "THE COLORED RACE"

In a final complement to the pedagogical works that compose *Still Woke!*—we conclude with a dialogue with each other conversing about ways we teach womanist *"Love"* for social justice "committed to survival and wholeness of entire people." Employing Alice Walker's revolutionary phrase to contextualize our dialogue, we ask each other a series of questions to map our evolution as "professors" of radical Black feminist-womanist thought. In doing so, we chart our individual academic her(stories) and (his)stories intricately related to the self-transformative legacy of esteemed, radical Black/women *and* men of color activists, scholars, and teachers. They planted in us a radical vision of *higher education*. It would be this seed of hope in our unwavering, soulful labor in the college classroom that would come to represent the legacy of their steadfast, untiring struggles against systemic and institutionalized oppression. In solidarity with our contributors, we openly articulate and share in our interview with each other and teachers and students dedicated to liberation from *all* forms of domination—including imperialism, patriarchy, sexism, capitalism, ableism, and homophobia.

As a collaborative radical pedagogical project—co-edited by two Black feminist-womanist thinkers *and* pedagogues—it has been an extraordinary journey of self-reflection and visionary sharing with individuals who teach, instruct, and profess the transformative power of critical consciousness in the classroom. As every contributor to this volume illustrates, feminist and womanist teaching is not only about being conscientious, educationally prepared, and professionally responsible—it is also about embracing the wholeness of the human experience and teaching for freedom and social justice. In sum, it's about being *Still Woke!* In the dialogue that follows, we talk about pedagogy rooted in the mind, body, and "Spirit" of womanism. As we share in the Foreword to this body of contributors—in solidarity with Alice Walker's definition of a womanist—we follow her path to critical consciousness on the path to freedom for all oppressed people. Here we go—

Cheryl: Teaching against the Hegemonic Narrative

In our ongoing conversation about radical Black feminist pedagogy, Gary asked me, "What was, has been, or is the most challenging aspect of your teaching related to feminist and womanist theory and methodology in the classroom?" This question requires a deep reconnection to my pedagogical history and memory. I have very proudly spent my entire academic career in Africana Studies, a discipline that was formally established on university campuses during the Black student movements of the 1960s.

From its inception, Africana Studies brought revolutionary and liberatory knowledge to the academy by boldly asserting its importance as a systematic and "conscious inquiry into the history, culture, and sociopolitical condition of African and African American people.[1] However, like most academic disciplines, Africana Studies was grounded in patriarchal beliefs and perspectives that revered and privileged the thoughts of Black men. In the early 1990s, I entered a very traditional, conservative, Africana Studies department as a Black feminist anthropologist, whose scholarship and teaching were informed by both intellectual and activist engagements. As a new faculty member, my struggles in the department involved addressing deeply engrained patriarchal practices that influenced curriculum development. Black women, as thinkers and creators of knowledge, were invisible in the department's core courses. Understanding that my task was not only to teach but also to "reexamine and transform inherited practices that stand in the way of justice,"[2] I made significant revisions to the courses assigned to me. In an introductory course that included African history, the complex creation of the African diaspora and Black struggles for freedom in the Western world, I expanded and enriched the curriculum by including Black women's voices and interweaving knowledge of Black women's intellectual and activist traditions.

There was one course on Black women in the United States that had been developed and framed in the "great Black women" historical context. As a Black feminist scholar, I found that approach very problematic and limited. I agree with Beverly Guy-Sheftall who argues that this approach in Africana Studies was simply to record the fact that Black women were present in history.[3] My syllabus on "Black Women in America" included theoretical and cultural considerations of Black womanhood from historical and contemporary perspectives. As my students were introduced to the concepts of feminism and intersectionality, they were also required to critique all forms of discrimination, including racism, sexism, classism and homophobia.

My very traditional colleagues at that time did raise eyebrows about my "radical" pedagogical practices. However, I must also say that there was student push-back to my curricular choices. One day a group of undergraduates came to my office and wanted to know why I had included the writings of Black lesbians in their reading assignments. I appreciated their courageous questions and I discussed the critical role of Black lesbian scholarship in the development of both Black Studies and Women's Studies. While this group of students may not have been convinced of the value of the course, I am certain that there were students who gratefully received the knowledge I had to share.

I also felt that it was important to provide a global perspective on Black women's lives. This led to the development of two courses, "Women in Africa and the Diaspora" and "Women of Color, Activism and Social Change." Both of these graduate courses were cross-listed with Women's Studies. In both courses, students learn about Black women's thorny relationships with feminism, racism within the feminist movement and the reconceptualization of feminism by Black women and other women of color. Some white women students (who were Women's Studies majors) really struggled with the analyses of racism that were presented in these courses. However, I have always attempted to remain receptive to students' critiques and I invited students to confront these issues in class or in individual meetings with me.

Ultimately, when I think of major challenges in my feminist and womanist teaching, I remember Black feminist scholar, teacher, and former president of Spelman College, who recalled: "As my interests in Black and Women's Studies merged, one of the earliest and most painful realizations I had was that in Black Studies it was hard to find women and in Women's Studies it was hard to find Black folk."[4] Over the years, my greatest challenges have been to address both of these invisibilities and, most importantly, teach for justice.

Gary also asked me: "What has been or is the best class you have taught related to your area of specialization?" In addressing this question, I must confess that on the first class meeting of every semester, regardless of what I am teaching, I tell my students that it is my favorite course! Saying this to my students is my way of bringing love, hope, and encouragement into the learning environment. I want my students to know that I value the curriculum I am about to experience with them, and I value their participation in my class. That being said, I must admit that I am always excited to teach the course "Black Women in America" to undergraduate students. The readings, films, discussions, and activities associated with that course can be transformational for students. Most of the students enter the course without ever being challenged to think seriously about Black women's lives—and many of these students are indeed, Black women! One of the most important ideas that emerges from this course is that, as a community of learners, we can discuss Black women's struggles with racism, sexism, classism, homophobia, and other social issues without creating narratives of victimhood. Students learn that these social issues are realities that are confronted and changed by Black women every day. Finally, I encourage students to use the knowledge gleaned in this course to learn more about Black womanhood and the ways in which we continue to redefine the parameters of our lives.

The third question that Gary asked is one that we each are excited to discuss: "How have you connected your work in the classroom to a larger community outside of the academic arena?" During my graduate study in anthropology, I began learning and conducting ethnographic research in a range of settings. These research experiences not only prepared me for the projects I would later conduct as a Black feminist anthropologist, but they also inspired me to learn as much as I could in order to teach qualitative research methods. As a faculty member in Africana Studies, I developed courses on activist community research for both undergraduate and graduate students. These courses engaged students with neighborhoods and communities outside of the university and became a powerful vehicle for teaching students how to ask questions and apply theoretical analyses to real-world issues. In one of my first articles about engaged pedagogy, I wrote:

> By eliciting support from community activists and leaders and through various levels of engagement with relevant local agencies and organizations, the class is a community-focused experience in which students are actively involved in self-exploration and self-education. The students also learn to test self-generated theories on African diaspora life and, from these theories, develop scholarly analyses of Black life in local communities.[5]

In this course, "African American Community Research," students explore such concepts as reflexivity, activist ethnography, and Black feminist epistemology—which "provide a critical framework for analyzing the interlocking hierarchies involved in issues of race, ethnicity, gender, class, sexual identity, religious/spiritual practices, and other sociocultural phenomena that must be addressed in African American community research."[6] While all the students' topics do not necessarily center women and gender issues, feminism—as theory and practice—is one of the foundations on which this course is built. As Davis and Craven contend, "Feminism is a prescriptive project, with a social justice vision that attempts to explain, in analytical terms, power differentials of a number of processes including colonialism, capitalism, militarism, ableism, homophobia, and others."[7]

In 2017, I taught this course to a small interdisciplinary group of graduate students who were at various stages of their research lives. Each of the students was very eager and receptive to develop solid ethnographic research skills that would eventually guide them in the thesis or dissertation work. Working together as a learning community, we went on field trips to a local African American research library and the site of Tampa's first historically Black community. We met with community activists, who discussed critical issues affecting the lives of people in their neighborhoods. Most importantly, we had many methodological discussions and we thought very carefully about how our community experiences aligned with the research literature. My students ended the course with skills that would allow them to pursue their own research projects with confidence. They also made connections with local leaders who view engaged pedagogy as useful and relevant to strong communities. So, for me, teaching community research is also teaching for freedom and justice.

Gary: I Profess My Black Pro-Feminist-Womanist Manhood

In this section, I respond to several questions Cheryl posed to me as co-editor of *Woke!* She asked me: How do male students typically respond to your discussions about Black men as feminists? What pedagogical strategies help male student to understand a Black man's decision to identify as a feminist or womanist? Do you believe that every class you teach can be taught from a feminist or womanist perspective? Why or why not? What relationship does your pedagogical approach have to do with larger communities outside your academic classroom?

In *Feminist Solidarity at the Crossroads: Intersectional Women's Studies for Transracial Alliance* (2012), I write:

> For me representing myself publicly as a feminist black man is all about the power of the personal in relation to the political. At the same time, it is a standpoint that clearly positions me at the margin of traditional heteronormative notions of black male identity. I have come to accept myself as a 'marginal

man.' Often, as I have written 'teaching as a pro-feminist man,' positions me at
the quintessential 'black male outsider.'[8]

Identifying myself as a Black male pro-feminist-womanist professor in the
college classroom is about my personal, social, political, *and* spiritual revolutionary journey toward owning my self-consciousness. As I have written
many times, the writings of bell hooks and a number of other black/feminists
and womanists of color—including Alice Walker—transformed my thinking
about what it means to be a *black* man holistically "[c]ommitted to survival
and wholeness of entire people, male *and* female."[9] You ask, how does this
positionality represent itself particularly related to male students' response to
the pedagogical politics associated with my identity? Having begun teaching
at the New School University in NYC as a "pro-feminist" in the early 1990's,
I would go on to writing about my impact on female *and* male-identified
students in the classroom—especially related to issues of race. In *Black Male
Outsider, a Memoir: Teaching as a Pro-Feminist Man* (2008), I talk about
teaching Black feminist literature in classes where the few male students
(almost always white) in them would rarely speak out:

> White [male] silence in the classroom not only threatened to disrupt class dis-
> cussion, its seemingly arrogant posture attempted to silences the voice(s) of
> students of color—as well as my own. For white [male] students to break silence
> on race opens space for a critical dialogue aimed to 'decenter' whiteness as *the*
> signifier of white supremacy. In my experience, far too many white [male] stu-
> dents claimed silence as a way to deal with race. *Of the white males who took my
> classes over the years (and the numbers [have been] consistently small, indeed),
> few possessed the courage to openly disclose their feelings about being white
> and male.*[10] (Emphasis added)

It is interesting to point out how issues of *race* connected to white, heterosexual male privilege(s) often determine whether white male students remain
in undergraduate African American literature classes I teach—even though
my course syllabi explicitly promote a pro-feminist-womanist pedagogical
approach. Before discussing the response of male students of color who take
my classes, I further reference white male students who feel *victimized* about
my teaching the connection between hetero-patriarchy, white supremacy, and
economic status. In a section of *Black Male Outsider* titled "White Males
Who Pass (out of Whiteness): Not the Right Kind of White Man"—I write:

> Over the years, for every white male who enrolled in my classes and remined
> to the end of the semester, there [would be at least] one who dropped them after
> the first or second class session. Why? Any number of reasons. But what I know,
> based upon my experience with white males I have taught, is that many feel they

are the targets of my critique of white supremacist capitalist patriarchy. No matter how much I have attempted to prove them wrong, many of them refuse to see themselves as anything but *victims* as 'straight white middle- (and upper-) class males.' Considering the feminist critique of the paradigm of power signified in the image of an elite, white heterosexual male identity, is there any wonder that a black-lash against feminism (of any color) would manifest itself in the antiracist pro-feminist classroom. In my classes, many straight white males who have internalized a victim mentality buckle under the pressure of suddenly being seen and engaged (often for the first time) as 'white' males.[11]

Yet, as I have argued previously,

There have, however, been those rare white male students (straight and gay) who have remained in my classes, not only bearing the weight of racial visibility but also discovering in memoir writing that critical self-examination in the contest of feminist anti-racist pedagogy can en(gender) feelings of liberation for white men in terms of class *and* sexuality. . . . [S]ome white males in my classes over the years have been openly willing to call into question their identity and to admit to possessing a fractured sense of who they are.[12]

Now for a decade, having taught African American literature and biblical studies at the University of South Florida, my scholarship about teaching students of varying races/ethnicities, genders, sexualities, cultures, abilities, and economic status continues to compel female *and* male students to embrace visionary feminist and womanist thought. As I have stated, particularly in my undergraduate courses, few male students (across race and ethnic differences) enroll in my courses. Those of color are few, indeed. However, one of the first courses at taught at USF was in the Department of Women's Studies, chaired by Kim Marie Vaz. One of the courses she invited me to was titled: "Men and Sexism." Writing about teaching this course in *Feminist Solidarity at the Crossroads*, I state:

First and foremost, as a man who for many years consciously understood the meaning of the word 'sexism,' both in theory and in practice, I wholeheartedly immersed myself (mind, body, and spirit) into the conceptualization of this course. Even before thinking about its goal, objectives, and outcomes, however, I wrestled with the course title. While it directly communicated the subject of the class, it might be misconstrued by some students (both female and male) that we would spend the semester bashing men. In a culture of male supremacist thinking rotted in patriarchal ideology, the term 'sexism' [can especially problematic for male students—white and of color].[13]

Related to Black/males of color who enrolled in my "Men and Sexism" class, I required all students in it to read bell hooks' book *We Real Cool: Black Men and Masculinity* (2004). Recalling one of the most memorable aspects of her critique of sexism in Black communities specifically, I remark:

> Hooks calls for us [black males] to claim 'the presentation of an alternative black man seeking freedom for self and loved ones, a rebel black man eager to create and make his own destiny.' Black men embracing emancipator ideas of masculinity linked to feminist personal and political transformation initiate a process of self-recovery and male healing from the wounds of patriarchy. . . . Committing ourselves to the liberation of all who struggle under the weight of oppression, we come to know the real power of the 'revolutionary manhood' hooks envisions and that pro-feminist black men have begun to recover.[14]

In sum, while the title of the course was offsetting to many of the students in it, by the end of the semester, many of them became critically aware of the oppressive realities bound up in sexist ideas of manhood and masculinity. One of the largest undergraduate courses I have ever taught, the majority of the students in it both female *and* male supported my call for them to stand against sexism. I still remember the transformative power of the students who remained in the class:

> In this class of fifty-two students, the majority of whom were female, three of them were black. Of the five males enrolled, two of them were black. Almost all of the students agreed that the name of the course more than likely turned males away. Males in the class, as well as a majority of the females, said the course title sounded accusatory—that all men were 'bad guys.' As we moved through the reading in *Men and Feminism: Reconstructing Gender Relations* (1998) and our engagement in class dialogue, by the end of the semester, students not only understood the systemic nature of sexism, but also comprehended its institutionalization in a culture of patriarchy where women just as men are susceptible to the internalization of sexist ideology. Both male and female students all agreed that while a course titled "Feminism and Me" [as I imagined it] carried it own potentially ideological baggage of exclusion, it was not to them as off-putting as the existing one.[15]

In an undergraduate course I teach called "The Bible as Literature," in 2018, Cheryl, you will recall that you helped me to add a community service component to it. Teaching the course from a pro-feminist and womanist standpoint, I wanted to collaborate with a progressive, multi-racial community church that would be open to my students sharing their written interpretations to the politics of gender, class, sexuality, and (dis)abilities as represented in biblical narratives. Arranging sessions during the semester in which my students and I would attend certain meetings of the church's Bible Study—as organized by the church's Black female pastor—we would partake in a visionary, life-transformative womanist-centered experience. In dialogue with members of the congregation during a series of its Bible study, not only by end of the term had our meetings been spiritually enriching for my students, they reaffirmed my belief that a womanist pedagogical approach to the study of "the Bible as literature" could have a significant liberatory impact on the lives of folks outside the college classroom.

Of the twenty-eight students who studied with me in "The Bible as Literature," fourteen of them were black/students of color. The class included six males, three of them black/of color. For me personally, it was profoundly evident that collectively the female *and* male students' dialogues (through paper presentations and introductions of each other) with the church's Bible Study members made a lasting impression on many of them—as their feedback enhanced the minds and hearts of my students. During each "talk-back" period during the sessions of the Bible Study we attended at the church, its members complimented and encouraged the students to keep moving forward in their support of social justice and human rights. More often than not, my students were simply amazed with how accepting their works on the Bible were received.

In recalling my journey toward becoming a Black man teaching as pro-feminist and womanist professor, I hold on to the memory of my mother's struggle to survive as a Black woman simultaneously contesting racism, sexism, and classism. I grew up watching the intensity of her stand against male domination and oppression—in and outside the "Black community." In truth, she is the primary, fundamental reason why I am who I would come to be—from a student to a teacher of womanism. In "To Be Black, Male, and Feminist: Making Womanist Space for Black Men on the Eve of a New Millennium," *Feminism and Men*, I write about my first life-changing experience in 1996 with a group of young, pro-feminist Black men:

> To know that one is not alone in a time of struggle is a knowledge to be cherished. When I recently came to know and interact with young black men at Morehouse College who had founded the organization Black Men for the Eradication of Sexism, I found myself struggling to under the historical importance of that moment. On the weekend of September 28 and 29, 1996, a year after the Million Man March, they (we) made history. At the conference entitled 'Black, Male and Feminist/Womanist,' devoted entirely to the subject of *black* men's relation to feminism/womanism, African American men had organized to declare publicly their commitment to eradication of sexism.[16]

HOLDING UP THE BANNER OF FREEDOM
IN AND OUTSIDE THE CLASSROOM

Narrating (her)stories and (his)stories—as "woke" radical teachers confronting *and* contesting systemic and institutionalized oppression—we collectively join with our contributors to embody the visionary legacy of Black feminism *and* womanism. Thus, together we demonstrate how the classroom can be/work as a life-saving space for en(Spirit)ed self-transformation. Acknowledging disciplinary boundaries many of us pedagogically transgress is one thing; acknowledging how our personal identities—and often our actual physical bodies radically represent what we teach—is quite another. This particular challenge has called for us to share our personal (her)stories and (his)stories with exceptional vulnerability. Narrative vulnerability acts as strategic tool to reveal the willing sacrifices we offer in sharing our classroom experiences. In doing so, we create *room* for critical self-consciousness not only for our students, but for ourselves. In this visionary space, our pedagogical labor works for liberatory ideas of freedom *and* justice for all historically marginalized "Folk."

To the readers of our personal narratives and pedagogical strategies—including students in higher educational settings, along with teachers across instructional levels and disciplinary boundaries—we join together acknowledging that students cannot be challenged to transform their thinking without evoking passions and emotions that stretch us as well. In unity and solidarity, our voices speak to the complex dynamics of critical self-reflections that arise in our classes. Addressing them in our essays, we candidly admit our failures, successes, and personal ways of engaging them. Thus, envisioning the classroom as a space of liberatory transformation for students *and* teachers, we actively labor in pedagogical solidarity to promote the struggle for *pro*-feminist-womanist education. As stated in the Introduction to *Still Woke!* together we continue the liberating and life-saving legacy of insightful, passionate, scholarly, and creative discussions about the politics Black feminist-womanist pedagogy that began in the academic establishment of Black women's studies. Firmly grounded in Black feminist-womanist theory and practice, this book honors the *herstorical* labor of Black/women of color intellectual activists who have unapologetically held up the banner of freedom in academia.

BIBLIOGRAPHY

Alexander, M. Jacqui. *Pedagogies of Crossing: Meditations on Feminism, Sexual Politics, Memory and the Sacred.* Durham: Duke University Press. 2005.

Cole, B. Johnnetta. *Conversations: Straight Talk with America's Sister President.* New York: Doubleday. 1993.

Davis, Dana-Ain and Christa Craven. *Feminist Ethnography.* New York: Rowman and Littlefield, 2016.

Guy-Sheftall, Beverly. "Black Women's Studies: The Interface of Women's Studies and Black Studies." *Phylon* XLIX (1 & 2): 33–41. 1992.

hooks, bell. *We Real Cool: Black Men and Masculinity.* New York: Routledge, 2004.

Lemons, Gary L. *Black Male Outsider, a Memoir: Teaching as a Pro-Feminist Man.* New York: State University of New York Press, 2008.

————. "To Be Black, Male, and Feminist: Making Womanist Space for Black Men on the Eve of a New Millennium." In *Men and Feminism: Reconstructing Gender Relations,* edited by Steven P. Schacht and Doris W. Ewing, 43–66. New York: State University of New York Press, 1998.

————. "'Women's Studies Is Not My Home?' When Personal and Political Professions Become Acts of Emancipatory Confession." In *Feminist Solidarity at the Crossroads: Intersectional Women's Studies for Transracial Alliance*, edited by Kim Marie Vaz and Gary L. Lemons, 166–81. New York: Routledge, 2012.

Rodriguez, Cheryl. "African American Anthropology and the Pedagogy of Activist Community Research." *Anthropology and Education Quarterly* 27(3):414–31. 1996.

Walker, Alice. *In Search of Our Mothers' Gardens: Womanist Prose.* New York: Harcourt Brace & Co., 1983.

NOTES

1. Johnnetta. B. Cole, *Conversations: Straight Talk with America's Sister President* (New York: Doubleday, 1993), 28.

2. Jacqui M. Alexander, *Pedagogies of Crossing: Meditations on Feminism, Sexual Politics, Memory and the Sacred* (Durham: Duke University Press, 2005), 93.

3. Beverly Guy-Sheftall, "Black Women's Studies: The Interface of Women's Studies and Black Studies," *Phylon* XLIX (1 & 2): 33–41, 1992: 37.

4. Cole, *Conversations* 29.

5. Cheryl Rodriguez, "African American Anthropology and the Pedagogy of Activist Community Research," *Anthropology and Education Quarterly* 27(3): 414–31, (1996): 416.

6. Ibid., 423.

7. Dana-Ain Davis and Christa Craven, *Feminist Ethnography* (New York: Rowman and Littlefield, 2016), 147.

8. Gary L. Lemons, "'Women's Studies Is Not My Home?' When Personal and Political Professions Become Acts of Emancipatory Confession" in *Feminist Solidarity at the Crossroads: Intersectional Women's Studies for Transracial Alliance*, eds. Kim Marie Vaz and Gary L. Lemons (New York: Routledge, 2012), 169–70.

9. Alice Walker, *In Search of Our Mothers' Gardens: Womanist Prose* (New York: Harcourt Brace & Co., 1983), xi.

10. Lemons, *Black Male Outsider, a Memoir: Teaching as a Pro-Feminist Man* (New York: State University of New York Press, 2008), 128.

11. Ibid., 139.

12. Ibid., 139.

13. Lemons, *Feminist Solidarity*, 176.

14. Ibid.,176.

15. Ibid., 175.

16. Lemons, "To Be Black, Male, and Feminist: Making Womanist Space for Black Men on the Eve of a New Millennium" in *Men and Feminism: Reconstructing Gender Relations,* eds. Steven P. Schacht and Doris W. Ewing (New York: State University of New York Press, 1998), 43–44.

Index

About the Contributors

Cheryl R. Rodriguez is professor of Africana studies and anthropology at the University of South Florida. She is co-editor of the book *Transatlantic Feminisms: Women and Gender Studies in Africa and the Diaspora* (Lexington Books). A Black feminist ethnographer and community anthropologist, she has authored several articles on Black feminist anthropology as theory and methodology. Her research and teaching focus on the cultural, social, and political lives of Black women in America with a particular focus on Black women's activism and community-building in Tampa, Florida.

Gary L. Lemons is professor of English at the University of South Florida. He teaches African American literature and biblical studies rooted in Black feminist-womanist theory, criticism, and theology. He received his PhD in literature and an advanced certificate in museum studies from New York University in 1992. Lemons' publications include: *Black Male Outsider, a Memoir: Teaching as a Pro-Feminist Man*; *Womanist Forefathers: Frederick Douglass and W.E.B. Du Bois*; *Feminist Solidarity at the Crossroads: Intersectional Women's Studies for Transracial Alliance* (co-editor Kim Marie Vaz); *Caught Up in the Spirit! Teaching for Womanist Liberation*; *Building Womanist Coalitions: Writing and Teaching in the Spirit of Love*; *Let Love Lead: On a Course to Freedom* (co-authors Scott Neumeister and Susie Hoeller); *Hooked on the Art of Love: bell hooks and My Calling for Soul Work*; and *Liberation for the Oppressed: Community Healing through Activist Transformation, a Call to CHAT*.

Vincent Adejumo is currently a senior lecturer of African American studies and affiliate senior lecturer of political science at the University of Florida, as well as the founder of the Olu Institute of Learning, Inc. He received a BS in business administration in 2008 from Florida State University. In 2015, he received his PhD in policy and administration from the University of Florida. He currently teaches introduction to African American studies, *The Wire*, mentoring at-risk youth, Black Wall Street, and Black masculinity. Adejumo was selected as professor of the year by the UF Black Student Union for the 2015–2016 school year. He was also selected as the professor and advisor of the year by the UF College of Liberal Arts and Sciences for the 2017–2018 school year.

Kendra N. Bryant is assistant professor of English and the composition director at North Carolina A&T State University, Greensboro. She obtained her PhD in English rhetoric and composition from University of South Florida, Tampa, 2012. Since then, she has taught composition at Florida A&M University, Tallahassee; University of North Georgia, Watkinsville; and Florida International University, Miami. With twenty years of teaching experience, four of which were spent in the high school English language arts classroom, Kendra has published peer reviewed essays in journals like *CLAJ, Journal of Basic Writing,* and *Studies in Popular Culture.* She is also the editor of *Engaging 21st Century Writers with Social Media,* IGI-Global Publishers, 2016. Her interests include composition theory, twentieth-century African American literature, and the Black arts movement. Kendra can be reached at drknbryant.com.

Paul T. Corrigan, PhD, teaches at the University of Tampa. His published essays have appeared in *Pedagogy, Profession, Reader, TheAtlantic.com,* and *Building Womanist Coalitions: Writing and Teaching in the Spirit of Love.* He is currently working on a book project on antiracist reading.

Roderick A. Ferguson, PhD, is the William Robertson Coe professor of women's, gender, and sexuality studies and American studies at Yale University. He is the author of *One-Dimensional Queer* (Polity, 2019), *We Demand: The University and Student Protests* (University of California, 2017), *The Reorder of Things: The University and Its Pedagogies of Minority Difference* (University of Minnesota, 2012), and *Aberrations in Black: Toward a Queer of Color Critique* (University of Minnesota, 2004). He is the co-editor with Grace Hong of the anthology *Strange Affinities: The Gender and Sexual Politics of Comparative Racialization* (Duke University, 2011). He is also co-editor with Erica Edwards and Jeffrey Ogbar of *Keywords of African American Studies* (NYU, 2018). He is the 2020 recipient of the Kessler Award from the Center for LGBTQ Studies (CLAGS).

Hanna Garth, PhD, is assistant professor of anthropology at Princeton University with affiliations in African American studies, and the program in Latin American studies. She is a sociocultural and medical anthropologist who studies food access and the global food system. She studies these questions in Latin America and the Caribbean, and among Black and Latinx communities in the United States. This work has looked at the ways macro-level changes and shifts in local food distribution systems impact communities, families, and individuals. She has conducted over ten years of research on household-level food access in Eastern Cuba and published the book Food in Cuba: The Pursuit of a Decent Meal . In addition to her work in Cuba she has an ongoing research project in Los Angeles, California. Based on this work she co-edited the volume Black Food Matters: Food Justice in the Wake of Racial Justice with Ashanté Reese.

M. Thandanbantu Iverson, PhD, is a retired senior lecturer, emeritus, from the labor studies department of the Indiana School of Social Work (IUPUI). Born in 1947, Iverson was reared in a segregated working-class neighborhood of Columbus, Ohio. An honors graduate of Hiram College and Clark Atlanta University, he received his doctorate in 2006, having examined the workplace and union resistance strategies of African American women healthcare workers in Gary, Indiana. He is a veteran trade unionist and human rights educator—having participated in the Black student, Black power, Vietnam antiwar liberation support, new left, human rights and liberation theology movements. Iverson continues his labor education and social movement-building efforts in Metro Denver.

Marquese McFerguson, PhD, is assistant professor of intercultural communication within the School of Communication and Multimedia Studies at Florida Atlantic University. His scholarship and teaching examine how individuals in society communicate, perform and (re)imagine identity across a diverse number of cultural intersections including race, class, gender, and sexual orientation. His research agenda is centered on building bridges of understanding across cultures by examining how racialized identities are produced/portrayed by media makers and interpreted/performed by media audiences. His research about representation and media-created scripts is guided by feminist, aesthetic, and narrative sensibilities and situated within the interdisciplinary fields of communication studies and African American studies. He is also an award-winning slam poet and teaching artist who has performed at academic institutions and performance venues throughout the United States and United Kingdom.

Scott Neumeister is literary scholar, author, TEDx speaker, and mythic pathfinder from Tampa, Florida, where he earned his PhD in English from the University of South Florida in 2018. His specialization in multiethnic American literature and mythology comes after careers as an information technology systems engineer and a teacher of English and mythology at the middle school and college levels. He is coauthor of *Let Love Lead: On a Course to Freedom* with Gary L. Lemons and Susie Hoeller, as well as a facilitator for the Joseph Campbell Foundation's Myth and Meaning book club at Literati.

Quynh Nhu Le, PhD, is associate professor of English literature at the University of South Florida. She is author of *Unsettled Solidarities: Asian and Indigenous Cross-Representations in the Américas* published by Temple UP in 2019. The book received the Association for Asian American Studies' Humanities and Cultural Studies: Literary Studies Book Award for 2021. Le's writing has appeared in interdisciplinary journals such as *Amerasia Journal*, *Journal of Asian American Studies*, and *Dance Chronicle*. Her work engages with the connections in Asian American studies, Native American/Indigenous studies, critical ethnic studies, settler colonial studies, critical refugee studies, and theories of affect and embodiment.

Maggie Romigh grew up in Brunswick, Georgia. She earned a BA from Eckerd College in St. Petersburg, Florida, in 1999 and an MA from New Mexico Highlands University in 2003. She received her PhD in literature at the University of South Florida in 2021. Romigh has published magazine articles, poetry, creative non-fiction, reviews, a critical essay entitled "Luci Tapahonso's 'Leda and the Cowboy': A Gynocratic, Navajo Response to Yeats's 'Leda and the Swan,'" and, most recently, an essay entitled "Separate Pathways, Same Mountaintop." Her conference presentations have focused on the literary works of Native American and African American literature. She has been a college instructor for over twenty years.

La-Toya Scott received her PhD in literature at the University of Florida in 2022. During this year, she accepted a post-doctoral fellowship at Rutgers University. Her research interests include African American literature, Black slave narratives, ethnic and cultural studies, womanism, and Afrofuturist safe spaces. La-Toya has published a collaborative digital webtext in *Peitho*, the lead journal for feminist rhetoric in composition studies. She also has a forthcoming article in *Supernatural Studies: An Interdisciplinary Journal of Art, Media, and Culture*, which explores safe space creation in HBO's *Lovecraft Country*.

www.ingramcontent.com/pod-product-compliance
Lightning Source LLC
Chambersburg PA
CBHW022306280326
41932CB00010B/999